WRITERS
and
POLITICS

WRITERS
and
POLITICS

by
George Woodcock

BLACK ROSE BOOKS

Montreal/New York

BLACK ROSE BOOKS No. T151
Paperback ISBN: 0-921689-82-9
Hardcover ISBN: 0-921689-83-7

Canadian Cataloguing in Publication Data

Woodcock, George, 1912 -
  Writers and politics

Originally published under title: The writer and politics.
ISBN: 0-921689-83-7 (bound) --
  ISBN: 0-921689-82-9 (pbk.).

  1. Politics and literature. 2. Literature and society. I. Title.
II. Title: The Writer and politics.

PN56.P54W66 1990   809'.93358   C91-090031-0

Library of Congress Catalog No. 90-83626
Cover design: Pierre-Paul Pariseau

Editorial Offices
BLACK ROSE BOOKS
3981 St-Laurent
Boulevard, Suite 444
Montréal, Québec
H2W 1Y5 Canada

Mailing Address
BLACK ROSE BOOKS
P.O. Box 1258
Succ. Place du Parc
Montréal, Québec
H2W 2R3 Canada

U.S. Orders
BLACK ROSE BOOKS
340 Nagel Drive
Cheektowaga, New York
14225

Printed and bound in Québec, Canada
on acid-free paper

Contents

PREFACE TO THE ORIGINAL EDITION   vii

I. INTRODUCTION TO THE NEW EDITION   1

II. THE WRITER AND POLITICS   10

III. THE FUNCTION OF THE POLITICAL MYTH   28

IV. PROUDHON AND HIS MUTUALIST THEORIES   42

V. ALEXANDER HERZEN   56

VI. THE SCIENTIFIC CONTRIBUTION OF PETER KROPOTKIN   80

VII. GEORGE ORWELL   111

VIII. GRAHAM GREENE   125

IX. IGNAZIO SILONE   154

X. ARTHUR KOESTLER   175

XI. KAFKA AND REX WARNER   197

XII. THE ENGLISH HYMN   207

XIII. HENRY BATES ON THE AMAZONS   227

XIV. THE PEROXIDE SAINT   240

[v]

Preface to the Original Edition

THE essays in this volume cover what may appear to be a wide variety of subjects, but I have felt justified in presenting them together because, except perhaps in the last three essays, which form a group on their own, there emerges a consistent and clearly perceptible theme.

That theme is social, and in a sense Utopian. It recognises the paramount need for a change in social structure, in order to promote the freedom of individual development, and in it is implicit the idea of an organic society from which such a freedom would emerge. Whether the individual essays are sociological or literary in character, they tend towards that conception of a society, which is unreal in the sense that it exists only in mind and desire, but which is also real in the sense that it provides an aim towards which our efforts as individuals and as members of society can be directed.

This book, therefore, embraces a social approach to literature and thought, an approach which takes into account the society where writers work and live.

Its attitude is, however, very different from that of the social literature of the 1930's, which was dominated by the political ideology of Marxism. The typical writers of that era found their social mission in the worship of a class and a collective state. But the social theme of the essays which are now presented is the recognition that, beneath all the collective institutions and concepts, individual man is the one fundamental concern of society, and that our social efforts are valid only in so far as they tend to assist man's tendency towards individuation.

The individual and the social are mingled inextricably in the life of man and equally in the work of the writer. His writing is his own product, and arises always from an individual impulse, from an inner apprehension of some truth concerning life. Even writing that does not originate genuinely from within, comes in its own spurious way from the individual character of the writer. We live in society, but as individuals, and society in the last analysis is no more than the sum of our individual actions. Therefore, society can only provide the frustration against which the mind rebels or − and this only in a vicarious manner − the achievement by which it is inspired. The force that is thus canalised and directed by social influences is that of the individual human spirit struggling to express itself.

It is possible, with some ingenuity, to argue that every act of our lives is socially conditioned. Our habits, our speech, our very methods of thought are the products of social intercourse, but they are also the common products of men who remain individual under all the conditioning to which they are subjected by tradition and environment.

We may observe the same social taboos and totems, but our lives and fortunes show an almost endless variety, so that even in the most stultifying of uniform occupations, even in the army or in prison, we contrive to present patterns of living which in their minor qualities show an infinity of variations. We may speak and write in the same tongue, but each of us does so in his own way, and, in spite of all the unifying influence of modern conditions, the convincing and accurate imitation of another writer's style is an extremely difficult task. We may think according to the same general laws, but the results of our thought show such a rebellious anarchy of ideas that the dictator can never hope permanently to

P R E F A C E

suppress the insurgence of intellect and imagination against any long-sustained attempt to impose from above a standard pattern of thought.

From this it emerges that to talk of society without recognising that it lives only by the infinity of individual impulses, is even more foolish than to consider man as entirely devoid of social attributes. The duality of individual and society is indeed to be regarded with suspicion, but it is no solution of our problems to accept the loss of the individual in a totalitarian social structure. Society must always be regarded as only a means to enrich the life of the individual. Here we might do well to recall the sound words of William Godwin, a defender of individual freedom who has been too long neglected:

"The wealth, prosperity and glory of the whole are unintelligible chimeras. Set no value on anything but in proportion as you are convinced of its tendency to make individual men happy and virtuous. Benefit by every practicable means man wherever he exists, but be not deceived by the specious idea of affording services to a body of men for which no individual man is the better."

I can think of no maxim that more justly deserves to be kept ever in the mind of the writer who concerns himself with social problems, and I hope that in the essays which follow I shall not be found to have departed materially from the good sense of this conception of the function of society in the lives of men.

I

Introduction to the New Edition

THE *Writer and Politics* was published more than four decades ago,
and the essays it contains were written in the mid-1940s when I was
beginning to establish a modest name in the English literary world;
in 1949, a year after it was published, I became lost to that world
by moving to Canada. It is many years since I last read the book,
and now, looking at it almost half a century after its appearance, I
am perhaps more surprised by the continuities in my ways of
writing and thinking that it reveals than by the changes. Still, a
collection of a young man's essays in some ways resembles those
volumes of last works and fragments that are often published after a
writer's death, for both contain much that is tentative — ideas in
the young man's book that wait for complete development, and
sketches in the old man's book that there was no time to develop;
what was to become, and what might have been.

Of course I see in *The Writer and Politics* what one would
naturally expect, a young man exploring the possibilities of the essay
in its historical and literary forms and in the process developing a
critical insight and a sense of form. It seems to me that already in
this book, written in my early thirties, I am starting to speak in my
own voice, and I am surprised to detect so little of the stylistic
influence of writers who did influence my thoughts greatly at this
period, particularly Herbert Read and Albert Camus and George
Orwell, who is the subject of one of these essays.

[I]

Over the years since then my style has indeed changed, become less cautious and more colloquial, and I have broadened my fields of interest enormously, living in Canada and travelling out into the great world of Asia and South America, of Europe and the scattered ocean realms of the South Pacific, a process that began once I had withdrawn from close immersion in the English literary world in 1949.

Still, in many ways my directions of interest have remained surprisingly constant. Three of the essays — those on Proudhon and Kropotkin and George Orwell — were the sketches out of which I would write books: *Pierre-Joseph Proudhon, The Anarchist Prince* and *The Crystal Spirit*. Two of these books — those on Proudhon and Kropotkin — would be pioneer works on their subjects in the English language. The essay on George Orwell was the first substantial piece ever written on him. The same was the case with the essay on Greene, whom the literati were only beginning to take seriously in the 1940s.

Of the other critical and appreciative studies, that on Kafka and Rex Warner strikes me as shallow because the parts of the equation — Kafka and Warner — were really too far apart in both literary quality and imaginative complexity to make a really valid comparison. The pieces on Ignazio Silone and Arthur Koestler, which strike me as more substantial, fit into a general pattern that recurs throughout *The Writer and Politics:* the free left as distinct from the authoritarian left. Both Silone and Koestler in recent years have lost much of the allure they held in the 1940s. In the case of Koestler I think this is because he was a writer of scanty imaginative power but some historical sense who wrote a few *romans à thèse,* such as *Darkness at Noon* and *Arrival and Departure,* that were timely but soon outlived their topical relevance. Silone, I think, was more imaginative, and more interesting in his ability in novels like *Fontamara, Bread and Wine* and *The Seed Beneath the Snow,* to relate his political ruminations to a

[2]

nostalgically remembered and clearly Italian rural society in the
Abruzzi. When I recently re-read his novels, I found them a little
naive in their moralising. Still, they seemed like extremely appealing
novels of southern Italy under the Fascist regime, and so thought
my Aburzzi-born Italian tailor in Vancouver.

Having re-read all these critical essays, I now feel that the one
on Graham Greene was perhaps the best. I was confronting a mind,
and a realm of experience, much farther removed from my own
than those of Orwell and Koestler, and I am surprised now at the
understanding I showed of the relationship between Greene's
Catholicism and the imaginative world of his fiction. Now I wonder
why I did not write a book on him as well as on Orwell.

One group of essays in *The Writer and Politics* plunges back with
a pleasant atavism into my life long before I began to think of
becoming a writer. These are the three piously reminiscent pieces at
the end of the book; now I would put them at the beginning.

All three dip back into memory, and in this sense they
collectively aniticipate my first volume of autobiography, *Letter to
the Past*. They are connected with my remote childhood, when my
English years were divided between the school holidays in
Shropshire, when at my grandparents' insistence I attended a rather
severe Anglican Low Church, and the rest of the year in
Buckinnghamshire, when each Sunday I went to a ritualistic High
Church. I was dedicated doctrinally to neither, for I was convinced
I had received a Satanic revelation in childhood and was probably
committed to the Devil, but I liked the Anglo-Catholic liturgy and
the ritualistic anthems as much as the thundering evangelical hymns,
and to this day — near Buddhist that I now am — I often sing
those grand old tunes again when I am travelling on a long car
journey. Dolled up with a bit of sociological chatter, my essay on
"The English Hymn" really celebrated those exalted but
unconvinced days. There is, incidentally, a small error in the essay,
picked up by George Orwell, himself a great hymn-lover; his

correction appears in a letter to me reproduced in Volume IV of his *Collected Essays, Journalism and Letters.*

"The Peroxide Saint" relates to the same period, and to the stream of missionaries who would visit my grandfather's house in Shropshire, often staying to Sunday dinner after a mid-day sermon. Most I found dreary, but a few had a gift of describing exotic lands, and it was out of these occasional accounts and of the missionary narratives on my grandparents' bookshelves — the only books I was allowed to read on Sunday apart from the Bible and *Pilgrim's Progress* — that I formed my first image of some of the regions, like south India and the South Seas that I would later visit. There seemed a strange fatality in the 1970s about my arriving at Tanna in the New Hebrides which had been the stamping ground of John G. Patom, the formidable and highly self-dramatising Scottish missionary who had imposed Presbyterian morality — and clothing — on this island of "naked cannibals" in the mid-Victorian age, and whose sensational memoirs formed my favourite summer Sunday reading. He was "the Peroxide Saint" of my essay's title because he actually used the chemical to give his hair and beard a blond aura, and so set a fashion that persists among the native people of Tanna to this day. But by the time I arrived in the 1970s, peroxide was perhaps the only remnant of Paton's triumph that remained, for his Presbyterian mission, after a century of domination, had collapsed under the onslaught of native credulity in the powerful cargo cult called Jon Frum. Remembering those missionaries of my boyhood, I could not help but rejoice.

"Henry Bates on the Amazon" represents another habitat of my childhood imagination that has been changed in reality even more utterly than Paton's Tanna, and even more irrevocably. Bates went in the 1840s with Alfred Russell Wallace to collect natural history specimens on the high Amazons; after parting with Wallace, he stayed there almost twenty years. He wrote of his experience in a remarkable travel book, *The Naturalist on the River Amazons,* which evokes the great South American rain forests as they were even before the earliest of their exploiters and transformers, the rubber gatherers, had arrived in any numbers. Not only did Bates describe the teeming variety of animal and plant life in the Amazonian forest, he also protrayed an extraordinary free river life that, even now, when I read of it again, sounds as near natural anarchism as man had ever reached. Such a life was possible only in a situation of natural abundance which the population was never large enough to challenge completely. For me, in childhood and long afterwards, Batcs on the Amazons projected an idyllic, almost utopian existence, and with the unhistoric mind of a child I believed it still existed there, and that I had only to go one day to Bates's longtime base on Ega on the upper river to find it unchanged and live there happily ever after.

I can only bless the series of apparently accidental inverventions that have always prevented me in later years whenever I planned a visit to the real Amazons, changed and ravaged as they are. I am glad to have retained in my mind an image of that idyllic life, even if it no longer exists, because it gives me a sense of human possibilities. I shared my interest in Bates with some of my contemporaries, for John Middletoj Murray, who pulbished my piece originally in *The Adelphi,* admired him greatly, and Orwell wrote, when he read my essay: "All those nineteenth century books about S. America have a wonderful Arcadian atmosphere."

If these final essays count in the context of my general *oeuvre* as autobiographical exercises, recalling childhood past, two of the earlier essays relate much more closely to my state of mind when I was writing *The Writer and Politics,* and in their own way echo forward strongly to my present state of mind. They are the opening essay on "The Writer and Politics," and the piece, somewhat later in the book, on Alexander Herzen. They reflect my personal concerns and parallel the concerns of the generation of English writers who emerged at the end of the 1930s and began to be recognized in the 1940s. In some ways we were very close to our immediate predecessors in the 1930s, since we too tended to move on the left. What made us different from that brief generation was that the Moscow trials of the mid-1930s, and the attempt by the Stalinists to gain control by ruthless methods of the Loyalist forces in the Spanish Civil War, had disillusioned us with the orthodox Communism that beguiled our predecessors. Indeed, by this time the predecessors, like Auden and Spender, had mostly shaken themselves free of their late obsession, and it was only a few eccentrics like Randall Swingler and Jack Lindsay who still adhered to the old party lines.

Of course even in the 1930s some writers had already been led by experience to reject fashionable Communism, as Orwell did through the accident of getting into a dissident Marxist militia in Spain which the Communists set out to eliminate. Younger writers adopted a variety of left-of-centre courses that took them away from orthodix Stalinism, which in any case became involved in the war on the same side of the western allies, when all the old Leninist talk about revolutionary anti-militarism and defeatism vanished overnight. Some of us veered to the Trotskyists; others adhered to the Independent Labour Party, the revolutionary breakaway from the Labour Party; yet others were militant pacifists seeking to create intentional communities, as Middleton Murry put it, "in the interstices of the totalitarian order," for by then we had decided that all war-directed societies were indeed equally totalitarian; and some, like me, moved from militant pacifism and the intentional communes to involvement in the small anarchist movement which in those days consisted of rapidly ageing veterans from Kropotkin's time, a few working class syndicalists, mostly in Glasgow, some young and largely ex-pacifist militants, and a few writers and painters like Herbert Read, Alex Comfort, Jankel Adler, Augustus John and me.

But there was a distinct difference between our political loyalties and those that the Communists had demanded of their intellectual supporters, and which some of the other leftist groups expected even if they could not enforce them. When I did work with militant anarchist groups I found that there was a perceptible moral pressure towards doctrinal conformity; I was even told that an intellectual was in some ill-defined way less than a militant and that I would be best employed fabricating simplistic messages for the workers as Kropotkin was held to have done.

It was this situation that led me, as I drew farther away from the organized groups, to write "The Writer and Politics" to define the position of the writer as anarchistic because of the nature of his occupation, but for that very reason as independent of party imperatives. By a coincidence that was not entirely accidental, because we were seeing a great deal of each other then, Orwell wrote a very similar essay entitled, "Writers and Leviathan" which appeared in 1948, round about the time my book was published. In his piece he rejected the demands of political leaders to dictate to writers what they might say, but he did not deny the writer's responsibility to write politically. Indeed, he has often said that no writing could be unpolitical, but the direction of its politics must come from the writer's own perceptions, and even when moved by sympathy with a particular movement, he must consider himself not as a soldier in the ranks, where the mass would submerge him, but as a *fran-tireur,* a guerilla operating on the verges of the main army.

All this betokened a rejection on our parts of deep involvement in political parties or similar movements. We became free-wheeling radicals, and our encounters with activists, even when friendship was involved, tended to become uncomfortable. I know that Julian Symons, who then considered himself a Trotskyist, had difficulties with the "official" Trotskyists who suspected him as an intellecutal, and I, to a lesser degree, had them with the anarchists; they were not improved when I became disillusioned with the old-style revolutionary line and began to develop my own ideas of a new society growing up through the development of mutual aid tendencies still surviving in the old society.

It was this sense of being faithful to the old leftist ideals, yet disagreeing on means with those who claimed to be the spokesmen of such ideas, that led me to the admiration for Herzen that I think glows through my essay on him, which I now regard as my favourite piece in *The Writer and Politics.* Herzen, of course, was a marvellous writer, whose *My Past and Thoughts* remains the best of all Russian autobiographies. But in the context of our times he was especially interesing as a kind of ancestor in disillusion, who kept his faith with the cause he believed in,who worked through his own writings and the expatriate journals he published to weaken the mental grip of autocracy in his country, and yet who came, as so many of us would do ninety years or so later, to distrust political parties and political leaders. I still see in Herzen a predecessor in the balancing of political attachment and detachment. And I still hold, after forty more years of experience as a free-running radical, to what I have said in "The Writer and Politics" about the writer's role. I have let those insights guide me as I do to this day, fighting on where I can for freedom and justice, choosing my own ground and my own means and rejecting orders and any organization but that of my own mind. How can I speak for the freedom of others without asserting and sustaining my own first of all?

November, 1990

II

The Writer and Politics

ONE of the problems which afflict the writer most persistently in
our present society is his relationship to the structure of that society,
and, in particular, his relationship to movements which aim at
changing such a social structure in order to eliminate some of the
evils it inflicts on humanity. To put the problem in another way,
most writers are deeply concerned with politics, and are equally
aware of the difficulty of reconciling political methods and actions
with the values which govern, or should govern, their approach
towards their vocation in writing. Even the writer who pretends
to eschew political thinking and to devote himself to his art exclu-
sively, is motivated in his actions by the importance which politics
holds in the world where he works. The conscious avoidance of
becoming implicated shows that in such a writer's mind politics
has a place, even if an unpleasant one. The ivory tower is as much
a symptom of inescapable social problems as the air raid shelter is of
the inescapable evils of war.

   This century is distinguished from its predecessors not merely in
the fact that it is a time of ineluctable social disturbance, affecting
the life of literally every individual, but also in the fact that, while
the writer cannot avoid developing some kind of social consciousness, either positive or negative, he finds his values as an artist, as
an intellectual, so strongly opposed to those of society in general
that it is almost impossible for him to engage in politics in any

ordinary sense of the term. (By politics in this instance I mean the kind of activities which are carried on by political parties and which are coloured by the methods and ideologies of those parties, whether of the left or the right.)

In the nineteenth century it was still possible for the writer to avoid a strong social conscience, provided he had an easy income and little contact with the working class. But even then it was becoming difficult for a writer who had become socially aware to reconcile political action with the standards and values he wished to observe in the practice of his vocation. William Morris, for instance, could not work on amicable terms for any length of time with the various sections of the embryo labour movement with whom he associated, precisely because his consciousness of values and his social vision were irreconcilable with the political attitudes and tactics of his associates.

This was in contrast with the situation of writers in the eighteenth and even in the early years of the nineteenth century. Dean Swift could act as a political pamphleteer without finding anything inconsistent between his writings on social matters and his literary work. Indeed, it is in Swift's polemical writings that we find some of his finest work from a literary point of view. Similarly at the time of the French Revolution it was possible for a *litterateur* like Godwin to play a leading rôle in social activity by writing a treatise on Political Justice. At the same period Hazlitt could write political commentary and literary essays without realising any deep incompatibility between these two activities. To us who read them to-day the works of Godwin and Hazlitt appear as unified bodies of writing. That is to say, there is no fundamental dichotomy evident in the work or outlook of these men. The values which Hazlitt observed in writing on the politics of his day belonged to the same unity as those in his superb essays in Shakespearean criticism. Between Hazlitt the politician and Hazlitt the literary essayist there appeared no mental hiatus like that which divided the Spender

[11]

of *Forward from Liberalism* from the Spender of *The Still Centre*. For Hazlitt there was never any problem of making a choice between politics and literature, like that which has faced many contemporary writers. He saw the two forms of writing merely as differing expressions of the same attitude towards the world.

In contrast with the career of Hazlitt which, however unhappy, was complicated by no doubt as to what was the right way for him to use his abilities, let us portray briefly the miserable record of contemporary British writers in their attempts at social activity.

Many of our poets and novelists, particularly in the generations that immediately preceded the war, were involved in sincere and serious attempts to use their powers of thought and writing in order to assist the establishment of social justice. They had their embroilments in politics, ran uneasily in the party packs, and endeavoured to sink their individualities in the collective baying of slogans for such futilities as the Popular Front. Very soon, however, they realised their incompatibility with their party associates and left the razor games of politics for those with thicker skins.

Bred in a liberal tradition of honesty and fair-play—and one cannot deny the negative virtues of the conscientious liberal— they were astonished and hurt to discover the palpable dishonesty and bad faith of "left wing" politics. Imbued with the intellectual's respect for independence of thought and speech, they resented the scarcely hidden forces which tried to keep them to the "party lines". Having at least some concern for truth as a social and individual virtue, they regarded with distaste the cynical cult of falsehood and distortion displayed by the party bosses and propagandists. Moreover, their troubles came not from one side only. Attacked by their fellow writers for deserting the detachment which had been regarded for so long as incumbent on the intellectual, they were at the same time attacked by their political associates because they could not bring themselves to adhere unquestioningly to a body of dogma with which they did not wholly agree.

An inevitable disillusionment commenced. The failure of the Popular Front, the betrayal of the Spanish Revolution, the vacillations and dishonesties of the Communist Party, as well as the personal discomfort of their own effort to balance on the fence between individual detachment and collective faith in dogma, led cumulatively to a state of disgust with left-wing politics. A few minor figures, for personal or profitable reasons, relinquished their literary pretensions and toed the line as party propagandists. These, however, were unimportant, and the Communists became, to all intents and purposes, detached from the intellectual world of Britain.

The revulsion of feeling against the Communists became a revulsion against political parties in general. To the innocent eye of the 1930's the Communists had, indeed, seemed the white hope of the social struggle. They formed the only really vocal group of any size that showed signs of vitality and talked what sounded like a revolutionary language. Furthermore, their opportunities for class betrayal had so far been small in this country, and the true record of their activities in Russia and other countries was yet known to few people, even among writers. The remaining parties had nothing to attract the intelligent, and when the doubts of the intellectuals made them withdraw their adhesion from the Communists, they saw no other political movement that seemed to deserve their attention. Indeed, many of them were too deeply disillusioned to search any further.

Returning to the point of departure, the intellectuals remained, as indeed they could hardly avoid remaining in such a society, deeply concerned with the social problem and, since their unfortunate experiences with political organisations, with the relationship of the individual writer to the achievement of social change. In a negative way, their attitude is perhaps less muddled than it was ten years ago. They have repudiated political methods, and have realised once again the need for individual freedom as the basic factor in social organisation. On the other hand, they have done little in a positive direction. Incapable of initiating any united actions or of manifesting any strong individual attitude, they have adhered vaguely to minor currents of thought which have little or no contact with the rest of the population and whose lack of a positive purpose makes them valueless as a means to social change or regeneration.

The experiences of English writers in their travels with politicians were, of course, largely shaped by circumstances peculiar to this country. English writers have little experience of revolutionary ideas and methods and show, usually, an undeveloped attitude towards politics. This is the result of a century or more during which a clever governmental system has maintained a political equilibrium unknown elsewhere in Europe. Only recently has the social struggle here gained the significance which it has held in France since 1789 and in the other continental countries for many decades. That a significantly large section of English writers should realise the complete rottenness of the present social system is something which happened only once before, for a comparatively brief period at the end of the eighteenth century. It is therefore not surprising that the writers of the thirties should have shown the political inexperience which led them as innocents into the hands of the party leaders. This lack of a developed social sense will also help to explain the fact that, after their disillusionment, few of them attempted to discover alternative methods to achieve the social change they still admitted to be necessary.

Nevertheless, their experience was one which, in general, writers of all countries have undergone in their relationship with political movements during recent years.

Mayakovsky and Yessenin, two of the greatest of recent Russian poets, supported the October Revolution with violent enthusiasm. They threw themselves unreservedly into the struggle and gave the Bolsheviks their complete support. But when the " revolution " was accomplished, when the party was seated in power, they saw a reality that mocked their vision of a better society. They found themselves in a land where petty bureaucrats harried them eternally and a party line was set as a measure for their poetic inspiration. Their faith was destroyed so completely that they were driven, Yessenin first, Mayakovsky a few months afterwards, to the actual physical self-destruction of suicide.

Elsewhere in Europe and America sincere and intelligent writers were driven, if not to physical suicide, at least to a realisation of the impossibility of their achieving anything by working with the existing political parties. Men like Gide and Silone had to dissociate themselves from the parties and policies they had supported in the past. They found that the sectarian structures of these movements made it impossible for any man to express independent thought while remaining within them. They found also that the parties which pretended to be revolutionary, in fact worked in such a way that their efforts could not possibly produce a revolutionary society. They realised the corruption implicit in power politics, and rejected it. But they did not cease to be sincere revolutionaries, or to work for a social change that would bring freedom and justice to mankind. The books which Silone wrote after he left the Italian Communist Party are among the greatest contributions any writer has made towards the struggle for freedom.

Politicians and professional " revolutionaries " have been quick to make use of the secession of writers from party groups in order to discredit them. In party circles we are always told that the intellectuals are corrupted by their bourgeois environment. They are supposed to be interested only in their careers, and to have no real concern for the future of the workers. They are held to be out of touch with reality (only Marxists, of course, can be realistic). They are all reactionary at heart, tainted with individualism and mysticism. They are the kind of people who can be expected to co-operate with " Fascism ". And, lastly, they are really of no use to the workers or to the revolutionary movement, and their departure is to be regarded with joy. This kind of calumny, combined with the difficulty with which state-educated workers follow the theorisings of many writers, has been very effective in dividing the intelligentsia from those workers who also are desirous of a radical social change. The very word " Intellectual " has become a term by which left-wing politicians try to discredit each other and any common rival. The effect of this policy has been to strengthen the hold of leaders over parties and political groups, because any person who takes an independent stand and refuses to follow the party line can be discredited as an "intellectual", who is out for his own ends and has nothing in common with the workers. I have actually seen this method at work in many left-wing movements. The demagogic use of such a line of argument is obvious. It serves effectively to keep the rank and file segregated from any individual writer who may think on original lines, and so it preserves the party dogma—and, incidentally, its dogmatists—from the effects of free criticism.

The facts of the situation, however, seem to be contrary to the arguments of the politicians. It is the object of this article to show that the reason why writers or intellectuals [1] cannot co-operate with political groups lies in faults inherent in the nature of party organisations and not in that of the writer *per se*.

In making this statement I do not mean that every writer is perfect. Unfortunately there is a minority of whom the current accusations against intellectuals are true. Some writers are blinded by money, or by their bourgeois environments. Some are interested in their careers to the exclusion of any consideration for the welfare of humanity. Some build for themselves private worlds of unreality

[1] By the terms " writers " and " intellectuals " I mean those men who write freely and according to their conception of the truth. I do not mean the hack journalists who willingly submit their work to the dictates of authority or money. Nor do I mean those pseudo-intellectuals who are concerned with self-advancement or personal fame, and whose mimicry and charlatanry help to discredit all intellectuals in the eyes of ordinary people.

in which they turn away from the cruelties of the public world. A very few, like Henri de Montherlant and Drieu de la Rochelle, have been led by some psychological perversity to support Fascist or reactionary politicians.

But, in spite of this, the number of writers—as distinct from hack journalists—who have deliberately betrayed the oppressed or acted in a socially reactionary manner is extremely small. Many have chosen to dissociate themselves completely from politics and to write according to their artistic impulses. Many more have become so disheartened with their political experiences that they have given up social activity in despair. But only the meanest sophistry could class such attitudes as betrayals, and those writers who have acted deliberately against the interests of the working class or against a genuine revolutionary ideal are few indeed in comparison with the great legion of men of working-class origin who, as party and trade union leaders, have been corrupted by privilege and have oppressed and attacked the workers who brought them to power. On the other hand, many writers have sacrificed their careers and their lives to work for social justice, and their danger to tyranny is shown by the number of intellectuals who have been martyred for their criticism of authority.

The really independent writer, by the very exercise of his function, represents a revolutionary force. I do not here refer specifically to the part taken by writers in preparing an indictment of modern society on which the revolutionaries have built their case. This is indeed important if one considers the value of the social criticism of men like Marx, Godwin and Kropotkin, or even of Defoe, Swift and their like. But I consider that the man who is ready to apply to any subject on which he writes a standard of values based on a sincere conception of the truth is bound to act in his writing against injustice and falsehood, even if he does not write for the specific purpose of expediting social change. The novelist who shows the hollowness of middle-class life, the poet who displays without comment the spiritual agonies of war, as well as the painter who shows on his canvas a symbol of the schizoid futility of a modern city, are all playing their part in subverting a corrupt society. To display the truth, even a limited aspect of the truth, is to elevate a criterion against which falsehood must be judged and condemned. In this way, any honest artist is an agitator, an anarchist, an incendiary. By expressing an independent standard of values he attacks the principle of authority ; by portraying the truth according to his own vision he attacks the factual manifestations of authority. This is why governments try to discourage the independent artist who refuses to become a hack, writing or composing or painting according to safe conventions in the interests of banal propaganda. In Russia the imposition of " Social Realism ", in Germany the campaign against " Degenerate Art ", were really attacks on the independent artist because the truths he told were subversive to authority. In such societies the writer or painter who in some way manages to express himself fearlessly becomes as much an agent of revolution as the most devoted revolutionary militant.

And here, I think, lies the real reason for the difficulty which most writers experience in associating themselves with political movements. The conscientious writer, the sincere artist, the true intellectual, are all capable of acting in a revolutionary manner so long as they are allowed to think and speak without compulsion or restriction. This applies as much to specifically social writing or painting as it does to the anarchic and subversive elements in such of their work as might be termed " pure art " or " detached thought ". As long as they work according to an internally valid creed, their work will have real significance and will contribute spontaneously to the destruction of falsehood. When, however, they are subordinated or themselves attempt to subordinate their work to an external system, they become afflicted with the schizoid frustration which we have noticed as characteristic of the attitude of the modern intellectual when confronted by social issues. The unity which should characterise a writer's work is replaced by a duality comprised of, on one side, the values which he has realised are valid within himself, and, on the other, the values of an external code to which he is attempting to mould his work. In so far as he subordinates the internal to the external values, his work loses significance. Instead of being subversive, he becomes subservient, an intellectual slave instead of a liberator of the mind.

If we return to our historical survey, we shall see this all the more clearly. It was with the rise of disciplined revolutionary parties at the time of the French Revolution that the split between the intellectual and political groups became evident. The Jacobins aimed at an authoritarian state under a party dictatorship imposing uniformity of opinion, and their political associations tended to take on the same authoritarian and dogmatic character.

Previously, the structure of political parties and groups had been sufficiently lax to admit a wide freedom of opinion. Doctor Johnson could claim to be a Tory and at the same time attack both patriotism and slavery. But the Jacobin societies tended increasingly towards set codes of opinion from which a departure became heretical. Godwin, realising this trend, kept aloof from the more highly organised political groups. He worked for social change as an individual co-operating with other individuals. In *Political Justice* he makes a clear statement of his objections to political associations, as distinct from small free groups of individuals :

" If once the unambitious and candid circles of enquiring men be swallowed up in the insatiate gulf of noisy assemblies, the opportunity of improvement is instantly annihilated. The happy varieties of sentiment which so eminently contribute to intellectual acuteness are lost. Activity of thought is shackled by the fear that our associates should disclaim us. A fallacious uniformity of opinion is produced which no man espouses from conviction, but which carries all men along with a resistless tide. Clubs, in the old English sense —that is, the periodical meetings of small and independent circles

—may be admitted to fall within the line of these principles. But they cease to be admissible when united with the tremendous articles of confederacy and committees of correspondence. Human beings should meet together not to enforce, but to enquire. Truth disclaims the alliance of marshalled numbers."

Godwin admitted that it might be necessary to associate in numbers at times of emergency and for the attainment of specific purposes. On critical occasions he himself willingly co-operated with other radicals, as when he played a leading part in thwarting the government during the State Trials of the members of the London Corresponding Society. But he held that such alliances should be temporary and should not be allowed to harden into associations with permanent codes determining the ideological beliefs which each of their members should hold.

Godwin's premonitions were well founded. The members of the political societies, who borrowed ideas from Godwin when it suited them, abused him for his condemnation of permanent associations, and during the political development of the nineteenth century their ideas gained the ascendancy, with results fatal to the social welfare of Europe.

It was with the rise of the Blanquist conspiratorial societies and, later, the organised Marxist parties, that political activity assumed the character it maintains to-day. These parties aimed at becoming highly disciplined groups which would attain control of society either by forceful *coup d'état* or by sheer weight of numbers in electoral campaigns. In order to achieve this they deemed it necessary to have not only an agreed common objective, but also a uniform means of attaining it. The members of the party were expected to think, believe and act alike. The founders and leaders imposed their ideas on the followers, and later these ideas crystallised into dogmatic systems which bound the thought of party adherents. These political systems of thought became all-pervasive, so that if a man joined a party he was expected automatically to believe the same as his fellows on a vast number of points. At best, every individual had to mould his ideas to those of the majority. At worst he had to accept the *ukase* of some central committee, which in its turn might be dominated by an individual politician whose ideas it voted into party decrees.

The effects of such conditions on the integrity of political life and of the individuals involved therein were disastrous. A man who deliberately accepts the intellectual domination of another soon loses any real sense of the truth. So does the man who imposes on others his own ideas. Falsehood in social life, cynically administered by the political leaders and blindly accepted by their dupes, was the inevitable result of such a situation.

The technique of propaganda adopted by the new parties and the need to reach some lowest common denominator by which their ideas could be administered to a great number of the population led to a further weakening of the truth by the presentation of a world of black and white generalisations, and by the replacement of fact and reasoned argument by the myth, the slogan and the symbol. Political parties, like churches, began to play mostly on the emotions, to use symbols in order to induce people to accept their political dogmas in the same way as the churches used symbols to bring about the adoption of their theological dogmas. The use of symbol and myth by left-wing political groups is a subject which is worth a detailed study, but this would lead too far from the main trend of argument for me to pursue at present. It is sufficient to say that the attempt to attain uniformity of thought, and the methods of propaganda used by politicians, have led to an acceptance of generalisations which tolerates falsehood, and an intellectual sectarianism intolerant to any form of thought which does not fit into the rigid pattern of dogmatic orthodoxy.

To this tendency towards falsehood we must add the corruption of moral attitude which results from the hierarchical constitution of most political groups. Such a form of organisation gives opportunities of power, internally when the party is out of place, externally if it governs. This power, and the privileges attendant on it, make it impossible for even the most sincere of political leaders to remain completely honest in his actions. When in opposition to the government he is concerned not so much with the statement of the truth as with the tactics of gaining power. To this end all his actions become subordinate. The welfare of humanity, to which he pays lip-service, is shelved until the struggle for power is ended. His own authority within the party is justified on the ground that only by keeping its disciplined structure can the party hope to gain the position where its ideals of helping humanity can be fulfilled. When, however, the leader has gained power, his ideals are never realised. Power and privilege are pleasant and readily corrupting to those who have sought them for long. Moreover, he who holds them is subject to rivalry and must fight to retain his position. He struggles to keep power, and in struggling, increases his own preoccupation with it. It becomes the major end. The excuse for his actions is always that he must preserve from attack the ideals and the freedom for which he fought. But in reality these are never achieved, while tyranny and falsehood grow up in their name.

This is a rake's progress followed by all political leaders. Their success in gaining and keeping power depends not on their honesty of purpose but on their faculties of fraud and cruelty. In politics the keenest liar and the most ruthless fighter will always defeat the man whose actions are inspired by any such values as truth, justice or freedom. Consequently, political movements become dominated by men whose actions are governed rather by expediency than by principles. A leader is chosen for his ability to conduct political manœuvres, not for his moral rectitude, and in the discussions of parties, tactics is always more esteemed than morality.

Thus the values on which a free and harmonious society can be built, and with which the true intellectual is concerned and governed, are not in general to be found in political groups. The desire to impose uniformity within the group tends to destroy honest and detached judgment. The needs of propaganda encourage an acceptance of something less than the exact truth, which soon approximates to a tolerance of falsehood. The tactical necessities of the struggle for power and the hierarchical internal structure of parties tend towards a disregard of the necessary moralities of human intercourse, towards political fraud and the intolerance and suppression of opposition. All parties are liable to these disorders of falsehood and power-seeking. They are the inevitable consequences of structure and methods, and no body that aims at a wide measure of internal uniformity is free from them. Even anarchist groups, when they have become highly organised movements concerned mainly with the tactics of struggle and the propaganda of generalisations, symbols and slogans, have suffered in some degree from these faults and have become proportionately less valuable as agents of the anarchism they desire.

Some years of concern with the problem of attaining social justice, and of practical work towards that end in conjunction with political and revolutionary groups, have led me reluctantly to accept Godwin's ideas concerning parties and associations. The only kind of group that is not liable to become corrupt or to demand of its members at least some relinquishment of private judgment is the small, loosely connected group of individuals whose object is the ascertainment and publication of social truths. And, indeed, this is the only kind of group that is really necessary for the attainment of freedom. Fundamentally, the problem of the social revolution is the problem of education. When the people have learned the need of freedom, they will act and struggle in spontaneous co-operation without permanent political organisations to lead them. But, on the other hand, they will not learn the need for freedom merely from social teachings.

Here we reach a further limitation of the politician's outlook. Generally, the most sincere social propagandist sees only a very

THE   WRITER   AND   POLITICS

limited facet of truth, the truth as it applies to men living in society.
For this reason, he seeks to find social and external causes and
remedies for every evil. But the universe and man have many more
aspects than those which confront the sociologist. Man is a social
being only by default. His most important qualities are individual,
and society becomes alive only in so far as it contains living individuals. The anarchists have rightly stressed in their teachings, if
not always in their practice, the supreme value of the individual
above society. The corollary of this belief is that man is governed
by laws which are not completely social. Or rather, perhaps, that
the laws and values which govern society must be transmitted
through the individual man and must be part of the system of values
which that man realises from within himself and not from external
society.

The social problem is fundamentally an individual problem for
each man to solve personally. Society will be free only when each
individual knows the meaning of freedom, harmonious only when
each individual realises his own harmony, integrated only when
each individual has become integrated within himself. Anarchism
is only secondarily a social teaching. Its primary object is the
realisation by the individual of his own nature. And for this
reason it may well be that those who are concerned with the study
of man as an individual and who wish to make articulate the values
that arise from within men, are contributing as much towards
eventual anarchy as those whose concern is primarily with man as
a social being. For instance, it is probable that a psychologist
may, by making freedom an internal reality, give at least as much to
the future harmony of mankind as the social theorist who aims at
making freedom an external reality.

From this point of view, we should treat with less impatience
those who claim that social peace will come only from a "change
of heart" within men. But this does not mean that social development should be disregarded. Indeed, the duality of individual and

society is largely unreal, as is any other fragmentation of the wholeness of life. Perhaps the most effective approach to the problem of man's future is one that recognises both the internal values which must govern men's actions and the external world where those actions can be enacted without disturbance of social harmony. But it is obvious that such a comprehensive view cannot be gained within the confines of a dogma-ridden political movement.

Most of the valuable social thinking has always been done outside the limits of social organisations, by individual writers and philosophers. These men were able to do this precisely because they could view society in a detached manner, and apply to it, not the criteria which had been forced upon them through external creeds, but the standards which they had tested by their own thought. The example of these writers, such men as Tolstoy, Godwin, Kropotkin, John Stuart Mill, Gerrard Winstanley, shows that the individual writer can play a more important part in social evolution than the politician or the politician's dupe. The very nature of political groups, as we have seen, makes it impossible for the writer to remain within them and keep his integrity. Either he must secede and do what he can individually, or he must stay and degenerate into the inanity and corruption of the party hack writer.

Nevertheless, the writer who is forced to end his connection with organised political activity need not become socially useless. Indeed, as we have already shown, as an individual he can do more towards the achievement of a true revolution in the basic nature of society. This fairly obvious fact has been ignored by many people because in our age social activity has become so much the usurped province of the political party. It was so little realised, for instance, by the English writers of the 1930's, that once they ceased to associate with political groups, they abandoned their duty to speak as socially articulate persons. They certainly failed to realise that every word they spoke as individuals would be worth ten they had spoken as party members or followers. The limit they have reached in their effort to re-establish the writer's duty to proclaim values is marked by Spender in an essay on " The Creative Arts of Our Time " :

" In a world of transition in which the values and standards of the past are giving way to new standards, even the meanings of words become lost in the uses of self-interested advertisers and rulers who have no object except to put their own interests in the most flattering light.   If words expressing ideas have been used often enough to express debased or even quite contradictory meanings, finally the word loses all meaning, and the idea itself is in danger of becoming lost or treated as meaningless.   The task of the poet is to organise words in such a way that their meaning is clear and unmistakable.   This is betrayed if the poet takes over the propaganda of political parties and uses words in false contexts. For if the meanings are allowed to become lost, the living values become lost or unrelated to the past contexts in which they have expressed something real."

This is excellent, so far as it goes.   The preservation of the truth of words and ideas we have already shown to be necessary for any movement of thought that would affect decisively the social and moral development of humanity.   To dissociate from and expose falsehood in writing and thought is an obvious duty of the sincere writer.   Indeed, it is the only duty which he can be said to incur. And so long as he defends the truth, in no matter how limited a field, he is helping to undermine the fabric of falsehood and injustice.   Hazlitt boasted that he " never wrote a line that licked the dust ".   Had he done nothing more than that, had he never written with positive social purpose, still his fearless expression of the truth wherever he found it would have been a defiance of authority and would have served a revolutionary purpose.

Nevertheless, while the duty of the writer is perhaps limited to adherence to sincerity and truth in whatever he writes, he has the ability, if he desires, to do far more.   For it is the writer who can express most capably those internal values which we have already seen to be the basis of social as well as individual life. It is the writer who can examine the inner heart of man and express the natural laws that govern his life, the universal harmonies upon which freedom and justice can be built. His work need not be philosophical. He can write on the most humble function or relationship in life and yet write with validity, if he observes sincerely his own values. Nor need he necessarily write fine literature or pitch his thought in a high register. If he feels a need to abandon his former standards of literary writing, as Tolstoy did, in order to write humbly and simply to be intelligible for uneducated men and women, then he is quite justified in following such an impulse. What is not justified is to write obediently, according to some external creed or compulsion, as writers do who act to the dictates of political parties.

To-day we are perhaps too sadly aware of the nature of politics to wish to claim, like Shelley, the doubtful honour of being the "unacknowledged legislators of the world". The task of the writer is not to make laws, or to elaborate dogmas. It is the humble task of realising and portraying the truth. It is a task of revelation, and true revelation is no more than making men aware of the natural and harmonious laws that already exist within them.

This function does not mean that the writer steps aside from the crude realities of life. On the contrary, it is these very crude realities which he must elucidate and give meaning. Nor does it in any way confer on him a mantle of "chosen" or "elect". The writer is a man who has been given, perhaps by chance of birth or circumstance, a happy gift of expression by which he can communicate to his fellows what wisdom he has gained. But just as, according to Coomaraswamy, each man is an artist, so each man, potentially at least, is capable of wisdom. The writer can give nothing—he can only awaken what has been given already.

[27]

III

The Functions of the Political Myth

THE political myth might be described as a projection into the past or, more often, the future, of a mirage based on the desires of a section of the people, which is used to induce them to follow some political group or embrace some programme, under the illusion that they will attain what they have seen in the mirage. Political myths, like religious myths, have about as much basis in reality as fantasies in general. They are almost always incapable of achievement, but they can lead men to act in such a way that actual social changes are precipitated through their agency. Occasionally, they have produced good changes, but in general their influence has been to obscure the social vision of those who succumbed to them, and in this way to open the path to political tactics, based on deliberate deception, which aimed at the anti-social acquisition of power.

The political myth began with Plato, whose efforts were comparatively harmless because his ideas were embraced by only a few of his contemporaries. It has been used ever since by all those brilliant political tacticians who have wished to gain a mass following for their own schemes. One of its most recent manifestations was the series of racial myths by which the Nazis led the German people into the misery of war and defeat.

In examining the myth, we should be careful to distinguish it from the falsifications of historical events which might be called political legends. The differences are relatively clear. As an example of the political legend, or a series of political legends, I will quote a small passage of falsified history which appeared in a Belgian Trotskyist paper, in October, 1945. It referred to accusations of fomenting a dock strike, which at that time had been levelled against the Trotskyists by rival legend makers, and it had no doubt emanated originally from some British source.

" The weekly, *Sunday Dispatch,* devotes the whole of its front page to the Trotskyists and describes our comrade Jock Haston, general secretary of the Party, as a ' particularly dangerous man '. This is not at all surprising. Though they have not instigated the strike, the Trotskyists are the only political party which has entirely solidarised itself with the strike and which has done everything in its power to help the strikers morally and materially to defend and spread their movement. Already during the war, in 1944, our comrades were the only people who supported the miners' strike in Wales. At that time comrade Haston had been put into prison but was liberated owing to the pressure of the workers."

Here are three evident falsifications. Firstly, the Dock strike was supported, not only by the Trotskyists, but also by the I.L.P., the Anarchists, a large section of the Labour Party and even some Communists. Secondly, the I.L.P., Anarchists and a section of the Labour Party also supported the South Wales miners. Thirdly, the release of Haston and his fellow Trotskyists in 1944 had nothing whatever to do with pressure from the workers, of whom only a very small minority have shown them any sympathy. In fact, the sentence was quashed by the Court of Appeal on a technical legal point.

I would mention that I have taken this quotation, not because of its source, but because it seemed a good example of political legend. Even worse falsifications of history can be found in the Stalinist accounts of the Russian revolution, from which Trotsky's name has been expunged, or in the Communist accounts of events in Spain, some of the most flagrant of which are quoted in George Orwell's *Homage to Catalonia*.

To show the difference between the political legend and the myth, I will quote the Marxist myth of the end of the capitalist order, which, again, I use more for its brevity and conciseness than for any other reason. It occurs in *Das Kapital*.

" Along with the constantly diminishing number of magnates of capital, who usurp and monopolise all the advantages of this process of transformation, grows the mass of misery, oppression, slavery, degradation, exploitation ; but with this too grows the revolt of the working class, a class always increasing in numbers, and disciplined, united, organised by the very process of capitalist production itself.

" The monopoly of capital becomes a fetter upon the mode of production which has sprung up and flourished along with it and under it. Centralisation of the means of production and socialisation of labour at last reach a point where they become incompatible with their capitalist husk. This husk is burst asunder. The knell of capitalist private property sounds. The expropriators are expropriated."

If we compare these two passages, the specific character of the political myth and its essential difference from the ordinary political legend or historical falsification become clear.

In the first passage we have a known series of facts, which have been taken by individual propagandists and *changed* quite deliberately in order to convey a different impression. This is a case of events *which have actually happened* being described in such a way as to create in the reader's mind the impression of something *which never really happened*. In other words, it is a question of plain lying about the facts in order to make the reader think something to the advantage of the writer. In this process desire plays a large part, but it is the active desire of the writer to impose his ideas, his will, his version of history upon the reader.

The immorality of such a procedure is evident. To justify it we have to admit that lying is permissible in political action. Occasionally there have been hard-boiled politicians who have stated this in writings not intended for the masses. Lenin's statement about truth being a *petit-bourgeois* virtue, and some of the advocacies of deception by Nazi leaders are modern examples. But, in general, the doubtful morality of such deceptions is recognised tacitly by the pretence of each political group that its own version of history is pure, but that all other versions are corrupt. The fact remains that, whether we justify it or not, historical falsification is plain and open lying.

The political myth, on the other hand, presents a much more ambiguous case, as will be seen from the second quotation. This, clearly, is not a lie about anything which has actually happened, for it concerns the future. Here, immediately, we can perceive two important characteristics of the political myth. It is never laid in the present, but almost always in the future, or rarely, in a remote and unhistorical past. Because of this, it cannot be checked by reference to any known or provable facts. Therefore, while it cannot be proved to be true, it equally certainly cannot be proved untrue. From these circumstances it gains two advantages. If it should ever come to be true, its creator, or his heir, can assume the privileges of a successful prophet. And, if it should not come true, it can usually be projected farther into the future—although there are limits beyond which a myth becomes stale and ceases to hold the imagination of the people, and at this point has to be replaced by another myth.

For the main driving force of the myth is the desire of the people. It may be created by some individual to further his own ends, or those of his party, but it will only succeed if it projects the unconscious or partly conscious desire of those who are to be led ; it is kept alive by this popular desire and by the idea that the group who propagate it are in fact providing a means for the attainment of such wishes.

Thus, the Christian myth of the kingdom of God—sometimes on earth, sometimes in heaven—represented the desire of slaves to escape from earthly kingdoms into realms where, in this life or after death, they would be free from oppression and would stand equal among the saints. For centuries the poor were content to wait in their misery, but eventually they became a little weary. The second coming of Christ, the kingdom of God on earth, seemed indefinitely delayed, and there was a depressing lack of travellers' tales about the realm beyond death. It became reasonably evident that, even if the myth were realisable, the Churches, who had used it for centuries to their own advantage, were unlikely to bring it to fulfilment. So men began to abandon Christianity and search for new myths.

One of these was the already-quoted Marxist myth of the downfall of the capitalist order. A circumstance which made Marx's myth less effective than its Christian forerunners was that he was only half-consciously a myth-maker. He was also a sociologist, concerned with the interpretation of actual social events, and he was foolish enough to link his myth too closely with such events. Consequently, when society began to develop in ways he had never anticipated, when fascism supervened and the great middle class began to absorb whole sections of the former proletariat, when the very places where capitalism appeared to have been overthrown turned out to be the least pleasant for the ordinary freedom-loving man, his myth was somewhat discredited. It no longer corresponded with or represented a means to achieve popular desires, and Marx's followers have since been forced either to repeat their story to a vanishing audience, or to create new myths —which among the Stalinists have reverted to more primitive desires, the desire for motherhood and protection instead of the desire for freedom represented in the original Marxist myth.

From this brief discussion we can discern a number of points concerning the myth, which it may be well to itemise.

1. It is not concerned with the present and is laid, usually in the future, but always, even if in the past, at some period outside history.

2. Not being dependent on ascertainable facts, it cannot be proved true or untrue.

3. If not immediately fulfilled, it can be projected farther into the future. Human hope and patience make the successful myth a long-term asset.

4. It is rooted in the desires of the people. It may be contrived by an individual, but unless it represents the satisfaction of some popular yearning, it will never make good.

5. It is subject to decay in time. People will not wait indefinitely for fulfilment, and the discredited myth has to be replaced by something new.

6. The more nearly related to actual circumstances, the less hardy is a political myth. If linked too closely to events, its achievement may be made impossible by the course of history.

The advantages of myths in governing and in gaining and holding power have long been recognised by political writers. Plato decided to base his ideal society on a myth of the Earthborn, and stoutly maintained the right of the ruler to fabricate such a myth— *even if he knew it to be false.* In *The Republic* he says : " Then it pertains to the guardians of the city, and to them alone, to tell falsehoods, to deceive either enemies or citizens for the city's welfare." Later he remarks : " Well, then, can we contrive anything in the way of those necessary lies of which we spoke a little while ago, so that by means of one noble falsehood we may convince, preferably the rulers themselves, but in any case the rest of the citizens?" He then goes on to describe the myth of the Earthborn.

Plato's myth failed because it did not correspond with the desires of his contemporaries. He would perhaps have been a more successful politician if he had adapted his myths to the mental currents of his age instead of merely interpreting his own fantasies of an ideal past.

Between Plato and the modern world lies the great revolution of Christianity, which gave a new dynamic to European thought by orientating men's ideas away from the Golden Age in the past to the Kingdom of Heaven in the future. The myth now represented, not a nostalgic wish to rebuild a past which had never existed, but a forward-looking desire for a future which, because it was a future, might fulfil the most extravagant desires. For centuries the great myths of Christianity dominated the whole of society, and even so practised a politician as Dante saw his ideals in terms of Christian mythology.

It was not, however, until the Renaissance that another thinker came forward with the same magnificent cynicism as Plato to observe the value of myths in the governing of men. This was Nicolo Machiavelli, whose almost disarming candour detected and extolled the uses of religion as an aid to political power. "Those Princes and Commonwealths," he declares, "who would keep their governments entire and incorrupt, are above all things to have a care of Religion and its Ceremonies, and preserve them in due veneration . . ."

Following Machiavelli, many of those theorists for whom social action is concerned mainly with the seizure of power have advocated in some manner the use of the myth. During the period of the German romantic philosophers there occurred a deliberate and wholesale creation of myths, racial and nationalistic myths, myths of the state and the people, by such writers as Hegel, Fichte and Schelling. Of this school, Schopenhauer, a philosopher who was not led and did not lead others into the mists of mythological invention, remarked : " . . . these so-called philosophers do not attempt to teach, but to bewitch the reader."

Hegel and his fellows did not attempt to portray any ascertainable reality, but presented a number of unprovable concepts which were myths in every true sense. Mr K. R. Popper, in his excellent attack on historicist philosophies, *The Open Society and its Enemies*, shows how Hegel's myth of " Spirit " was transformed into the Nazi myth of " Blood " and the Marxist myth of " Class ", and so became a dynamic element of change in social history. Incidentally, the passages from Hegel given by Mr Popper present such a clear example of the way in which the myth moves on a plane outside all rational discussion, that they are worth quotation at length :

" The Nation State is Spirit in its substantive rationality and immediate actuality ; it is therefore the absolute power on earth. . . . The State is the Spirit of the People itself. The actual State is animated by this spirit, in all its particular affairs, its Wars and its Institutions. . . . The self-consciousness of one particular nation is the vehicle for the development of the collective spirit ; . . . in it, the Spirit of the Time invests its Will. Against this Will, the other national minds have no rights : *that* Nation dominates the World."

If we attempt to analyse these sentences into concrete social terms, they are revealed as empty and meaningless abstractions. Yet the fact remains that such statements make a successful appeal to the desire for identification with a greater whole, for immersion in a victorious collectivity, which is present in many people and is related to their fear of freedom and responsibility. Foolish as they may seem, phrases and myths very similar to those concocted by Hegel played a decisive part in the Nazi assumption of power in Germany and the German campaign of conquest and expansion.

When we pass from Hegel to Marx, we must observe one point concerning the myth—that it need not be consciously fabricated in order to deceive and defraud the people. It is possible for a social thinker to create a theory in which he honestly believes and which has at the same time all those desire-fulfilling qualities which make it a successful political myth. I consider that Marx was one of these almost unconscious myth-makers and that, despite the petty dishonesties in which he sometimes indulged during his polemics with opposing theorists, he quite sincerely believed that his prophesies of the end of capitalism were destined to be fulfilled. He really believed in the bursting of the husk, and the knell of capitalist private property. But a political myth is no more effective for being sincerely believed by its originator. Indeed, it is usually less so, for it is too closely connected with contemporary realities to have that longevity and tenacity which is the characteristic of the successful myth, and which comes from its having the least possible connection with social reality.

This was realised by one of Marx's more unorthodox disciples, Georges Sorel, who became the leading theorist of the political myth. Sorel was an engineer who, in his retirement, became interested in social matters and attached himself to the syndicalist movement which was then arising in France. Sorel affected to despise politicians and intellectuals. Nevertheless, he saw more clearly than any previous social theorist the power of the myth in affecting the social actions of men, and realised its formidable nature as a political weapon. In his book, *Reflections on Violence*, he develops at some length his theory of the political myth, with special application to the general strike, regarded by his fellow syndicalists as a practical method of social struggle, but by Sorel as a potent myth, by which, independently of its achievement, the working classes might be led to action and produce a somewhat mystically conceived social regeneration.

According to Sorel, men engaged in any dynamic social move-ment "always picture their coming action as a battle in which their cause is certain to triumph." Such "groups of images" he calls *myths*, and contends that they cannot be analysed, but " must be taken as a whole, as historical forces, and . . . we should be especially careful not to make any comparison between accomplished fact and the picture people had formed for themselves before action." He then puts his idea of the myth beyond reasoned thought by an admission which is strikingly similar to those of the Nazi and Fascist theorists :

" In employing the term myth, I believed myself that I had made a happy choice, because I thus put myself in a position to refuse any discussion whatever with the people who wish to submit the idea of a general strike to a detailed criticism, and who accumulate objections against its practical possibility."

But, despite his expressed distaste for realistic discussion, Sorel has a number of shrewd observations on the nature of myths which are worth our consideration.

In action, according to Sorel, we create " an imaginary world placed ahead of the present world composed of movements which depend entirely on us." Such artificial constructions generally vanish rapidly from our minds, " but when the masses are deeply moved, it then becomes possible to trace the kind of representation which constitutes a social myth." In other words, the myth is a fantasy which happens to offer fulfilment to the desires of many people. Without the existence of myths, according to Sorel, it is useless to expect any widespread action on the part of the workers. He claims that " Utopian " ideas, based on a discussion of practical realities, have no such motive power as myths.

" A myth cannot be refuted, since it is, at bottom, identical with the convictions of a group, being the expression of these convictions in the language of movement ; and it is, in consequence, unanalysable into parts which could be placed on the plane of historical descriptions."

Later, in his discussion of the specific myth of the general strike, Sorel becomes more explicit in his views on the power of the myth to produce action by the presentation of social issues in a way which will deeply impress the minds of the people :

" Oppositions, instead of being glozed over, must be thrown into sharp relief if we desire to obtain a clear idea of Syndicalist movement ; the groups which are struggling one against the other must be shown as separate and as compact as possible ; in short, the movements of the revolted masses must be represented in such a way that the soul of the revolutionaries may receive a deep and lasting impression.

" These results could not be produced in any very certain manner by the use of ordinary language ; use must be made of a body of images which, *by intuition alone,* and before any considered analyses are made, is capable of evoking as an undivided whole the mass of sentiments which corresponds to the different manifestations of the war undertaken by Socialism against modern society."

From this passage it is again clear that the myth-maker takes his arguments completely out of the realm of reason and objective truth—indeed, that he no longer uses arguments in any real sense, but merely images and generalisations which make an emotional appeal to the irrational elements in the human mind. The lack of any connection with objectivity is made even more clear in later passages, where Sorel denies that there need be any accuracy whatever in the content of the myth. What is important to him is not whether it has any real connection with the future, but its effect on men's actions in the present, which need never achieve or approach what the myth promises. It is sufficient, for Sorel, if the myth makes men eager to act :

" The myth must be judged as a means of acting on the present ; any attempt to discuss how far it can be taken literally as future history is devoid of sense. *It is the myth in its entirety which is alone important ;* its parts are only of interest in so far as they bring out the main idea. No useful purpose is served, therefore, in arguing about the incidents which may occur in the course of a social war,

and about the decisive conflicts which may give victory to the proletariat ; even supposing the revolutionaries to have been wholly and
entirely deluded in setting up this imaginary picture of the general
strike, this picture may yet have been, in the course of the preparation for the Revolution, a great element of strength, if it has
given to the whole body of revolutionary thought a precision and
a rigidity which no other method of thought could have given."

The major weakness of Sorel's position is, of course, that the
myth may be used by any clever demagogue for moving the people
to action, no matter what his actual objectives may be. Nothing is
easier, as has been proved time and again in the history of political
struggle, than to lead a people to a given situation by inducing
them to struggle for a promise of its opposite. Thus almost all
tyrants who have ruled with a mass following have established their
government by inducing the people to struggle for freedom. The
Bolsheviks gained power by using the potent promises of " Land
to the peasants, factories to the workers," and " All Power to the
Soviets". When, by such means, they had induced the Russian
workers to support them, they proceeded to enact the opposite of
their promises, by putting the factories and the land under state
control and by making the Soviets into powerless bodies of yes-men.

Sorel may have been sincere in his revolutionary desires. But it
was the ruling classes, not the workers, who benefited by his revela-
tions concerning the myth, and put them into practice. The Italian
Fascists, in particular, made free use of his ideas in order to persuade
the people into allowing them to take power on promises that would
not be kept. Nor is it likely, in the long run, that any truly revolutionary end will be achieved by the use of the myth.

For, in the last analysis, human life and relationships are not
governed by generalised ideas, by all-embracing promises, but by
the factual details of production and every-day intercourse. It is
on these details that the essential life of the community proceeds,
and that real social advances are made. A change in a method of

production, a new source of power used rationally, is much more likely to lead to increased freedom and well-being than any political myth.

It is true that myths stir the people to action. They lead them forward in emotional surges which have little reasonable in them, but which undoubtedly precipitate certain changes. Yet, because the mood of a people led by a myth is essentially irrational, the social changes that occur are moulded and turned to their own account by men who have contrived to retain their powers of calculation. The people die in the streets for an unrealised myth, but the politicians and parties gain power and privilege by the changes that are brought about.

While the myth remains a potent factor in society, there is little chance of men becoming free from the power of the demagogue who is capable of creating myths or of adapting them to his own ends. It is only when people can see political realities in a rational manner, and can mould their desires for the future according to practical standards, that they will begin to distinguish between really productive social advancement and the kind of action which results from accepting the impulse of certain images and emotional stimuli presented in the shape of a political myth. Then we may hope to see an end to the era of the demagogue, and the beginning of a society of co-operation between equals.

But we must not for a moment suppose that the power of the political myth will be easy to break. The average man is uneducated in the details of social life, and accepts the promise of a myth-maker because he knows no better, and also because it seems to promise fulfilment for his desires. The myth appeals to emotional impulses which are all the stronger in rationally undeveloped people.

The conquest of myths is a work partly for the psychologist and partly for the teacher. The psychologist has still much work to do in studying the action of such irrational appeals among the masses. He and the teacher (with whom we might include the serious social student) can between them decide how his discoveries can be used to counter the appeals of unreason and induce people to accept the reasoned statement of facts. Education in social details and in rational methods of thinking is equally necessary. (Lenin remarked to Clara Zetkin on one occasion that the Bolsheviks owed their success largely to the illiteracy of the peasants.) Lastly, the rejection of the myth should not mean the abandonment of planning for the future. Without provisional planning, there would be little guide to reasonable action. But our plans should be concerned, not with abstractions, but with concrete facts, with people and things, with probabilities which can be proved or amended in accordance with experience. And, above all, we should be careful to avoid the deceptive use of symbols and images.

In such a way, the people could be brought into a direct contact with the working of their own society, and, by participating in the details of social activity, could gain an experience in co-operative action which would provide a much more reliable force towards real social revolution than the most formidable and seductive myth.

IV

Proudhon and his Mutualist Theories

WE live in an age that tends to be dominated by totalitarian and mutually exclusive systems of thought, by dogmas and orthodoxies which contend for our loyalties with a ferocity that destroys the standards of individual responsibility. We are offered political and economic panaceas based, not on human needs, but on abstract systems that attempt to fit all social phenomena to uniform formulæ and to suppress the influence of any heterodox thought. Organised parties dominate the stage of social action ; the individual voice, if it is raised at all, is soon drowned in disciplined condemnation. Yet it is only by keeping our minds open for these individual voices, by hearing them when they speak in our own age and by recovering what they have said in the past, that we can preserve the independence of our minds and so salvage our freedom from the steady movement towards totalitarian forms of organisation and thought in which the world is involved to-day.

One such individual voice in the past was that of Pierre-Joseph Proudhon. Proudhon founded no party, left no organised movement to carry on his work, and established no ideological orthodoxy to struggle for complete domination over the human mind. His friend and disciple, Alexander Herzen, the Russian revolutionary, said of him : " Such men stand much too firmly on their own feet to be dominated by anything or to allow themselves to be caught in any net." Nor did Proudhon try to weave a net for other men.

To an English tourist who once said : " I like your system very much," Proudhon replied angrily, " But I have no system ! " He was right. He was in no way a system builder—if by such a name we understand the founder of a political orthodoxy like Marxism— but a conscientious enquirer into social principles who endeavoured to interpret his discoveries so that they would provide a practicable means of harmonising human activities. He had a distaste for rigid patterns of social life, and instead tried to discover the roots of social morality, to enunciate general principles of life in society, and to show how they could operate in his own age.

Yet, while Proudhon did not attempt to found a political orthodoxy, his influence on social thought, although not obvious, has undoubtedly been greater than that of any nineteenth-century social thinker, with the sole exception of Marx. To-day, when experience leads us to question many of the basic teachings of Marxism, it is to ideas derived from Proudhon that the politically conscious are beginning to return.

Proudhon, unlike the other great rebels and reformers of the nineteenth century, was a man of the people by origin and nature. He came of a Burgundian peasant family, and was born in 1809 in a suburb of Besançon. His parents both worked in a brewery which, together with their home, was destroyed during the siege of Besançon in 1814. The elder Proudhon later became a cooper and afterwards set up as a brewer on a very small scale, but he was never successful in business because, according to his son, he insisted on dealing honestly and charging no more than a just price for his products. Thus, he failed utterly to raise his children above the poverty into which they were born, and this became an example to young Pierre-Joseph of how a corrupt society treated those who tried to live by honest means.

When he was eight, Proudhon was already at work, cleaning the house or tending cattle in the hills above the city. At that early period he had already developed a desire for knowledge, but he received no regular schooling until his twelfth year, when he was sent to the day school in Besançon. He studied under great difficulties, owing to the poverty of his parents ; he frequently had to borrow books from the more prosperous boys, and went to school ill-clad and shod in wooden sabots, which aroused the derision of his class-mates. But he persevered, and supplemented his school work by private studies and reading in the town library.

Meanwhile, the fortunes of his family continued to decline, and one day, when he returned home loaded with prizes for distinctions he had gained at school, there was neither food nor money in the house. It had become obvious that his family could no longer maintain him, and Pierre-Joseph decided that he must begin to earn his living. At nineteen he became apprentice in a printing works, and mastered his trade thoroughly, not only gaining a full knowledge of printing, but also acquiring Latin, Hebrew and a mass of theological knowledge as a result of correcting the proofs of religious books.

He was always proud of his technical proficiency as a manual worker, and regarded with pity those of his fellow intellectuals who had never proved themselves as craftsmen. He began life as a trained craftsman, and he never forgot his allegiance to the class in which he was born and began his long career.

In 1836 he started a printing business, in partnership with some workmates. But he proved no better business man than his father, and, on the suicide of a partner in 1838, the works was closed at a loss.

Already, his experiences had given him an extensive knowledge of the injustices afflicting the poor, and imbued him with a desire to rectify them. But his first literary production, in 1837, was an essay in philology. Largely through this, he was successful in competing for the three-yearly pension of 1,500 francs a year offered by the Besançon Academy for aspirants to a learned career. In his letter of application, Proudhon made a characteristic statement of his desire for the amelioration of the class from which he sprang. " Born and brought up in the working class, belonging to it still, to-day and forever, by feelings, intellect and habits, and, above all, by the community of interests and wishes," he promised to work " by philosophy and science, with all the energy of his will and all the powers of his mind, towards complete emancipation of his brothers and fellows." At the instance of his sponsor, he slightly mitigated the terms of his application, but he adhered to it in his actions from that time onwards.

He went to Paris, where the first product of his study was an undistinguished essay on *The Usefulness of the Celebration of Sunday*. Then, in 1840, he produced the work that contained the first statement of his characteristic doctrines and established him as a social theorist. It was the essay entitled *What is Property ? or an Inquiry into the Principle of Right and of Government*.

This work opened with a statement of the most uncompromising nature :

" If I were asked to answer the following question : *What is slavery ?* and I should answer in one word, *Murder*, my meaning would be understood at once. No extended argument would be required to show that the power to take from a man his thought, his will, his personality, is a power of life and death ; and that to enslave a man is to kill him. Why, then, to this other question : *What is property?* may I not likewise answer, *It is theft*, without the certainty of being misunderstood ; the second proposition being no other than a transformation of the first ? "

Proudhon's contentions regarding property were not so levelling as might appear from this opening. What he condemned unreservedly was the use of property by non-producers in order to live by interest. On the other hand, he regarded property—in the sense of the right of each worker or group of workers over houses, land, workshops, etc. needed for carrying on a productive life— as the necessary basis for the socialist commonwealth he envisaged.

[45]

Property in this very limited form seemed to him a guarantee of independence, and he really sought not its abolition, but its equalisation. Nevertheless, he became regarded as a rabid enemy of all property, and his statement that " Property is theft " was used for or against him by political partisans who did not trouble to find out what he really intended.

His essay brought him to the notice of the government, and the Minister of Justice considered a prosecution. He was dissuaded by an orthodox economist, Blanqui (who seems to have had no connection with the celebrated conspirator of the same name), on the grounds that Proudhon was not an agitator, but a serious student of social questions.

Proudhon followed his first essay with a *Letter to M. Blanqui*, in which he elaborated his theories, and a third memoir, the *Warning to Proprietors*, published in 1842, in which he returned to attack the existing system of ownership with such vigour that a prosecution was initiated against him in Besançon. Proudhon carried himself so well that the jury acquitted him on the charge of sedition, and he walked out of the court a free and notorious man.

During the ensuing years he lived a hard and penurious life as a journalist, a " ghost " writer, and, for some years, the travelling representative of a river transport business—an occupation which bred an enduring prejudice against the railways as the destroyers of older and cheaper means of communication.

He had gained, by his writing and prosecution, a growing reputation in radical circles, and was regarded as a promising, but unorthodox, social theorist. However, he remained aloof from any political group, and as early as 1840 criticised the sentimental Jacobinism of the majority of the radicals, whose romantic visions of 1789 would, he foresaw clearly, end in defeat for the revolution and misery for the workers, as in fact happened in 1848. For this reason, and because of his steadfast opposition to the ideas of a revolutionary dictatorship, he was distrusted by the neo-Jacobins of the Mountain and also by the regimented conspirators who followed Blanqui. Nor was he popular among the orthodox socialists of the time, for he had criticised the community theories of Saint-Simon and Fourier because of their danger to individual freedom of development.

When his *System of Economic Contradictions or the Philosophy of Poverty* appeared in 1846, it was greeted by a fervent attack from a new enemy, Karl Marx, whose *The Poverty of Philosophy* signalled the beginning of that long struggle between Marxists and libertarian socialists which split the Labour movement throughout the nineteenth century. Undoubtedly, Marx's attack had a basis in personal jealousy over Proudhon's better reputation in radical circles as a writer on economics ; but it would be foolish to accept this as the only cause and to ignore the fact that, despite the often exaggerated Hegelianism common to both of them, the ideas of Proudhon and Marx defined a fundamental split between moral and material views of history and society, between the almost religious attitude towards freedom and mutual trust of the anarchist and the unprincipled expediency of the authoritarian politician.

In 1847 Proudhon returned to Paris, where he hoped to start a newspaper to expound the economic revolution which he regarded as the only means of eliminating for ever the evils of a society ridden by privilege and authority. He regarded political revolutionism with great scepticism, and declared of the republican deputies : " They are worth a hundred times less than the conservatives, for they are hypocrites into the bargain."

Nevertheless, during the February Revolution of 1848 he placed his knowledge as a printer at the disposal of the insurrection, and even helped to build the barricades. But he remained pessimistic of the eventual result of this easy political triumph. On the day after the rising he alone had a sufficiently clear head to see that the revolution was chaotic in its lack of any plan of action. " It must be given a direction and already I see it perishing in a flood of speeches." His insight was uncannily accurate, as subsequent events very soon demonstrated.

But the revolution at least brought him the means to express his ideas to the people ; on the third day a group of friends offered to provide him with the means of publishing a newspaper, and he was able to start *The Representative of the People*. He rapidly gained an attentive body of readers for his " mutualist " teaching of a social system based on contract rather than force, and for his independent criticism of the political scene. The circulation of his journal rose to 60,000, and even to 100,000 for particularly sensational issues. The rise of his influence was shown by the fact that in June he was elected to the Assembly at a Paris by-election with 77,000 votes.

But his career in the Assembly permanently disillusioned him with such political institutions. He refused to support any party, and when he put forward his own proposals for the equalisation of property and the abolition of government, the Assembly voted almost unanimously a resolution declaring his proposition to be " an odious attack on the principles of public morals." Proudhon and one other deputy were the only dissentients. His journal was suppressed again and again by the government, but he was equally unpopular with the Mountain, whose authoritarian ideas he criticised. He even fought a duel with the Jacobin journalist, Felix Pyat. In an attempt to initiate the economic revolution, he began to organise a " bank ", by which producers could exchange their products, in the hope of undermining the money system, but, as soon as he had gained sufficient support, he was sentenced to three years' imprisonment for an attack on Louis Napoleon Bonaparte, the newly elected president. He escaped to Belgium, but returned secretly to Paris and was denounced by a police spy.

The conditions of his imprisonment were light. He could write, receive friends daily, edit his newspaper, which was eventually destroyed by the consumption of its funds in a series of enormous fines, and was even allowed to marry. In prison he at last had the leisure to digest his thoughts and prepare some of his more important works. *The Confessions of a Revolutionary* and *The General Idea of the Revolution in the Nineteenth Century*, which more than any other book gives a complete picture of his social and economic ideas, were compiled during his stay in prison and published in 1849 and 1851 respectively.

His imprisonment ended in 1852. He now found it difficult, under the Bonapartist dictatorship, either to earn a living or to maintain his attacks on existing society. The press was closed to him, and the government steadily refused to allow him to publish a review of his own. A pamphlet entitled *The Social Revolution Demonstrated by the Coup d'Etat* was regarded as sufficiently dangerous for the police to forbid Proudhon to write any further political works.

In order to earn money, he compiled *The Manual of the Stock Exchange Speculator*, which discussed the merits of the various companies quoted in the Paris Bourse. Into this curious volume he contrived to insert occasional fragments of his social ideas, but in general he found such work extremely uncongenial.

At this period he seems also to have considered making literature his career. His French style was clear and eloquent, and his ideas on writing and the arts as vigorous as they were unorthodox. For instance, he recognised the genius of Courbet, and demanded the rejection of artistic conventions in favour of the direct interpretation of nature. Many writers, including Saint-Beuve, one of the greatest French essayists, thought very highly of his work, and tried to persuade him to take up criticism. But Proudhon could not long suppress his social ideas, and in 1854 he commenced his great work on justice.

Because of recurrent illness, he wrote slowly, but by 1858 he had finished this three-volume treatise, *Justice in the Revolution and the Church*, which embodied all his social ideas and mounted a great attack on the Church. The authorities immediately took action. Five days after publication the book was suppressed, and at a subsequent trial Proudhon was sentenced to three years' imprisonment and a large fine. He fled to Belgium, where he remained in exile until an amnesty in 1862 enabled him to return to Paris.

During his exile he published *War and Peace*, in which he showed that no justice could ever be obtained by military means. Shortly after his return he wrote *The Federative Principle*, in which he criticised the creed of nationalism that then afflicted the revolutionary movement and found its strongest expression in Polish nationalism and the movement for Italian unity. Proudhon condemned all these attempts to build up new centralised states, and advocated instead the establishment of federated commonwealths, in order to reverse the career of imperialism which he saw with a clearly prophetic eye would be the development of the new national states.

In his last few years Proudhon was again supported by many of the militant workers, and the lack of a newspaper did not prevent his views from becoming known. While the orthodox Left continued to recognise the Empire by serving as deputies, Proudhon demanded a complete boycott of the governmental machine, and the development by the workers of their own movement, clearly opposed to the ruling class and basing their actions on mutual aid and moral integrity. During his last illness he still continued work on his study of *The Political Capacity of the Working-classes*, but it was incomplete on his death in January, 1865.

Proudhon's main and most influential ideas can be classified under three headings : anarchism, mutualism, federalism. All of these teachings are discussed adequately in *The General Idea of the Revolution*, but are elaborated in such later works as *Justice in the Revolution and the Church* and *The Federative Principle*.

Proudhon's anarchism is based on a recognition of the integrity of each individual in his own right. A man can be free only if he decides for himself on all vital questions. Society may be justified in protecting itself, but beyond that it has no right of judgment or any legitimate power to dictate the actions of men. Any over-riding authority, any general constitution or legal code is un-justifiable because it cannot be based on the agreement of each individual.

In place of government, Proudhon advocates a system of social interconnection between men bound by individual contracts, for which they are responsible to each other and not to authority. As far as possible, men should control their own affairs; where co-operation is necessary, as in the management of large concerns like factories and railways, the workers should be linked in syndical organisations for control and operation. For municipal affairs the people should be grouped in towns and villages, where they would administer, again by contract, all those matters which concern them immediately. In place of the state there would be a federation of towns and provinces, to administer the very few matters really requiring common action. As far as possible, all social functions should be decentralised. In time political life would be extirpated, and the economic organisation of goods and exchange would take its place as the basis of social intercourse.

The elements of Proudhon's conception of contract are given in a condensed passage, in which he shows how it leads to the achieve-ment of the true revolution, the reign of Liberty, Equality and Fraternity.

" That I may remain free; that I may not have to submit to any law but my own, and that I may govern myself, the authority of the suffrage must be renounced : we must give up the vote, as well as representation and monarchy. In a word, everything in the government of society which rests on the divine must be suppressed, and the whole rebuilt upon the human idea of CONTRACT :

" When I agree with one or more of my fellow citizens for any object whatever, it is clear that my own will is my law; it is I myself, who, in fulfilling my obligation, am my own government.

" Therefore if I could make a contract with all, as I can with some; if all could renew it among themselves, if each group of citizens, as a town, country, province, corporation, company, etc., formed by a like contract, and considered as a moral person, could thereafter, and always by a similar contract, agree with every and all other groups, it would be the same as if my own will were multiplied to infinity. I should be sure that the law thus made on all questions in the Republic, from millions of different initiatives, would never be anything but my law; and if this new order of things were called government, it would be my government.

" Thus the principle of contract, far more than that of authority, would bring about the union of producers, centralise their forces, and assure the unity and solidarity of their interests.

" *The system of contracts*, substituted for the *system of laws*, would constitute the true government of the man and of the citizen; the true sovereignty of the people, the REPUBLIC.

" For the contract is Liberty, the first term of the republican motto : we have demonstrated this superabundantly in our studies on the principle of authority and on social liquidation. I am not free when I depend upon another for my work, my wages, or the measure of my rights and duties, whether that other is called Majority or Society. No more am I free, either in my sovereignty or in my action, when I am compelled by another to revise my law, were that other the most skilful and most just of arbiters. I am no more at all free when I am forced to give myself a representative to govern me, even if he were my most devoted servant.

" The Contract is Equality, in its profound and spiritual essence. Does this man believe himself my equal; does he not take the attitude of my master and exploiter, who demands from me more than it suits me to furnish, and has no intention of returning it to me ; who says that I am incapable of making my own law, and expects me to submit to his ?

"The contract is Fraternity, because it identifies all interests, unifies all divergences, resolves all contradictions, and in consequence, gives wings to the feelings of goodwill and kindness, which are crushed by economic chaos, the government of representatives, alien law.

"The contract, finally, is order, since it is the organisation of economic forces, instead of the alienation of liberties, the sacrifice of rights, the subordination of wills."

This society of mutual contract, or mutualism, could be attained, in Proudhon's view, gradually and without violent revolution. He envisaged the breaking down of unequal property by the abolition of usury and the establishment of "banks" through which the individual producers could exchange their products. Just value relationships would be established, so that eventually the operations of the exchange banks would eliminate money and replace political administration by simple exchange book-keeping. With the abolition of interest, rent could become part of the purchase price of premises, and so, over a period of years, each man would gain control of his home and means of production, each group of workers would gain control of their factory or public utility.

But there was one initial destructive step which Proudhon regarded as essential—the abolition of law as a coercive force.

"Remember, that there is but one way to do justice ; it is that the culprit, or merely the defendant, shall do it himself. And he will do it when each citizen shall have appeared at the social compact ; when, at this solemn assemblage, the rights, the obligations and the functions of each shall have been defined, guarantees exchanged, and assent signed.

"Then justice, springing from liberty, will no longer be vengeance ; it will be reparation. As there will be no more opposition between social law and the will of the individual, litigation will be cut off, there will be nothing for it but acknowledgment. . . .

"The complete, immediate, abolition of courts and tribunals, without any substitution or transition, is one of the prime necessities of the Revolution. Whatever delay may occur in other reforms, if social liquidation, for example, should not take place for twenty-five years, or the organisation of economic forces for half a century, in any case the suppression of judicial authority cannot be postponed."

Proudhon, if he were not as sanguine of an early revolution as some of his contemporaries, had an easy confidence in its eventual accomplishment through the processes of history. Like Marx, he was influenced to a certain extent by Hegel's historicist ideas, and decorated his writings with occasional ill-digested Hegelian texts, such as :

". . . after liquidation, reconstruction ; after the thesis and antithesis, the synthesis."

Such theories led him to believe that the reaction of his time would eventually breed the revolution. But his Hegelianism was never thorough. Nothing could have been further from Proudhon's attitude than Hegel's *Junker* doctrines of the nature of the state.

Proudhon's teachings left an international heritage, and have not ceased to echo in the world to-day. His denunciation of the state was taken by Bakunin as a text for the anarchist doctrines whose adherents gained ascendancy in the First International in all the Latin countries. His federalism and decentralism inspired the workers of the Paris Commune, provided a basis for the ideas of Pi y Margall, the precursor of the great Spanish federalist and anarchist movements, and were interpreted by the scientific brain of Kropotkin in treatises which even to-day are respected by the most advanced sociologists. Syndicalism had its first expression in Proudhon's suggestion of the formation of workers' groups to administer public utilities, and the first impetus of the Russian revolution among the peasants and many of the industrial workers came from the spreading of ideas of handing land to the peasants and factories to the workers, which undoubtedly owed much to Proudhon's influence on the earlier Russian revolutionaries, particularly Bakunin and Herzen.

To-day, much that Proudhon wrote remains valid. It is true, as many critics, following Engels, have been eager to indicate, that his teachings are those of a society of peasants and artisans, at a period when large-scale industry had embraced only a fraction of the population. To this extent they do not apply to our own day, and this affects particularly his proposals for exchange banks, which were based on the presupposition of a society of small proprietors and producers. Some different form of economic pattern would undoubtedly be necessary for an industrial society like our own, especially during the interim before economic decentralisation had shown any appreciable effect.

But the main teachings of Proudhon, his radical criticisms of the state and of coercive institutions, his prophetic condemnation of nationalism and centralisation, have been proved with bitter effect in our modern world of totalitarian wars and repressive state action. More and more we are led to despair of ever attaining peace and freedom by means of the economic and political institutions of capitalism and the state, institutions which are superimposed upon humanity instead of springing from the free will of all men. Proudhon's contractual and federalist theories provide the basic ideas for an alternative social pattern which might avoid the major temptations to strife and exploitation that exist in the world to-day and indicate the way to a social conception based, not on political abstractions, but on man's concrete needs.

V

Alexander Herzen

When we observe the famous revolutionary figures of the nineteenth century, we are impressed by the wide difference in approach to social problems between these men and the revolutionary intellectuals of our own time. The thinkers of the nineteenth century, the founders of social doctrines which still have the power to call men from the indifference of their ordinary lives, acted in an environment of confidence. Progress was inevitable. The social revolution would come, if not this year or next, at least in a measurable period of time. Capitalist accumulation, war, all the social calamities, merely speeded the day when exploitation and tyranny would vanish and freedom would be established permanently in the lives of men. Having few doubts, the revolutionaries worked for that day with a consistency, a self-abnegation, a Gargantuan energy at which we can only wonder.

For to-day we live in a world of uncertainty, and disillusionment. Progress is not inevitable, nor does it seem always desirable. And we perceive that the revolution is inevitably delayed, not merely by social conditions, but also by fears and faults within the individual which must be removed before a golden age of freedom will return among us. Consequently, while the social movements that were founded by idealists have become dominated largely by career " revolutionaries ", hard-headed opportunists who treat their activities as a kind of business for their own personal advancement, the genuine revolutionaries who remain are radically different in their attitude from their nineteenth-century predecessors.

They still believe that the revolutionary ideals are just and desirable, but they have been so disillusioned by the events of the intermediate decades, and particularly by the colossal betrayal of the Russian Revolution, that they are beset with doubts as to the possibility of their attainment, at least within a foreseeable length of time. Doubt and scepticism have become unhealthily dominant in their outlook, and have sapped not merely their faith in the future, but even their faith in themselves. Consequently, they are completely unable to summon the vast enthusiasm, energy and self-sacrifice that were shown consistently by men like Bakunin, Proudhon and Stepniak. The comparison is melancholy. A Koestler is an unsatisfactory substitute for a Kropotkin. Yet the change in the revolutionary character was implicit in the historical circumstances, and the study of an ironic figure like Alexander Herzen will show that, even in the great era of the revolutionary upsurge, the disorders of doubt and disillusionment were already present.

It is because he suffered so much from these modern maladies, because he was so much the revolutionary *malgré lui*, that Herzen possesses an almost contemporary interest. In the history of Russian revolutionary activity he has a considerable importance, yet this part was rather thrust upon him by circumstances than assumed out of a feeling of considered responsibility, and if he seems to share in a lesser degree the nobility and greatness of spirit that characterised his friends Bakunin and Ogarev, it is because he found himself unavoidably entangled in the revolutionary movement. In his general outlook he approximated far more than any of them to the disillusioned revolutionary intellectual of our own day.

Herzen, like Bakunin and Kropotkin, was born of the propertied nobility of Tsarist Russia. His father, Ivan Yakovlev, was a nobleman, an ex-Guards captain, an owner of many souls, and a hypochondriac. Yakovlev, during a tour of Western Europe, had abducted a young woman from Stuttgart, and set up a household with her in Moscow. He never took the trouble to marry her, and to their eldest child, Alexander, he gave the name of Herzen to signify a child of love. Alexander was brought up in his father's household as if he had been a legitimate son, according to the custom of Russian landowners of the period. But it was a lonely and melancholy life for a child, as Herzen narrates in *My Past and Thoughts*, and we can already trace here the seeds of that chronic doubt which possessed his later life.

" It may well be imagined how drearily and monotonously the time passed in the strange convent-like seclusion of my father's home. I had neither encouragement nor distraction ; my father had spoilt me until I was ten, and now he was almost always dissatisfied with me ; I had no companions, my teachers came and went, and, seeing them out of the yard, I used to run off on the sly, to play with the house-serf boys, which was strictly forbidden. The rest of my time I spent wandering aimlessly about the big dark rooms, which had their windows shut all day and were only dimly lighted in the evening, doing nothing or reading anything that turned up."

Into this aimless life there burst suddenly, when Herzen was a boy of thirteen, the news of the first revolution in modern Russia, the rising of the Decembrists in 1825. This was a conspiracy of liberal officers against the bloodthirsty Tsar Nicholas I, and it was suppressed with great cruelty. These events impressed profoundly a whole generation of Russian youth ; for Herzen they meant a change of heart that eventually turned him from a Russian serf-owner into a lifelong revolutionary.

" The accounts of the rising and of the trial of the leaders, and the horror in Moscow, made a deep impression on me ; a new world which became more and more the centre of my moral existence was revealed to me. I do not know how it came to pass, but though I had no understanding, or only a very dim one, of what it all meant, I felt that I was not on the same side as the grapeshot and victory, prisons and chains."

Not long afterwards, Herzen met his lifelong friend, Nicholas Ogarev. " He, too, had broken loose from the grim conservative shore, and we had but to shove off more vigorously together." Up to this time Herzen had been able to discuss his liberal sentiments only with occasional tutors, but now, with the sympathetic agreement of a friend of his own age, he developed his ideas rapidly, and soon went beyond Decembrist constitutionalism to the republicanism of the French Revolution.

In 1829, he entered Moscow University, an island of advanced thought in the great slough of Russian autocracy. He joined vigorously in the discussions on social topics, and soon discovered the ideas of socialism which were already assuming prominence in Western political thought. His memoirs convey a vivid impression of the intellectual ferment among the students and young intellectuals of Moscow, always in advance of bureaucratic St Petersburg.

The circle which Herzen and Ogarev gathered soon began to show signs of brilliance which attracted the ready suspicions of the authorities, and in 1834, after Herzen had left the university, most of them were arrested on a charge of " conspiracy". The main excuses for this action seem to have been the discussions on socialism which had taken place, and also certain satires and scurrilous songs concerning the Tsar, said to have been sung at a party where Herzen was not even present. The prisoners stayed for nine months in the cells of the Third Division, the notorious Tsarist political police. Then after " investigations ", three were sent to the deadly fortress of Schusselburg, a number were released, and six, including Herzen and Ogarev, were exiled to provinces remote from the capital.

Herzen was sent to Perm, where he received a post in the local administration. A short time later he was transferred to Vyatka, and then to Vladimir. The only hardships of his exile seem to have been the boredom of official work and the absence of Moscow intellectual life. But even in these outlying places there was the company of other exiles, and particularly of the Polish revolutionaries, for whom Herzen developed a lasting respect. He also enjoyed at least one sentimental affair with a married woman, and towards the end of his exile he carried out the feat of entering Moscow secretly and eloping with his cousin Natalie, whom he married in Vladimir.

In 1840 he was allowed to return to St Petersburg. There he resumed contact with the remaining members of his circle, and also with the young radicals who had become active in Moscow during his absence, notably Vyelinsky and Bakunin. Moscow thought had left its old allegiance with the French socialists and was floundering in German philosophy. Hegel was the reigning god, and even Bakunin was at this time a sturdy defender of that philosopher. Herzen, with his ironical and practical mind, provided a counterbalance to this tendency, and helped to re-establish a concern with social problems. His efforts did not go unperceived, and shortly afterwards, on a trivial excuse, the Third Division obtained his exile to Novgorod.

In Novgorod he did what was possible in his official position to help the peasants and curb the cruelties of the landowners, but after a year he resigned in disgust and was allowed to return to Moscow. His remaining years in Russia were unhappy. He was still subjected to police spying, and began to feel the intellectual frustration of life under the Tsar. His father's death in 1845 left him economically independent, and a year afterwards he set out on his long-anticipated foreign tour. On January 21st, 1847, he crossed the Russian frontier. Perhaps even then he half expected there would be no return, as he watched his old nurse and his tutor Sonnenberg, " that symbol of the parental home, that comic figure from the days of childhood", waving farewell in an " endless plain of snow ".

Driving across northern Germany, Herzen began to express his liberal opinions to a fellow passenger on the stage coach. He was disconcerted to find that his first acquaintance in " free " Europe was a police spy, and this unpleasant discovery set the pattern for a life of exile in which political persecution was a recurrent feature. For Herzen, in spite of his material prosperity, shared with his fellow exiles the continual movement from land to land, and the persistent uneasiness that prevented his settling happily even where he was left in peace.

He hastened across Europe to Paris, that Mecca of nineteenth-century Russian radicals.

" In Paris—the word meant scarcely less to me than the word ' Moscow ' ! Of that minute I had been dreaming from child-hood. . . .

" I could not stay indoors ; I dressed and went out to stroll about the streets . . . to look up Bakunin, Sazonov : here was Rue St Honoré, the Champs-Elysées—all those names which had been familiar for long years . . . and here was Bakunin himself . . .

" I met him at a street corner ; he was walking with three friends and, just as in Moscow, discussing with them, continually stopping and waving his cigarette . . .

" I was beside myself with happiness ! "

In the enthusiastic round of new experiences, places and friends, Herzen forgot for a while the police spy on the German stage-coach. He manifested a generous solidarity with the revolutionary causes that were then preparing for their brief triumph of 1848. From France he proceeded to Italy, where he found a popular agitation at work in all the great cities, and mingled with the gay and noisy crowds whose demonstrations frightened the petty Italian potentates into granting constitutional governments.

The news of the February revolution in France drew him away

from his Italian pleasures, but by the time he reached France the reaction had begun. At a republican demonstration in Marseilles he was already disgusted to see the National Guard stamping their gun butts on the toes of the onlookers.

In Paris Herzen showed himself in public among the revolutionaries, attended a number of banquets, and began to experience impatience with his comrades. He stayed in Paris for another year, attending conspiratorial meetings which came to nothing, assisting at the miscarriages of political magazines, and generally implicating himself in the vague and imprecise revolutionism of the period. He made some pleasant friendships, talked with Proudhon and a few other men of sound ideas, and began already to feel that attitude of ironic detachment which was to distinguish him so markedly from his great contemporaries.

Proudhon, then at the zenith of his reputation, was the one abiding influence on Herzen during this period. In 1849 Proudhon found himself unable to carry on his paper, *Le Voix du Peuple*, all the funds having been taken to pay the fines inflicted for Proudhon's frequent breaches of the rigid press regulations. Herzen provided a fund which enabled the paper to continue for some months, until the next great fine consumed the reserves. His estimate of Proudhon is interesting, if not wholly accurate.

" Reading Proudhon, like reading Hegel," he says, " cultivates a special faculty, sharpens the weapon, and furnishes not results but methods. Proudhon is pre-eminently the dialectician, the controversialist of social questions. . . .

" It is in the denial, the destruction of the old social tradition, that the great power of Proudhon lies ; he is as much the poet of dialectics as Hegel is, with the difference that the one rests on the calm heights of the philosophic movement, while the other is thrust into the turmoil of popular passions and the hand-to-hand struggle of parties.

" Proudhon is the first of a new set of French thinkers. His works mark a transition period, not only in the history of socialism but also in the history of French logic. He has more strength and freedom in his argumentative tenacity than the most talented of his fellow-countrymen. . . . Proudhon often presses on without hesitating to crush anything on the way, without fearing to destroy or to go too far.

" He has none of that sensitiveness, that rhetorical revolutionary chastity, which takes the place of Protestant piety among the French . . . that is why he remains a solitary figure among his own people, rather alarming than convincing them.

" . . . he has assimilated Hegel's dialectical method, as he has assimilated all the methods of Catholic controversy. But neither the Hegelian philosophy nor the Catholic theology furnished the content nor the character of his writings ; for him these were only weapons with which he tested his subject, and these weapons he mastered and adapted to his own purposes just as he adapted the French language to his powerful and vigorous thought. Such men stand much too firmly on their own feet to be dominated by anything or to allow themselves to be caught in any net."

It was just this destructive side of Proudhon that Herzen appreciated, because his own youthful Fourierism had given way to a scepticism that saw flaws in any Utopia. Just as Herzen lived like a temporary exile, although he never expected to go back to Russia, so he prepared for the revolution, although he had no confidence that it would take place and certainly no idea of the kind of society that would arise from it. Therefore he tended to overlook completely the constructive side of Proudhon's thought or, when he did consider it, to dismiss it as expecting men to do too much from their sense of duty. The creative Proudhon was perhaps too exacting for a man of Herzen's temperament, and in the end even the destructive elements he accepted willingly from Proudhon were vitiated by disillusionment.

In 1849 the persecution of foreign revolutionaries by the reac-

tionary French police led Herzen to leave Paris and to cross the
Swiss frontier with a Wallachian passport. This was the end of his
practical revolutionary experience. He was not cast for a sensational rôle in the social conflict ; neither prison nor barricades
again played any part in his career. From now, he was the quiet
theorist who provided the intellectual justification for more active
men to attack the tyrannies he hated, and his trials were the
unheroic ones of exile and instability in unfriendly lands.

The years of exile in Switzerland and Nice were largely dominated
by personal tragedies—his wife's unfaithfulness and subsequent
death in childbed, the death of his mother and son in a steamboat
disaster off the French coast. Meanwhile his activities had brought
him under the observation of the Russian secret agents, and he
received the usual summons to return. The reward for a man who
had twice earned exile at the displeasure of the Tsar, and who had
since implicated himself thoroughly in the revolutionary activities
of Western Europe, could hardly have been less than a long and
probably lethal imprisonment in one of the penal fortresses. Herzen
preferred his nomad exile, and ignored the summons. The Russian
Government then confiscated his property in Russia, but Herzen
very adroitly enlisted the international banker, Rothschild, on his
side, and, by a threat that he would sabotage certain loans, the
banker obtained a speedy release of Herzen's funds, which were
later to be used very effectively in carrying on propaganda against
the Tsar, and also in giving assistance to the many political refugees
who were less prosperous than Herzen.

He ensured himself against the Third Division by taking Swiss
citizenship, being accepted by the people of the tiny village of
Châtel in the canton of Freiburg, who celebrated the occasion by
making Herzen dead drunk.

His personal tragedies and the apparent triumph of reaction
everywhere on the continent led Herzen to seek refuge in the one
country that seemed to him to retain some real freedom—England.

He came a sad and disillusioned man. His personal life appeared to have been wrecked completely by the death of his wife, his public vocation by the apparently universal defeat of the revolution.

" I was humiliated," he tells us, " my pride was outraged, I was angry with myself. My conscience tormented me for the sacrilegious desecration of my grief, for the year wasted in petty agitation, and I was conscious of a terrible inexpressible weariness. . . . How I needed then a friend who, without judging and condemning, could have received my confession and have shared my unhappiness ! but the wilderness about me grew more and more desolate, there was no one near to me, not one . . . and perhaps that was for the best.

" I had not meant to stay more than a month in London, but little by little I began to understand that I had absolutely nowhere to go and no reason to go anywhere. Nowhere could I have found the same hermit-like seclusion."

He stayed in all more than twelve years in England, and during that time not only recovered partially from his personal malaise and social disillusionment, but also carried out the important work of his life.

He never really settled to the English environment. His life there was almost nomadic—he lived in no less than fourteen different abodes, some for as little as three weeks, none for as much as three years. He had little contact with English society. In those days the colonies of exiles were much more self-contained than they are in modern London, and the Germans, Frenchmen and Italians who inhabited Soho and the environs of Tottenham Court Road were regarded by the English, if not with hostility, at least with amusement. The London crowd might cheer a Garibaldi who symbolised the liberty which the nineteenth-century Englishman still regarded as a desirable attribute, but the more humble political exile, with his pidgin-English and his eccentric clothes, seemed a being from another world, to be tolerated, to be given sanctuary, but at the same time to be shunned. Few Victorian Englishmen would think of extending individual hospitality to the strangers whom their political tolerance admitted within their frontiers.

In consequence, the life of the exile in England was usually both lonely and dull. This was often aggravated by extreme poverty, for most of the exiles had lost everything in their flight from oppression. Moreover, as Herzen records, the exiles always looked forward to the revolution which would allow an early return to their native lands, and consequently rarely tried to extend their relationships beyond the cheap boarding-houses and taverns where their compatriots gathered. Herzen, although he was not poor and was naturally too pessimistic to expect an early return to Russia, shared the inability of his fellow refugees to accept England as a settled home, although at this time most of the continent was closed to him.

When Herzen first came to England there were few Russian refugees, and thus, even before he had undertaken the work that earned him an international reputation, he was known among London exiles as " the Russian revolutionary ". The fact that so few of his compatriots had settled in London made him seek the company of refugees of other nations, and he soon had a wide circle of friends among the French, Polish, Hungarian and Italian exiles, but not among the Germans, whom he disliked after the Russian fashion of the day.

At public meetings and political banquets he began to appear as the representative of Russian radicalism, and there was more than one moving scene on a London platform when a Polish representative and the Russian speaker (always Herzen) embraced to symbolise the mutual forgiveness of these two races commonly regarded as mortal enemies. On one occasion Mazzini and Garibaldi held a meeting of reconciliation in his house at Teddington, and he was among those who tended the deathbed of the Polish hero, Worcell.

Nor was he any less popular among the ranks of this revolutionary army of the unfortunate, for he rarely refused a request for assistance that he was able to grant, and he kept a number of his more unfortunate friends from the starvation that afflicted so many of the exiles.

Reading the chapters of *My Past and Thoughts* which deal with his English period, we have always the impression of an island within an island, of a refugee life hardly touched by the life of England around it. There is no commentary on English political life, and English social customs are mentioned only in so far as they affect the foreigner. Yet on a few occasions, when refugees became involved in English political events, Herzen was bound to acknowledge, however grudgingly, a certain impartiality in English judges, a lack of corruption among English juries, and an honest love of freedom and hatred of injustice among the English people of the time which makes melancholy reading when one thinks of the lethargy of their descendants to-day.

Certainly the most impressive passages of his English memoirs are those in which he describes his fellow exiles. His irony gave him a sense of proportion which enabled him to portray them in a true relationship to the circumstances that overpowered them, to show how few of them ever reached the heights they had imagined, and how many of them declined into pathetic Quixotes waiting on the edge of great moments. Yet he was sufficiently in sympathy with them to speak with genuine brotherhood and to respect the fortitude with which they endured their miseries and the inner greatness that was often exhibited by their behaviour at times of failure.

Herzen's own isolation was very much mitigated in the fourth year of his sojourn in England by the sudden arrival of Ogarev and his wife Natalie. Ogarev had freed his serfs, and had been deprived of his estates by legal trickery. For a while he operated a paper factory until, in 1855, it was burnt down, and he was left a pauper.

He and Natalie went to St Petersburg and, after great difficulty, obtained a passport and came to London in the spring of 1856.

The arrival of Ogarev awoke Herzen from the comparative inactivity of the past few years. Ogarev was in no way a dynamic figure, but his presence recalled the situation in which Herzen had developed his first revolutionary ideas, and acted as a stimulus to new activities.

Natalie Ogarev had already something in common with Herzen, for she had experienced a devotion to his dead wife, the other Natalie, and this emotional link led them into a passionate and unhappy love relationship. Natalie bore Herzen three children, who passed for Ogarev's, and the situation seems to have been recognised by all of them as inevitable. Ogarev, who eventually attained the most happy relationship of his life with a prostitute whom he rescued from the London streets, does not appear to have been greatly disturbed, and he continued in economic dependence on Herzen and his family for the rest of his life.

From this renewed association arose the venture for which the names of Herzen and Ogarev are celebrated, the founding of the Russian magazine *Kolokol* (*The Bell*). During his early days in London, Herzen associated in the founding of a Polish press. This led him to start a Free Russian Press, at first little more than the hobby of a tired dilettante, devoted to publishing occasional pamphlets which Herzen wrote on Russian political questions. From these publications he seems to have expected few results, but they actually created a minor sensation in Russia itself. It was the first time that publications in Russian openly attacking the Tsar had appeared, and when some hundreds of them crossed the frontier in the baggage of returning tourists, the Third Division became alarmed. Slight and superficial as they were, these pamphlets provided the first intellectual stimuli of the great Russian revolutionary movement of the later nineteenth century.

This unexpected success led Herzen to consider a journal

devoted to the liberation of the Russian people. The death of
Nicholas I provided an immediate excuse, and in August, 1855,
he published the first number of *The Polar Star*, named after the
short-lived Decembrist journal; Herzen was very conscious of
being the spiritual descendant of these martyrs for Russian freedom.

The Polar Star was an expensive volume with a literary tone,
and the three numbers that appeared at wide intervals before the
arrival of Ogarev, although they sold relatively well, did no more
than carry on the work already achieved by the pamphlets. Herzen
began to realise that a wider appeal was necessary if a real movement of opinion against the Tsar were to be fostered.

His approach to propaganda was somewhat equivocal. The
ironical side of his nature regarded the prospect of any real achievement with the greatest scepticism. But at the same time the spirit
of his idealistic youth had been aroused by the arrival of Ogarev,
and there were also certain political circumstances in the Russian
situation that seemed to justify optimism. Nicholas I, father of the
autocratic régime, was dead, and his successor, Alexander II,
appeared sympathetic towards the liberal cause—he had already
made a significant pronouncement in favour of the abolition of
serfdom. Russia had just been defeated in the Crimean war, and,
in the revolutionary tradition, Herzen regarded this as a propitious
sign for radical hopes. He had, therefore, some justification for
thinking that his efforts might be effective, and it was in this spirit
that he decided to start a popular journal that would be the nucleus
of a radical body of Russian opinion. But often during his venture
the ironic Herzen questioned pertinently the value of his
work.

The first issue of *The Bell* appeared on July 1st, 1857. It was
published regularly for exactly ten years, after which a few odd and
sporadic numbers appeared until its final demise in 1868. The
six numbers which appeared in 1870 were published by the
terrorist Nechaev, and had no connection with the original *Kolokol*.

THE WRITER AND POLITICS

The editorial policy of *The Bell* aimed at discussing the problems which would be uppermost in the minds of contemporary Russian liberals. In this aim Herzen was helped by his critical attitude towards the revolutionary movements of the West. In his youth, like most of his contemporaries, he had looked for revolutionary inspiration to Germany, France, Italy. He had regarded Russia as wholly benighted, and had seen the only possibility of regeneration in the injection of Western ideas. But his participation in the events of 1848–49, as well as his acquaintance with almost all the leading revolutionaries of the Forty-Eight, had led him to realise, and perhaps to exaggerate, the weaknesses of the western revolutionary tradition. He began to look back to Russia, to recollect his experience of the Russian people, and, with a clear insight, to perceive in the spontaneous social organisation and resistance to the state of the Russian peasant a force that might be even more powerful than the conspiracies and insurrections of professional revolutionaries.

This point of view was already expressed as early as 1851, in an article entitled *The Russian People and Socialism*. Herzen's thoughts in this essay anticipate in a striking way the ideas discussed by Kropotkin in *Mutual Aid* and *The Conquest of Bread*.

After discussing the artificial nature of existing Russian society, Herzen enunciates the thought that was to be maintained as a central belief by the great Russian Social Revolutionary and Anarchist movements until their extinction by the Bolsheviks in 1918 :

" Centralisation is alien to the Slav spirit—federation is far more natural to it. Only when grouped in a league of free and independent peoples will the Slav world at last enter upon its genuine historical existence. Its past can only be regarded as a period of growth, of preparation, of purification. The political forms in which the Slavs have lived in the past have not been in harmony with their national tendency, a tendency vague and instinctive if you like, but by that very fact betraying an extraordinary vitality and promising much in the future."

He goes on to defend the Russian peasant against accusations of dishonesty by pointing out that what appears to be dishonesty is in reality a natural reaction against the attacks made by the Government on the peasant way of life :

" Deprived of every possible means of defence, the peasant resorts to cunning in dealing with his torturers, he deceives them, and he is perfectly right in doing so.

" Through his aversion for private property in land, through his heedless and indolent temperament, the Russian peasant has gradually and imperceptibly been caught in the snares of the German bureaucracy and of the landowners' power. He has submitted to this humiliating disaster with the resignation of a martyr, but he has not believed in the rights of the landowner, nor the justice of the law-courts, nor the legality of the acts of the authorities. For nearly two hundred years the peasant's existence has been a dumb, passive obedience to the existing order of things. He submits to coercion, he endures, but he takes no part in anything that goes on outside the village commune.

" . . . Rejected by all, he instinctively understands that the whole system is ordered not for his benefit, but to his detriment, and that the aim of the Government and the landowners is to wring out of him as much labour, as much money, as many recruits as possible. As he understands this and is gifted with a supple and resourceful intelligence, he deceives them on all sides and in everything. It could not be otherwise ; if he spoke the truth he would by so doing be acknowledging their authority over him ; if he did not rob them (observe that to conceal part of the produce of his own labour would be considered theft in a peasant) he would thereby be recognising the lawfulness of their demands, the rights of the landowners and the justice of the law-courts."

This resistance to the state is based on the positive reality of the

commune which, according to Herzen, has bred the best elements
in Russian society. In the commune the peasant becomes a responsible and socially active person.

" The life of the Russian peasantry has hitherto been confined
to the commune. It is only in relation to the commune and its
members that the peasant recognises that he has rights and duties.
Outside the commune everything seems to him based upon violence.
What is fatal is his submitting to that violence, and not his refusing
in his own way to recognise it and his trying to protect himself by
guile. . . .

" There is a fact which no one who has been in close contact
with the Russian peasantry can doubt. The peasants rarely cheat
each other. An almost boundless good faith prevails among them ;
they know nothing of contracts and written agreements.

" The problems connected with the measurement of their fields
are often inevitably complicated, owing to the perpetual re-division
of land, in accordance with the number of taxpayers in the family ;
yet the difficulties are got over without complaint or resort to law
courts. . . . Petty disputes are submitted to the judgment of the
elders or of the commune, and the decision is unconditionally
accepted by all. . . .

" The Russian peasant has no morality except what naturally,
instinctively flows from his communism ; this morality is deeply
rooted in the people ; the little they know of the Gospel supports
it ; the flagrant injustice of the landowner binds the peasant still
more closely to his principles and to the communal system.

" . . . The communal system, though it has suffered violent
shocks, has stood firm against the interference of the authorities ;
it has *successfully survived up to the development of socialism in
Europe.* This circumstance is of infinite consequence for Russia."

This reorientation towards Russia, towards a country as yet
untouched by the revolutionary failures of Western Europe and in
which an indigenous tendency towards communism was already

in existence, gave the early numbers of Herzen's journal a realism of outlook unique among the political reviews of its time. Where a journal imbued with French socialism or German philosophy would have made little impression on the Russia of the 1850's, Herzen's attempt to find direct and practical solutions to Russian problems met a ready response.

The Bell, while it envisaged an ultimate solution of the Russian problem in a revolutionary society based on natural communism, federalism and free co-operation, had an immediate programme which made an appeal to a very wide section of liberal opinion. Its three urgent aims were the liberation of the serfs, the abolition of corporal punishment, and the abolition of censorship of the printed word. With the liberal professions of Alexander II, it did not seem at all impossible that these aims should be achieved within a measurable period.

The Bell had a phenomenal circulation, not only among the exiles, of whom there were yet comparatively few in Western Europe, but also within Russia, in spite of the difficulty of getting copies across the frontier under the vigilant eyes of the Third Division. For some years Herzen and Ogarev, through *The Bell,* wielded an influence on Russian opinion which is all the more remarkable when we consider that it resulted from the efforts of two exiles in a distant land, neither of whom had enjoyed any great celebrity before their departure from Russia.

The great success of *The Bell* enormously increased Herzen's reputation as an international revolutionary figure, and his various houses in London became places of pilgrimage for Russians who were touring Western Europe. Some were mere sightseers, others police agents, but many were genuinely interested in the revolutionary future of Russia and left Herzen to spread his doctrines at home or, having compromised themselves too openly, to join the growing groups of exiles in England and Switzerland.

The liberal movement seemed to have gained a triumph in

1861, when the abolition of serfdom was proclaimed. At that time the onerous conditions of redemption were not fully understood, and Herzen and his friends acclaimed the Tsar as a hero in the struggle against oppression. Herzen arranged a reception for the international exiles at his house in Paddington. The outside of the house was covered with banners and illuminated with seven thousand gas jets, and an orchestra was engaged to play, among other items, an Emancipation Fantasia by the exile musician, Prince Golitsyn. But the evening was spoiled by sinister news. Russian soldiers had fired on the Poles during a riot in Warsaw. The day of triumph was turned into bitter mourning. In the next issue of *The Bell* Herzen once again denounced the Tsar.

From this time Herzen began to return to the disillusionment that had characterised his early days in England, and his increasing personal distress was matched by a decline in the influence of *The Bell*. This was due very largely to the Polish rebellions which commenced at this time, and in which racial hatred was so far exploited by the reaction that many of the Russian liberals were carried away. Herzen clung steadfastly to his advocacy of Polish liberation, and for this reason his journal suffered a steadily increasing loss of support.

But before its final decline, *The Bell* was to receive a temporary stimulus from the arrival of Bakunin, who had escaped from his exile in Siberia.

" A new element, or rather an old element, the shadow of the 'forties, and most of all of 1848, risen up from the dead, came into our work, into our league that consisted of two. Bakunin was just the same ; he had grown older in body only, his spirit was as young and enthusiastic as in the days of the all-night arguments with Homyakov in Moscow. He was just as devoted to one idea, just as capable of being carried away by it, and of seeing in everything the fulfilment of his desires and ideals, and even more ready for every effort, every sacrifice, feeling that he had not so much life before him, and consequently that he must make haste and not let slip a single chance. He fretted against prolonged study, the weighing of pros and cons, and, as confident and theoretical as ever, longed for any action if only it were in the midst of the turmoil, in the midst of upheavals and menacing danger. . . .

" The European reaction did not exist for Bakunin, the bitter years from 1848 to 1858 did not exist for him either ; of them he had but a brief, far-away, faint knowledge. . . . The events of 1848, on the contrary, were all about him, near to his heart. . . .

" As soon as Bakunin had looked about him and settled down in London, that is, had made the acquaintance of all the Slavs and Russians there, he set to work. To a passion for propaganda, for agitation, for demagogy, to incessant activity in founding, organising plots and conspiracies, and establishing relations, to a belief in their immense significance, Bakunin added a readiness to be the first to carry out his ideas, a readiness to risk his life, and reckless daring in facing all the consequences.

" His was a heroic nature, deprived of complete achievement by the course of events. He sometimes wasted his strength on what was useless, as a lion wastes his strength pacing up and down in the cage, always imagining that he will escape from it. But Bakunin was not a mere rhetorician, afraid to act upon his own words, or trying to evade carrying his theories into practice. . . .

" Bakunin had many weak points. But his weak points were small while his strong qualities were great. . . . Is it not in itself a sign of greatness that wherever he was flung by destiny, as soon as he had grasped two or three characteristics of his surroundings, he discerned the revolutionary forces and at once set to work to carry them on further, to fan the fire, to make of it the burning question of life ? . . .

" Bakunin thought us too moderate, unable to take advantage of the position at the moment, and not sufficiently inclined to resolute measures. He did not lose heart, however, but was convinced that in a short time he would set us on the right path."

There was much to be said for both sides. Herzen's position as the detached intellectual had some value, and had undoubtedly played an indispensable rôle in the development of the Russian revolutionary movement. His voice had been necessary to stir the dormant consciences of the Russian intelligentsia, to bring to them the candid analytical opinions of a man who saw their situation both from the outside and with a sympathy unique among the inhabitants of Western Europe. But the situation in Russia was already passing beyond the mere stirring of consciences and the making of intellectual contacts. A movement for action was beginning to form within Russia, and it was necessary for it to gain direct inspiration and aid from the exiles of Western Europe. Here Bakunin's revolutionary instinct was correct. But he was wrong in supposing that this need cancelled out the function of the detached propagandist.

Moreover, Bakunin had misjudged Herzen's character when he imagined that his friend could be transformed for the rôle of a practical revolutionary. In character Herzen was no man of the barricades—not from any lack of genuine courage, but merely because intellectual activities were more congenial to his mind. Bakunin, having learned from experience was to assess Herzen in terms which, according to his own attitude, were reasonably just :

" Herzen has presented, and continues to sustain, the Russian cause magnificently before the public of Europe. But in matters of domestic policy he is an inveterate sceptic, and his influence on them is not merely not encouraging, but demoralising. He is, first and foremost, a writer of genius ; and he combines all the brilliant qualities with the defects of his profession. When liberty has been established in Russia, or when it begins to be established, he will be, beyond question, a powerful journalist, perhaps an orator, a statesman, even an administrator. But he decidedly has not in him the stuff of which revolutionary leaders are made."

The attempt to transform *The Bell* into a triumvirate was thus bound to fail, because of the incompatibility in character of these men, and from the beginning tension began to appear between them. Herzen's situation was rendered more delicate by two other circumstances. The first was that Ogarev, in so far as his weak character was capable of making decisions, tended to side with Bakunin. The second was that, since the emancipation of the serfs, the Russian liberal movement had begun to change character, owing to a split of the intelligentsia into an extreme section of "nihilists", from whom sprang later the anarchists, the terrorists, the People's Will groups and the Social Revolutionaries ; and a section representing constitutional liberalism which was frightened by the attitudes of the extremists into an approach towards conservatism.

The Bell found its support dwindling from both sides, and, although Herzen wished to retain its detachment of attitude, he was persuaded by the arguments of Bakunin and Ogarev to move to the left and support the new secret society, *Land and Liberty*, thereby making a clear break with the cause of constitutional liberalism and lining himself up with conspiratorial revolutionism. *The Bell* also supported the ill-fated Polish rebellion of 1863, but unfortunately the editors took for granted a measure of support from Russian officers and soldiers which did not materialise, and in the end *The Bell* had to endure the recriminations of the Russians for supporting the Poles, and of the Poles for promising support which did not exist.

Herzen, reviewing the situation afterwards, wished that his doubting mind had been more able to control the ease with which his revolutionary conscience was persuaded to act against his cautious " better judgment " :

" Here I must stop to ask a sorrowful question. How, whence did I come by this readiness to give way with a murmur, this weak yielding after opposition and a protest ? I had at the same time a conviction that I ought to act in one way and a readiness to act in quite another. This instability, this disharmony, *dieses Zögernde*, has done me no end of harm in my life, and has not even left me the faint comfort of recognising that my mistake was involuntary, unconscious ; I have made blunders *à contre cœur* ; I had all the arguments on the other side before my eyes . . .

" How many misfortunes, how many blows I should have been spared in my life, if at all the important crises in it I had had the strength to listen to myself alone. I have been reproached for being easily carried away ; I have been carried away, too, but that is not what matters most. Though I might be carried away by my impressionable temper, I pulled myself up at once ; thought, reflection and observation almost always gained the day in theory, but not in practice. That is just what is hard to explain : why I let myself be led *nolens volens.* . . .

" My speedy surrender to persuasion was due to false shame, though sometimes to the better influences of love, friendship and indulgence ; but why was all that too strong for my reason ? "

What a devastating familiarity there is in these sentences ! We see here portrayed, as clearly as it has ever been since, the schizoid tendency that is so evident in the minds of the revolutionary intellectuals of our own day. At Herzen's time such an attitude and the honesty to recognise and confess it, were rare enough. Yet it is all implicit in the duality of construction and destruction, of scepticism and faith, which dominates the outlook of the revolutionary, and which can only be resolved by a synthesis of these two apparent opposites in an attitude based on the wholeness of man's personality.

By 1864, when Herzen left England, *The Bell's* influence on Russian affairs was practically ended. Herzen carried on the journal for a few years in Geneva, in the hope that the presence of a large group of Russian exiles would help it to become integrated once again with the Russian revolutionary movement. But Herzen could not enter into the new spirit of the International, which was becoming the dominant influence in revolutionary affairs, and it rapidly became evident that the peculiar accident of circumstances that had made him the embarrassed father of the Russian revolutionary movement had finally passed away. Moreover, he was personally unhappy and involved in family tragedies which sapped any enthusiasm he may have been able to muster, while Ogarev was steadily declining to incapacity after a life of dissipation, and Bakunin was busy forming his anarchist movement within the International.

Herzen's personal problems dominated his life more and more in his last years, and in 1867 *The Bell* ceased regular publication. Herzen survived it another three years, until, in 1870, he was taken ill in Paris with inflammation of the lungs, and died after a short illness, exhausted and unhappy.

His work was unfulfilled. The early liberalism of Alexander had deepened into a tyranny of the traditional Russian kind, and there seemed slight prospect of the tiny revolutionary forces having any success. Yet it was perhaps better for Herzen to have died with his aims unfulfilled than to have lived to see what the revolution brought to Russia when it eventually occurred. Bolshevism, a totalitarian rule as foreign to the true Russian spirit as Tsarism itself, was far removed from the free federalist communism that Herzen envisaged as the most appropriate society for the Russian people. Faced with Russian Communism as it appears to-day, Herzen would have despaired, but none the less his curious double nature would probably have forced him to work against it. For in his ironic, unheroic way he was one of the staunchest fighters in the nineteenth-century struggle for freedom, and his contribution was unique and valuable precisely because his self-criticism rendered him singularly devoid of dogmatism, prejudice or any other of those defects of the mind that blind the judgment of the political enthusiast.

VI

The Scientific Contribution of Peter Kropotkin

I

TWENTY-FIVE years ago, in a tiny village near Moscow, died one of the most influential thinkers of the nineteenth century. This was Peter Kropotkin, the prince who put aside his privileges to move among the workers as a revolutionary prophet ; the scientist who renounced his beloved work to strive for the liberation of mankind and later returned enriched to become one of the founders of our modern science of sociology ; the anarchist who preached mutual aid and effectively confuted Huxley's theories of the struggle for existence ; the libertarian who saw the dangers of totalitarian tyranny implicit in Marxism and strove to implant the care for freedom among the workers of his time ; the veteran who, in his eightieth year, was among the few to denounce the attacks on liberty by which the Bolsheviks betrayed the original spirit of the Russian revolution.

In this study I am most concerned with Kropotkin as a scientist, for in this rôle he made his greatest contribution to human progress. Admittedly, it is impossible to dissociate his scientific work from the libertarian philosophy he maintained ; the two inevitably affected each other. But there was nothing terrifying or brutal about the anarchism which Kropotkin preached. It was essentially a doctrine of brotherhood, mutual aid and co-operation ; in his last great work, *Ethics*, he stressed the need to create a " human " morality that would transcend all partisan considerations and base itself on the natural solidarity of mankind. Such ideas reflected his personal qualities, for, as Herbert Read has said :

" Kropotkin, gentle and generous, infinitely kind and nobly wise, was not a terrifying man : he was a seer, a prophet, but above all a scholar. Others had given anarchism the fervour of a revolutionary faith, the imaginative force of a social vision. Kropotkin did not despise these qualities, but when in his eightieth year his pen fell from his failing hand, he had given that faith and that vision the dignity of a science and the scope of a philosophy of life."

Kropotkin's work made anarchism a doctrine which cannot be ignored, even to-day, by serious students of our social problems. But, independently of his own social creed, Kropotkin's treatises on sociology and ethics have undoubtedly made a great contribution to modern thought, a contribution which is worthy of consideration by those who are concerned for the future well-being of society.

Kropotkin began his career as a student of geography—a science which produced many of the early sociologists. He sprang from a noble family who lived in the careless extravagance customary to propertied Russians of the period. As a boy he entered the Corps of Pages at St Petersburg, which was usually regarded as the beginning of a career as courtier or general. But Kropotkin became interested more in natural history and politics than in the prospect of a high administrative career, and when he was asked to choose the regiment which he would join as an officer, he startled the authorities and his father by asking to be posted, not to the Imperial Guards, but to a Siberian regiment, the Mounted Cossacks of the Amur. This choice was determined by the knowledge that the Far East would provide a great field for the exercise of his scientific interests, and also that he might find in these regions some means of beginning those political reforms which he already believed to be necessary in the autocratic and inhuman social system of Tsarist Russia :

" I had read all about the Mississippi of the East, the mountains it pierces, the sub-tropical vegetation of its tributary, the Usuri, and my thoughts went further—to the tropical regions which Humboldt had described, and to the great generalisations of Ritter, which I had delighted to read. Besides, I reasoned, there is in Siberia an immense field for the application of the great reforms which had been made or are coming : the workers must be few there."

He could not have wished a better situation for an apprenticeship in natural history and in local administration. During his five years in Siberia he made three geographical expeditions, which were important both in increasing the available information concerning this vast land and in developing his own knowledge and resourcefulness. The first was along the Amur and its tributary, the Usuri—a distance of more than 2,000 miles, along which it was proposed to build a chain of settlements down to the Pacific coast. The second was to explore the ancient trade route across the north of Manchuria from Transbaikalia to Blagovéschensk on the Amur. He was the first European to visit this region. The third was up the Sungari to Kirin, in the centre of Manchuria. In these areas, where there was an abundant animal life, Kropotkin was able to make at first-hand those observations of natural co-operation among animals and primitive peoples which were to provide him with examples for his later work on mutual aid.

But his explorations were not the only valuable work which he was called to perform during his sojourn in Siberia. He was made the secretary of committees for reforming the prison and exile system and for preparing a scheme of municipal self-government for the Siberian communities. He pursued this work with enthusiasm, making tireless investigations, mixing with all classes of society, and discussing the problems of administration with people directly acquainted with the practical details. But his efforts were perpetually frustrated, for his reports, which recommended many reforms that would have been beneficial both to the exiles and to the peasants of this region, failed completely to dissolve the bureaucratic apathy of the government departments, away in St Petersburg. Kropotkin perceived a lack even of elementary humanity in the Tsarist governmental system, and felt himself driven steadily towards that revolutionary path which then attracted the best, the most vigorous and intelligent, of Russian youth.

Nevertheless, these years in Siberia certainly provided Kropotkin with a direct contact with the things about which he wrote that gave his work a kind of reality absent from so many of the other social writers of his period. He had actually seen mutual aid among animals and primitive peoples, had familiarised himself with the practical details of social administration, so that his works always seem so much nearer to the actual life of men than did the theorisings of those contemporaries who had never stepped far from the study or the reading-room of the British Museum.

In 1867 Kropotkin decided to leave the army and devote himself entirely to a scientific career. He returned to St Petersburg, and entered the university, learning mathematics among the younger students, and engaging vigorously in geographical studies. He became secretary of the physical geography section of the Russian Geographical Society, a position which brought him into close contact with many of the explorers, who, in an age before the rise of anthropology, were the main sources of information concerning the habits of primitive peoples. Kropotkin heard and remembered their experiences. But his principal work was on the mountain structure of Northern Asia.

He formed the correct opinion that the current maps of this area, which represented a series of mountain ranges, were inexact and that in fact the region was a great plateau from whose marshes the rivers of Siberia took their source. For years he worked on the information of travellers, collecting geological and physical facts, charting barometric observations, calculating altitudes. In his incomparable *Memoirs of a Revolutionist* (" a great book " as Lewis Mumford has called it), he tells us :

" This preparatory work took me more than two years ; and then followed months of intense thought, in order to find out what the bewildering chaos of scattered observations meant, until one day, all of a sudden, the whole became clear and comprehensible, as if it were illuminated with a flash of light. The main structural lines of Asia are *not* north and south, or west and east ; they are from the south-west to the north-east—just as, in the Rocky Mountains and the plateaux of America, the lines are north-west to south-east ; only secondary ridges shoot out north-west. Moreover the mountains of Asia are not bundles of independent ridges, like the Alps, but are subordinated to an immense plateau—an old continent which once pointed towards Behring Strait. High border ridges have towered up along its fringes, and in the course of ages terraces, formed by later sediments, have emerged from the sea, thus adding on both sides to the width of that primitive backbone of Asia."

In later years Kropotkin maintained that this was his most important contribution to science and—although his statement will be disputed by those who regard him as one of the pioneers of sociology—the patience, efficiency and clear-sightedness with which he carried out his research and reached his conclusions show that he was indeed inspired by the true scientific spirit. In another passage of his Memoirs he describes the joy he took in this work :

" There are not many joys in human life equal to the joy of the sudden birth of a generalisation, illuminating the mind after a long period of patient research. What has seemed for years so chaotic, so contradictory, and so problematic, takes at once its proper position within an harmonious whole. Out of the wild confusion of facts and from beside the fog of guesses—contradicted almost as soon as they are born—a stately picture makes its appearance, like an Alpine chain suddenly emerging in all its grandeur from the mists which concealed it the moment before, glittering under the rays of the sun in all its simplicity and variety, in all its mightiness and beauty. And when the generalisation is put to a test, by applying it to hundreds of separate facts which seemed to be hopelessly contradictory the moment before, each of them assumes its due position, increasing the impressiveness of the picture, accentuating some characteristic outline, or adding an unsuspected detail full of meaning. The generalisation gains in strength and extent; its foundations grow in width and solidity; while in the distance, through the far-off mist on the horizon, the eye detects the outlines of new and still wider generalisations.

"He who has once in his life experienced this joy of scientific creation will never forget it; he will be longing to renew it; and he cannot but feel with pain that this sort of happiness is the lot of so few of us, while so many could also live through it—on a small or on a grand scale—if scientific methods and leisure were not limited to a handful of men."

His map of the mountain formations of Northern Asia and an accompanying monograph were eventually published in 1873.

In 1871 he was sent by the Russian Geographical Society to examine the glacial deposits of Finland and Sweden. Here he experienced the conversion that changed completely the course of his life and made him abandon science temporarily, in order to work for those social changes which seemed to him of greater urgency. It was not that he had in any way lost his deep interest in scientific matters. Indeed, at this time he was considering the preparation of an exhaustive physical geography of Russia, dealing in a thorough and scientific manner with the natural phenomena of each region and investigating the incidence of such calamities as droughts and crop failures, to ensure an adequate prevision of such events where they were likely to occur.

But for some years he had become steadily more conscious of the need for activity to alleviate the appalling social injustices of Tsarist Russia. And during his journey in Finland, when he was detached from the daily preoccupations of study and secretarial work, he had time to reconsider his attitude towards his work and his social opinions. At first, he continued his scientific speculations, and began to evolve a theory concerning the Ice Age in Europe and its effect on the present distribution of fauna and flora. Then he thought that in his physical geography of this part of Russia he could tell the peasant how, by machinery and scientific manuring, his land could be made more fruitful. But how futile this seemed when the peasant could not even feed himself properly because of the burden of rent and taxes! Kropotkin began to feel he had no right to indulge his passion for scientific generalisations and speculations when the workers were still poor and downtrodden :

" But what right had I to these higher joys, when all round me was nothing but misery and struggle for a mouldy bit of bread ; when whatsoever I should spend to enable me to live in that world of higher emotions must needs be taken from the very mouths of those who grew the wheat and had not bread enough for their children ? From somebody's mouth it must be taken, because the aggregate production of mankind remains still so low.

" Knowledge is an immense power. Men must know. But we already know much ! What if that knowledge—and only that— should become the possession of all ? Would not science itself progress in leaps and cause mankind to make strides in production, invention, and social creation, of which we are hardly in a condition now to measure the speed ?

" The masses want to know : they are willing to learn : they *can* learn. There, on the crest of that immense moraine which runs between the lakes, as if giants had heaped it up in a hurry to connect the two shores, there stands a Finnish peasant plunged in contemplation of the beautiful lakes, studded with islands, which lie before him. Not one of these peasants, poor and downtrodden though they may be, will pass this spot without stopping to admire the scene. Or there, on the shore of a lake, stands another peasant, and sings something so beautiful that the best musician would envy him his melody for its feeling and its meditative power. Both deeply feel, both meditate, both think ; they are ready to widen their knowledge : only give it to them ; only give them the means of getting leisure. This is the direction in which, and these are the kind of people for whom, I must work. All these sonorous phrases about making mankind progress, while at the same time they pretend to push onwards, are mere sophisms made up by minds anxious to shake off a fretting contradiction.''

Kropotkin began to abandon his researches and to spend his time mingling with the peasants and industrial workers as a member of an underground circle bent on social enlightenment. His decision was put to the test before he left Finland, for while he was still there the Russian Geographical Society sent a telegram asking him to become their secretary. He had long hoped for this post, because he felt that it would give him the opportunity to carry on his scientific work with greater ease. But he was determined on his new course of action and calmly declined this long-desired position. It was not an unusual sacrifice for the age. Thousands of young Russian intellectuals, men of the noblest type, were so deeply conscious of the sufferings of the people that they were moved to act in a similar way. Many an aristocrat abandoned his wealth and title, many a promising scientist or author gave up his career to mingle with the people, to live their lives and work among them, and for their sakes to undergo the dreadful years of exile in Siberia. It was a generation whose kind have long been exterminated from the Russian scene, a generation of almost saintly revolutionaries whose sincerity and love for freedom made them among the first victims of the cynical Bolshevik commissars.

2

For a time Kropotkin seemed lost to science, as he engaged more deeply in his social activity, but his later history showed that he remained a scientist in his attitude to the discovery and use of knowledge. His need to express his social ideas led him to sociology, and he eventually produced some of the most important early writings in this science. As Herbert Read has remarked :

" Deeply as he was moved by his sympathy for the poor and oppressed, and however visionary his conception of the future, he realised that the truth in sociology as in geography or any other science could only be established by inductive methods."

For this reason he stands apart as one of the few social writers of the nineteenth century whose works still have a deep social relevance.

In 1872 he went to Switzerland. There he joined the International Workingmen's Association, and became a convert to socialism. But it was not the rigid state socialism of Marx. It was the free socialism, later to be called anarchism, which was advocated by another Russian aristocrat, Michael Bakunin, and his disciples among the watchmakers of the Swiss Jura. Kropotkin was quick to detect the dangers of state rule and economic domination implicit in the teachings of Marx. Moreover, unlike a number of scientists of our own day, he carried his scientific methods into every realm of knowledge with which he came into contact, and he soon detected the unscientific nature of Marxist sociology and the much-vaunted dialectic method. Of the latter he said :

" We have heard of late very much about the dialectic method, recommended to us by Social Democrats in order to elaborate the Socialist ideal. But we no more admit this method than would

natural science. The dialectic method reminds the modern naturalist of something very antiquated that has had its day and is forgotten,
happily long since forgotten by science. No discovery of the
nineteenth century, in mechanics, astronomy, physics, chemistry,
biology, psychology, or anthropology, has been made by the dialectic method. All the immense acquisitions of the century are due
to the use of the inductive-deductive method—the only scientific
method. And as man is a part of Nature, as his personal and social
life is a natural phenomenon, just as the growth of a flower, or the
evolution of life in societies of ants or bees, there is no reason why
we should, when we pass from the flower to man, or from a village
of beavers to a human city, abandon the method which till then
has been so useful, and look for another method in the realms of
metaphysics."

Kropotkin always opposed any idea of class-dictatorship or state-
control as envisaged by the orthodox socialists, and based his conception of a free society on the co-operative tradition which had
been developed by men like Robert Owen, Fourier and Proudhon
in the earlier part of the nineteenth century. In the last decades of
that century he represented the principal opponent of Marxist
influences in the socialist movement, and it is very probable that,
had his libertarian influence prevailed in Russia, the Revolution
would not have experienced its tragic decline into the present
merciless Russian dictatorship.

Returning to Russia, Kropotkin resumed his attempts to educate
the peasants and workers of that country. Like all his associates
he knew well the dangers of such work. But he persisted, and
eventually, in 1874, was arrested and imprisoned in the dreaded
Peter and Paul fortress. There he remained for two years, returning in confinement to his geographical studies ; he wrote a report
on his Finnish expedition and also a dissertation on his glacial
theories. Then, in 1876, he made his celebrated escape from the
fortress (described vividly in his Memoirs), and came to England.

For a short time he reviewed books for *Nature* and wrote notes for the *Encyclopædia Britannica*. Then he went on to Switzerland, and spent the next few years there and in France, editing in Geneva the newspaper *Le Revolté*. In 1881 he was expelled from Switzerland because of the scare caused by the assassination of the Tsar Alexander II (an affair in which he took no part), and in 1882 he was arrested in France and sent to Clairvaux prison on a faked charge. His arrest became the subject of angry protests from the scientific and literary worlds. Herbert Spencer, Swinburne and Victor Hugo were among those who demanded his release, and eventually, when public disapproval of his imprisonment had grown too great to be ignored, he was released in 1886. He returned to live permanently in England.

" We settled in a small cottage at Harrow. We cared little about the furniture of our cottage, a good part of which I made myself with the aid of Tchaykovsky—he had been in the meantime in the United States and had learnt some carpentering—but we rejoiced immensely at having a small plot of heavy Middlesex clay in our garden. My wife and myself went with much enthusiasm into small culture, the admirable results of which I began to realise after having made acquaintance with the writings of Toubeau, and some Paris *maraîchers* (gardeners), and after our own experiment in the prison garden at Clairvaux."

But the cultivation of his garden and the making of his furniture formed only one side of Kropotkin's life in England. His experiences had led him to realise the complementary natures of manual and intellectual work, and he balanced his craftsmanship with much writing and speaking.

He devoted himself first to the continuation of his anarchist teachings. He made lecture tours all over the country, and was one of the founders of the Freedom Press and of the periodical *Freedom*, still in circulation. But his scientific interests began to manifest themselves again, and the more

[90]

he investigated social questions, the more he realised the need to establish an independent sociology, concerned rather with the objective description of the faults in society and the formulation of the natural laws of social intercourse, than with supporting any partisan doctrine.

The three most important books of this period are *The Conquest of Bread*, published in 1888, *Field, Factories and Workshops*, published in 1899, and *Mutual Aid*, published in 1902. The first was intended to advocate anarchist ideas. The others were very careful scientific studies of social phenomena, and they have been acknowledged by many modern sociologists as among the classic forerunners of social science. Nevertheless, although Kropotkin in these later works carefully avoided mingling his anarchist views with the discussion of his investigations into social phenomena, he retained his consistently libertarian attitude, and always found that his studies reinforced the ideas he already held.

The Conquest of Bread, for all its intention to spread anarchist teachings, is a book infused with the scientific spirit and which should not be neglected by the student of social thought. Kropotkin's main thesis is that neither individualism nor State collectivism can attain a satisfactory society. We must base our economic and social affairs on a foundation of solidarity, of voluntary co-operation, rather than on the ruthless competition of one extreme or the restrictive regulation of the other. Kropotkin saw that *laissez-faire* capitalism of the nineteenth-century type resulted in continued injustices within society and had failed completely to solve the problem of an effective distribution of commodities. But he also saw that the Marxist ideas of state-socialism were unlikely to produce any solution of this problem, and that, so far as the working classes were concerned, the increased power of the state could only mean a steady diminution of their freedom, with no compensating increase in material prosperity. The accuracy of his premonitions has been proved by the examples of modern totalitarian states, where governmental control of production has been linked with tyrannies as oppressive as any in human history.

Kropotkin saw the solution to the more formidable social problems in the spread of voluntary co-operation as a principle of organisation. He viewed with approbation the success of such voluntary bodies as the Red Cross and the Life-Boat Institution, and indicated the efficient and valuable part which co-operative activities had played in society before the rise of the State. Even the international agreements between railways and post offices of various countries, working efficiently without over-riding authorities, impressed him as further examples of the power of co-operation to create social assets, and he looked forward to the day when the whole life of man would be organised on such a basis, and the need for the State itself would eventually vanish.

It is, however, in the latter part of *The Conquest of Bread* that Kropotkin presents the ideas which are most interesting from a sociological point of view. These include an attack on the ideas of production and consumption held by contemporary economists, an advocacy of industrial decentralisation, a denunciation of the " division of labour " system, and a dissertation on the value of intensive scientific methods in agriculture.

His main quarrel with the orthodox political economists was that they were concerned too much with current production instead of with the potential needs of consumption.

" If you open the work of any economist you will find that he begins with PRODUCTION, *i.e.*, by the analysis of the means employed nowadays for the creation of wealth : division of labour, the factory, its machinery, the accumulation of capital. Adam Smith to Marx, all have proceeded along these lines. Only in the latter parts of their books do they treat of Consumption, that is to say, of the means resorted to in our present Society to satisfy the needs of the individuals ; and even there they confine themselves to explaining how riches are divided among those who vie with one another for their possession.

" Perhaps you will say this is logical. Before satisfying needs you must create the wherewithal to satisfy them. But, before producing anything, must you not feel the need of it ? Was it not necessity that first drove man to hunt, to raise cattle, to cultivate land, to make implements, and later on to invent machinery ? Is it not the study of the needs that should govern production ? To say the least, it would therefore be quite as logical to begin by considering the needs, and afterwards to discuss how production is, and ought to be, organised, in order to satisfy these needs.

" But as soon as we look at Political Economy from this point of view, it entirely changes its aspect. It ceases to be a simple description of facts, and becomes a *science*, and we may define this science as : *The study of the needs of mankind, and the means of satisfying them with the least possible waste of human energy.* . . . In the series of sociological sciences, the economy of human societies takes the place occupied in the series of biological sciences by the physiology of organic bodies.

" We say, here are human beings, united in a society. All of them feel the need of living in healthy houses. The savage's hut no longer satisfies them ; they require a more or less comfortable solid shelter. The question is, then : whether, taking the present capacity of man for production, every man can have a house of his own ? And what is hindering him from having it ?

" And as soon as we ask *this* question, we see that every family in Europe could perfectly well have a comfortable house, such as are built in England, in Belgium, or in Pullman City, or else an equivalent set of rooms. A certain number of days' work would suffice to build a pretty little airy house, well fitted up and lighted by electricity.

" But nine-tenths of Europeans have never possessed a healthy house, because at all times common people have had to work day after day to satisfy the needs of their rulers, and have never had the necessary leisure or money to build, or to have built, the home of their dreams. And they can have no houses and will inhabit hovels as long as present conditions remain unchanged.

" It is thus seen that our method is quite contrary to that of the economists, who immortalise the so-called laws of production, and, reckoning up the number of houses built every year, demonstrate by statistics, that as the number of the new-built houses *is* too small to meet all demands, nine-tenths of Europeans *must* live in hovels."

In these simple terms Kropotkin made a criticism of orthodox economics which has been steadily reinforced by social and industrial developments in our own century. To-day, scientific development proceeds so quickly that it has become evident, as it was to Kropotkin, that the only real limit to possible production is the extent of human needs. Only the organisation of distribution stands in the way of an economy of plenty.

Another fallacy of the orthodox economists which Kropotkin attacked was the theory of over-production, held by Marxists as well as academicians. Kropotkin showed clearly that it was not a question of over-production. It was merely a question of the consumers being debarred by the financial system from ever satisfying the full extent of their needs, and if these barriers were dissolved we should in fact find that the present is by realistic standards a period of under-production. In view of the perennial appearance of this theory as an explanation of economic crises, it is worth recalling Kropotkin's able refutation :

" Is there a single economist, academician, or candidate for academical honours, who has not supported arguments, proving that economic crises are due to over-production—that at a given moment more cotton, more cloth, more watches are produced than are needed ! Have we not, all of us, thundered against the rapacity of the capitalists who are obstinately bent on producing more than can possibly be consumed !

" However, on careful examination, all these reasonings prove unsound. In fact, is there one single commodity among those in universal use which is produced in greater quantity than need be ? Examine one by one all commodities sent out by countries exporting on a large scale, and you will see that nearly all are produced in *insufficient* quantities for the inhabitants of the countries exporting them.

" It is not the surplus of wheat that the Russian peasant sends to Europe. The most plentiful harvests of wheat and rye in European Russia only yield *enough* for the population. And as a rule, the peasant deprives himself of what he actually needs when he sells his wheat or rye to pay rent and taxes.

" It is not a surplus of coal that England sends to the four corners of the globe, because only three-quarters of a ton, per head of population, annually, remains for home domestic consumption, and millions of Englishmen are deprived of fire in the winter, or have only just enough to boil a few vegetables. In fact, setting aside useless luxuries, there is in England, which exports more than any other country, one single commodity in universal use— cottons—whose production is sufficiently great to *perhaps* exceed the needs of the community. Yet when we look upon the rags that pass for wearing apparel worn by over a third of the inhabitants of the United Kingdom, we are led to ask ourselves whether the cottons exported would not, on the whole, suit the *real* needs of the population ?

" As a rule it is not a surplus that is exported, though it may have been so originally. The fable of the barefooted shoemaker is as true of nations as it was formerly of individual artisans. We export the *necessary* commodities. And we do so, because the workmen cannot buy with their wages what they have produced, *and pay besides the rent and interest to the capitalist and the banker.*

" Not only does the ever-growing need of comfort remain unsatisfied, but the strict necessities of life are often wanting. Therefore,

' surplus production ' does *not* exist, at least not in the sense given to it by the theorists of Political Economy."

These considerations on the nature of capitalist production led Kropotkin to the other investigations which he had sketched in *The Conquest of Bread*. As a true scientist, he did not merely make the statement that production could be increased immeasurably. Instead, he set about laboriously considering the nature of agricultural and industrial production, and eventually gathered so much information that he was able to prove his contentions without the least difficulty. In *Memoirs of a Revolutionist* he links this whole line of research with his thoughts on the myth of over-production :

" I thought . . . that under the present conditions of private ownership production itself had taken a wrong turn, so as to neglect, and often to prevent, the production of the very necessities of life on a sufficient scale. None of these are produced in greater quantities than would be required to secure well-being for all ; and the over-production, so often spoken of, means nothing but that the masses are too poor to buy even what is now considered as necessary for a decent existence. But in all civilised countries the production, both agricultural and industrial, ought to and easily might be immensely increased so as to secure a reign of plenty for all. This brought me to consider the possibilities of modern agriculture, as well as those of an education which would give to everyone the possibility of carrying on at the same time both enjoyable manual work and brain work."

All the questions involved in this study, the conditions of agricultural and industrial production, the decentralisation of industry, the evils of the division of labour, and the need for an integration both of town and country life and of brain and hand work, are discussed in the latter chapters of *The Conquest of Bread*, but Kropotkin was not content with a mere sketch of his ideas. He set to work on a treatise in the scientific manner and, after many years of painstaking research, produced a series of articles which appeared

in *The Nineteenth Century* and were later published in a volume
as *Fields, Factories and Workshops*. In the modern sociological
tendency towards the advocacy of an open and organic society
this was an epoch-making work, and it even had some prophetic
significance, as has been indicated by Lewis Mumford, who says :
" What was bold prophecy when he first published *Fields, Factories
and Workshops* has now become a definite movement, as the technical means of economic regionalism and the social impulses that
gave it direction have emerged. For the other side of the indus-
trialisation of agriculture, which has been so rapidly going on alike
under capitalism, co-operation and socialism, is the ruralisation of
industry."

Fields, Factories and Workshops opens with a passage on the
decentralisation of industry, in which Kropotkin points out how,
even in his day, the specialisation of various countries in industrial
production was being threatened by the steady spread of industry
in the countries which had formerly been consumers. The old
hegemony of England, Germany and America over the markets of
the world was breaking up—a process which has gone on apace
since Kropotkin's day—and he regarded this as an excellent tendency
in correction of the top-heavy structure of nineteenth-century
industrialism. Against the regional specialisation of industry, and
equally against that specialisation among individuals implied in the
theory and practice of division of labour, Kropotkin advocated the
integration of labour as the basis for a healthy social and individual
life :

" When we revert from the scholastics of our text-books, and
examine human life as a whole, we soon discover that, while all the
benefits of a temporary division of labour must be maintained, it is
high time to claim those of the *integration of labour*. Political
economy has hitherto insisted chiefly upon *division*. We proclaim
integration ; and we maintain that the ideal of society—that is,
the state towards which society is already marching—is a society

of integrated, combined labour. A society where each individual is a producer of both manual and intellectual work; where each able-bodied human being is a worker, and where each worker works both in the field and the industrial workshop; where each aggregation of individuals, large enough to dispose of a certain variety of natural resources—it may be a nation, or rather a region—produces and itself consumes most of its own agricultural and manufactured produce.

" Of course, as long as society remains organised so as to permit the owners of the land and capital to appropriate for themselves, under the protection of the State and historical rights, the yearly surplus of human production, no such changes can be thoroughly accomplished. But the present industrial system, based upon a permanent specialisation of functions, already bears in itself the germs of its proper ruin. The industrial crises, which grow more acute and protracted, and are rendered still worse and still more acute by the armaments and wars implied by the present system, are rendering its maintenance more and more difficult. . . .

" But we maintain also that any socialist attempt at remodelling the present relations between Capital and Labour will be a failure, if it does not take into account the above tendencies towards integration. These tendencies have not yet received, in our opinion, due attention from the different socialist schools—but they must. A reorganised society will have to abandon the fallacy of nations specialised for the production of either agricultural or manufactured produce. It will have to rely on itself for the production of food and many, if not most, of the raw materials; it must find the best means of combining agriculture with manufacture—the work in the field with a decentralised industry; and it will have to provide for ' integrated education ', which education alone, by teaching both science and handicraft from earliest childhood, can give to society the men and women it really needs."

The first part of Kropotkin's examination of the possibilities of integrated production is concerned with agriculture. Viewing the present situation, where most manufacturing countries grow insufficient food and import large quantities, he considers how it might be improved and, from a long series of conscientious investigations of potential production in agriculture, he reaches the conclusion that it is in fact possible for countries like England to grow enough agricultural produce to feed their present populations in plenty. His calculations are in no way speculative; they are based on the actual results of intensive cultivation which have been used regularly by market gardeners and even by peasants in certain parts of the world. Some years ago, when I was writing my booklet, *New Life to the Land*, I had occasion to investigate much of the information given by Kropotkin, and I found that, not only were his calculations based on practical methods of intensive farming used by growers with unexceptional soils and climates, but also that they have been reinforced by recent developments in agricultural technique. My own practical experience as a market gardener also led me to the opinion that there was nothing impossible in Kropotkin's suggestion.

Kropotkin was a very emphatic supporter of self-sufficiency, and in the following passage he discusses the possibilities and benefits of attaining this condition :

" Supposing, then, that each inhabitant of Great Britain were compelled to live on the produce of his own land, all he would have to do would be, first, to consider the land of this country as a common inheritance, which must be disposed of to the best advantage of each and all—this is, evidently, an absolutely necessary condition. And next, he would have to cultivate his soil, not in some extravagant way, but no better than land is already cultivated upon thousands and thousands of acres in Europe and America. He would not be bound to invent some new methods, but could simply generalise and widely apply those which have stood the test of experience. He can do it ; and in so doing he would save an

immense quantity of the work which is now given for buying his
food abroad, and for paying all the intermediaries who live upon
this trade.   Under a rational culture, those necessaries and those
luxuries which must be obtained from the soil, undoubtedly *can*
be obtained with much less work than is required now for buying
these commodities. . . . If we take, indeed, the masses of produce
which are obtained under rational culture, and compare them with
the amount of labour which must be spent for obtaining them
under an irrational culture, for collecting them abroad, for trans-
porting them, and for keeping armies of middlemen, we see at
once how few days and hours need be given, under proper culture,
for growing man's food."

Kropotkin then examines industry, and shows, with equal detail,
that, despite the spread of the large factory system, much industry
has been left to small localised workshops, and that such a method
has remained more efficient for many types of production.   Looking
into the future, he sees, accurately, that under the stimulus of modern
technics it will become possible for a decentralised and regional
industry again to take the place of the large-scale factory.   This
development has actually started in our own day, when, under the
necessities of war and with the assistance of universally disseminated
electrical power, a major decentralisation of industry has already
begun.   If this development were continued with the object of
promoting the integration of human lives, it would undoubtedly
lead to a much healthier community.   Kropotkin's theories of the
mingling of agriculture and industry are very similar to those
developed later by Patrick Geddes, Ebenezer Howard (the founder
of the garden cities) and Lewis Mumford, while they even find an
echo in some of the schemes for satellite towns which are being
prepared in post-war schemes of reconstruction.   On this subject
he says :

"The scattering of industries over the country—so as to bring
the factory amidst the fields, to make agriculture derive all those

profits which it always finds in being combined with industry and
to produce a combination of industrial with agricultural work—
is surely the next step to be taken, as soon as a reorganisation of
present conditions is possible. It is being made already, here and
there, as we saw in the preceding pages. This step is imposed by
the very necessity of *producing for the producers themselves* ; it is
imposed by the necessity for each healthy man and woman to spend
a part of their lives in manual work in the free air ; and it will be
rendered the more necessary when the great social movements,
which have now become unavoidable, come to disturb the present
international trade, and compel each nation to revert to her own
resources for her own maintenance. Humanity as a whole, as well
as each separate individual, will be gainers by the change, and the
change will take place."

Kropotkin is fully conscious that the kind of individual rein-
tegration which should emerge from such a change in the form of
society must imply, if it is to be fully successful, an " integration of
capacities," which will mean not only a replacement of the division
of labour by a variety of occupations, but also the combination of
hand work with brain work. To this end he advocates an integral
education, in which the old forms of academic education would be
replaced by new forms wherein mental and manual aptitude
would be cultivated at the same time. In this again, he anticipates
the work of modern educationalists, who have turned away from
academic and towards integral education in their progressive and
free schools.

From these changes, the intensification of agricultural production,
the mingling of industry and land work, the integration of various
faculties in work and education, the elimination of division-of-
labour systems and profit motives, Kropotkin foresees a steadily
improving society, where the resources of science will be used
unstintingly to increase production and reduce toil.

" But modern knowledge has another issue to offer to thinking

men. It tells them that in order to be rich they need not take the
bread from the mouths of others ; but that the more rational outcome would be a society in which men, with the work of their own
hands and intelligence, and by the aid of the machinery already
invented and to be invented, should themselves create all imaginable
riches. Technics and science will not be lagging behind if production takes such a direction. Guided by observation, analysis
and experiment, they will answer all possible demands. They will
reduce the time which is necessary for producing wealth to any
desired amount, so as to leave to everyone as much leisure as he or
she may ask for. They surely cannot guarantee happiness, because
happiness depends as much, or even more, upon the individual
himself as upon his surroundings. But they guarantee, at least, the
happiness that can be found in the full and varied exercise of the
different capacities of the human being, in work that need not be
overwork, and in the consciousness that one is not endeavouring
to base his own happiness upon the misery of others."

3

But these ideas of a co-operative society which Kropotkin put
forward in *The Conquest of Bread* and *Fields, Factories and Workshops* were always threatened by the arguments of those who maintained that men were incapable of co-operation and quoted in
support of their contention the theory of the Struggle for Existence
put forward by Thomas Henry Huxley and other neo-Malthusians,
as the logical development of Darwin's evolutionary teachings.
The opponents of a rational co-operative view of society justified
by this theory both the unlimited and rapacious competition of
laissez-faire capitalism and the rigorous oppression by the state of
those who did not fit in with the desired pattern of social hegemony.
Clearly, if any co-operative social action were to be maintained with
success, it must be supported by an effective answer to Huxley and
his followers. Kropotkin, with his early training in natural history,

was eminently capable of such a task, and he prepared a series of essays, which were published in *The Nineteenth Century* and later appeared as *Mutual Aid* in 1902.

Kropotkin shows, from his own observations and those of other scientists, that, far from the struggle for existence being the general rule in the animal world, the majority of animals, and particularly those which lived in groups, carried on their relations within the species on a basis of mutual aid, and at times of danger or need often showed a remarkable solidarity and self-sacrifice which was not at all in the spirit of the " Hobbesian war of each against all " postulated by the Huxleyans. The details and facts on which Kropotkin bases this contention are as abundant as those with which Darwin supported his original theory of the origin of species, and leave no doubt of the scientific validity of the mutual aid theory.

But Kropotkin further shows that, not only is mutual aid a rule among the majority of animal species, but also that the physically weaker species almost always owe their survival to this quality, and that, in fact, the social species, although they may be individually weaker than such solitary beasts as the larger carnivores, have a better chance of survival and evolution to a higher form. Undoubtedly, man owes his position in a great degree to the fact that his ancestors were a particularly social species who made up for their weakness by their capacity for co-operation. Contrary to some of the early speculations of man's origin, there is no evidence at all that he was ever other than a social species ; indeed, there is abundant indication among the relics of early man of his primeval sociability and co-operativeness. Kropotkin, it must be emphasised, does not deny that there is a struggle for existence. Indeed, he holds that in certain circumstances the presence of the competitive spirit was a valuable element in progress, and that its complete absence would be detrimental to progress. But he contends that everywhere it is balanced by the contrary principle of mutual aid, and that in evolution, at least in the evolution of the higher animals, mutual aid is the more important factor.

Kropotkin goes on to demonstrate how the element of co-operation lies at the basis of all human societies. In brilliant examinations of the life of savage communities, of barbarian villages, of mediæval cities and of our modern society, he shows the important part which mutual aid has played in the development of social activities, and its vital rôle as the principal and organic bond between human beings. Even to-day that principle survives as the most important factor in human intercourse :

" . . . neither the crushing powers of the centralised State nor the teachings of mutual hatred and pitiless struggle which came, adorned with the attributes of science, from obliging philosophers and sociologists, could weed out the feeling of human solidarity, deeply lodged in men's understanding and heart, because it has been nurtured by all our preceding evolution. What was the outcome of evolution since its earliest stages cannot be overpowered by one of the aspects of that same evolution. And the need of mutual aid and support which had lately taken refuge in the narrow circle of the family, or the slum neighbours, in the village, or the secret union of workers, reasserts itself again, even in our modern society, and claims its rights to be, as it always has been, the chief leader towards further progress."

Human nature is in fact such that in a natural state of existence men are led by feelings of personal responsibility to co-operate willingly with their fellows for the common good. This fundamental mutuality is the basis of every creed of social ethics, and, if it did not condition almost every act of our common lives, the most austere of tyrannies could not prevent the disintegration of human social patterns.

Mutual Aid is a book whose place in the history of sociology is undisputed. It finally placed beyond doubt the natural character of human co-operation, and helped to base social conceptions on a natural and organic rather than on an artificial and political basis.

4

The work of Kropotkin's last years had already been fore-shadowed in the closing passage of *Mutual Aid* :

" . . . it is especially in the domain of ethics that the dominating importance of the mutual-aid principle appears in full. That mutual aid is the real foundation of our ethical conceptions seems evident enough. But whatever the opinions as to the first origin of the mutual-aid feeling or instinct may be—whether a biological or a supernatural cause is ascribed to it—we must trace its existence as far back as to the lowest stages of the animal world ; and from these stages we can follow its uninterrupted evolution, in opposition to a number of contrary agencies, through all degrees of human development, up to the present times. Even the new religions which were born from time to time—always at epochs when the mutual-aid principle was falling into decay in the theocracies and despotic states of the East, or at the decline of the Roman Empire —even the new religions have only reaffirmed that same principle. They found their first supporters among the humble, in the lowest, downtrodden layers of society, where the mutual-aid principle is the necessary foundation of everyday life ; and the new forms of union which were introduced in the earliest Buddhist and Chris-tian communities, in the Moravian brotherhoods and so on, took the character of a return to the best aspects of mutual aid in early tribal life.

" Each time, however, that an attempt to return to this old principle was made, its fundamental idea itself was widened. From the clan it was extended to the stem, to the federation of stems, to the nation, and finally, in ideal, at least—to the whole of mankind. It was also refined at the same time. In primitive Buddhism, in primitive Christianity, in the writings of some of the Mussulman teachers, in the early movements of the Reform, and especially in the ethical and philosophical movements of the last century, and of our own time, the total abandonment of the idea of revenge, or of ' due reward '—of good for good and evil for evil—is affirmed more and more vigorously. The higher conception of ' no revenge for wrongs ', and of freely giving more than one expects to receive from his neighbours, is proclaimed as being the real principle of morality—a principle superior to mere equivalence, equity or justice, and more conducive to happiness. And man is appealed to, to be guided in his acts, not merely by love, which is always personal, or at the best tribal, but by the perception of his oneness with every human being. In the practice of mutual aid which we can trace to the earliest beginnings of evolution, we thus find the positive and undoubted origin of our ethical conceptions ; and we can affirm that in the ethical progress of man, mutual support—not mutual struggle—has had the leading part. In its wide extension, even at the present time, we also see the best guarantee of a still loftier evolution of our race."

Kropotkin devoted the remainder of his long life to the consideration of the problem of ethics and to the preparation of a great book on the subject which was to have been his *magnum opus*. Already, in 1892, he had published a pamphlet entitled *Anarchist Morality*, in which he sketched out a general basis for ethics, and in 1904–5 he published in *The Nineteenth Century* two essays, " The Ethical Need of the Present Day " and " The Morality of Nature ". But, as he was engaged on two other important books which lie somewhat outside the scope of the present study (*Ideals and Realities in Russian Literature* and *The Great French Revolution*) he had not started the actual writing of this work when the Russian Revolution began in 1917 and, although he was an old man of seventy-five, he hastened there to play what part he could in the regeneration of his country. It was a period of bitter disillusionment. He found that the most powerful group of revolutionaries had become dominated by those very authoritarian principles against which he had always striven to warn the workers, and, despite his efforts to avert the tragedy, the Bolsheviks made their way to power by force and fraud.

All those who defended individual freedom were persecuted, and many thousands of liberals, anarchists and social revolutionaries were shot and imprisoned. Kropotkin was not threatened, because of his great reputation in Russia and the outside world, but, after he was prevented from carrying on a survey of the industrial resources of the country, he saw quite clearly that there was nothing he could do to improve the condition of Russia, and retired . to a tiny village, Dimitrov, to write his book on ethics. He worked in great privation. Food and fuel were scanty, and, perhaps the greatest hardship of all, he had to work after nightfall with a meagre oil lamp, except when his friends sent him candles. He had few books, and checking references was often extremely difficult, while he had to type his own notes laboriously on a worn-out machine. Occasionally, he would play the piano for recreation.

" However," says Emma Goldman in *My Disillusionment with Russia*, " it was not his own discomfort which sapped his strength. It was the thought of the Revolution that had failed, the hardships of Russia, the persecutions, the endless *raztels*, which made the last two years of his life a deep tragedy. On two occasions he attempted to bring the rulers of Russia to their senses : once in protest against the suppression of all non-communist publications ; the other time against the barbaric practice of taking hostages. . . . But the protests had no effect. Thereafter Kropotkin felt that it was useless to appeal to a government gone mad with power."

He died on the 8th February 1921, leaving his work on ethics half completed, with even a sentence unfinished in his exhaustion. His funeral became the occasion for the last great demonstration in Moscow by the lovers of freedom against the tyrannies of the Bolshevik régime, as the great procession, led by the black anarchist flags and banners with slogans denouncing the tyranny, and surrounded by an unbroken line of students, moved through the Moscow streets. At his graveside the anarchist leaders made their last defiant speeches before they entered the dungeons from which they never emerged.

*   *   *   *

The portion of *Ethics* which Kropotkin left and which was published in England in 1924 consists of almost all the uncompleted first volume, in the form of a history of ethical ideas, of which Herbert Read says : " No better history of ethics has ever been written." The second volume was intended as an " exposition of the basis of realistic ethics, and its aims." Kropotkin sought to establish a system of ethics which would be divorced from the supernatural or the metaphysical ; in other words, a morality concerned for once with its real function, the relationship of man to man.

It is unfortunate that we have been deprived of this work, but from the first volume and from the previously published pamphlet and essays, we can at least reconstruct a general outline of Kropotkin's ethical ideas.

Kropotkin was quite convinced that ethics could become a science, and could be treated in a purely scientific manner :

" A system of ethics worthy of the present scientific revival, which would take advantage of all the recent acquisitions for reconstituting the very foundations of morality on a wider philosophical basis, and which would give the civilised nations the inspiration required for the great task that lies before them—such a system has not yet been produced. But the need of it is felt everywhere. A new, realistic moral science is the need of the day—a science as free from superstition, religious dogmatism, and metaphysical mythology as modern cosmogony and philosophy already are, and permeated at the same time with those higher feelings and brighter hopes which are inspired by the modern knowledge of man and his history—this is what humanity is persistently demanding."

[108]

Kropotkin regarded mutual aid, or solidarity, as the basis of morality, which thus exists as a factor even among the lowly forms of animal life. But, with the development of human consciousness, the growth of reason and imagination, there is added the element of sympathy, by which we try to put ourselves in the place of another person, and thus understand his needs and sufferings. It is from this kind of mutual sympathy, of putting oneself in another's position, that there arises the " Golden Rule ", which enjoins men to act to others as they would like others to act to them. But this rule is too vague to be an effective basis for a rational morality.

Therefore we must add justice, which is essentially the recognition of each man as an individual with equal rights to the satisfaction of his needs, to freedom of choice, and to an equal share in all the opportunities of the society with which he co-operates. It means even more than the mere recognition of such rights—it demands an active spirit of sociality which will attempt to ensure such equality.

But justice is not all. A living morality needs something that will carry men beyond the mere recognition of reciprocal equality, the giving to other men what is their exact due. For human society to grow, for the relationship of men to become fruitful, it is necessary for another quality, which Kropotkin called magnanimity, to be exercised. Men should learn to give their efforts freely in whatever way they have chosen to help humanity, and to go always beyond what justice itself might demand of them in their relations with other men. It is a mistake to think that such action necessarily means any kind of mystical self-sacrifice on behalf of others. On the contrary, pure altrusim as envisaged by the moralists does not exist, and the man who gives and continues to give does so because he finds that in this way he gains a greater personal fulfilment.

From all these qualities morality is built up :

" *Mutual Aid—Justice—Morality* are thus the consecutive

steps of an ascending series, revealed to us by the study of the animal world and man. They constitute an *organic necessity* which carries in itself its own justification, confirmed by the whole of the evolution of the animal kingdom, beginning with its earliest stages (in the form of colonies of the most primitive organisms), and gradually rising to our civilised human communities. Figuratively speaking, it is a *Universal law of organic evolution*, and this is why the sense of Mutual Aid, Justice and Morality are rooted in man's mind with all the force of an inborn instinct—the first instinct, that of Mutual Aid, being evidently the strongest, while the third, developed later than the others, is an unstable feeling and the least imperative of the three.

" Like the need of food, shelter, or sleep, these instincts are self-preservation instincts. Of course, they may sometimes be weakened under the influence of certain circumstances, and we know many cases when the power of these instincts is relaxed, for one reason or another, in some animal group, or in a human community ; but then the group necessarily begins to fail in the struggle for life ; it moves towards its decay. And if this group does not revert to the necessary conditions of survival and of progressive development—Mutual Aid, Justice and Morality—then the group, the race or the species dies out and disappears. Since it did not fulfil the necessary condition of evolution—it must inevitably decline and disappear."

This outline of Kropotkin's moral ideas is necessarily sketchy and incomplete. But he left the notes of his final volume, and it is to be hoped that they have survived and will one day be arranged and published to provide the crowning work of the career of this scientist devoted throughout his life to the cause of human freedom.

VII

George Orwell

THE English writers of the 1930's have worn badly in an ensuing decade, with perhaps three important exceptions—George Orwell, Herbert Read and Graham Greene. It is difficult not to connect this fact with their political records, for these three were the only writers of real significance who did not at one time or another become deeply involved with the Communist Party and suffer a subsequent disillusionment which drove them back to an unrealistic social isolation.

Of the three, all had been aware throughout the 1930's of the faults of both capitalist society and also of the ascendant Stalinism. Herbert Read was an anarchist, Graham Greene a Catholic of that socially conscious type which reached its best development in Eric Gill, and George Orwell an independent socialist with libertarian tendencies, whose peculiar experiences, particularly in Spain, led him early to a distrust for the Communists which has become his best-known single characteristic. Ask any Stalinist to-day what English writer is the greatest danger to the Communist cause, and he is likely to answer " Orwell ". Ask the ordinary reader what is the most familiar of Orwell's books, and he is likely to answer *Animal Farm*. Inquire in any circle of anarchists or independent socialists who regard opposition to totalitarian communism as an important task of the militant Left, and you will find Orwell's name respected as a writer who, when the communist cause was most popular in this country, did not hesitate to denounce the falsehood and disregard for elementary human liberties which are essential to Communist methods of political action. Indeed, it is perhaps because this anti-Communist side of Orwell's writing has been stressed so much both by his critics and by his friends that it is necessary to give a wider picture of his literary achievement and of the character of his writing.

Orwell is a writer whose work is essentially autobiographical and personal. Several of his books are devoted to the direct description of his own experiences ; in his novels can be seen clearly the influence of incidents which have occurred during his life, and in his political essays there is always a strong upsurge of personal likes and dislikes, of scraps of experience which have made some recent and powerful effect on his imagination. Indeed, the connection between Orwell's work and even the minor events of his life is so close that, for those who are friendly with him, it is an interesting pastime to trace recent conversations reproduced with considerable faithfulness in his articles in periodicals. I have met few writers whose work was so closely integrated with their daily action and observations.

For this reason, it is perhaps best to begin a closer study of Orwell's work with a biographical sketch which will help to show why he evolved differently from his English contemporaries.

Orwell was born into the impoverished upper-middle class, a particularly unhappy section of English society where a small income is strained to the utmost in the desperate struggle to keep up appearances, and where, from the very fact that social position is almost all these people possess, snobbery is more highly developed and class distinction more closely observed than anywhere else in the complicated hierarchy of English society. " I was very young," he tells us, " not much more than six, when I first became aware of class distinctions," and in *The Road to Wigan Pier* he gives a clear description of the whole attitude of this poor-genteel class, "the shock-absorbers of the bourgeoisie" as he calls them, towards the working class.

Later, Orwell was sent to Eton. He went there with a scholarship, and, as he tells us : " On the one hand, it made me cling tighter than ever to my gentility ; on the other hand it filled me with resentment against the boys whose parents were richer than mine and who took care to let me know it. . . . The correct and elegant thing, I felt, was to be of gentle birth but to have no money. This is part of the *credo* of the lower-upper-middle class. It has a romantic, Jacobite-in-exile feeling about it which is very comforting." It was the feeling of resentment that first made him think in revolutionary terms. He read the works of Shaw and Wells, the latter of whom was to become a great influence, and began to describe himself as a Socialist. "But I had no grasp of what Socialism meant, and no notion that the working class were human beings."

Up to this stage, Orwell's progress had much in common with that of his contemporary writers of the 1930's—the genteel middle-class home, the upper-class school, the continual struggle in youth between an ingrained snobbery and a sentimental revolutionism. But the difference lay in subsequent experiences. While most of the other public-school writers, who formed the backbone of the Communist support during the 1930's, went on to the universities, became schoolmasters, and gained a purely academic knowledge of social problems, perhaps ending by going to Spain as journalists or broadcasters, Orwell's life gave him the opportunity of seeing imperialism in action at close quarters, and of observing the troubles of the workers from among them, as well as experiencing the Spanish civil war in a more direct manner than most English writers.

At a little under twenty, he joined the Indian Imperial Police in Burma, then still administered as part of India. He worked in

this force for five years, during which he witnessed imperialism at
its worst, saw hangings, floggings and filthy prisons, and was forced
to assert a superiority over the Burmese which he never really felt.
All this is portrayed with great vividness in his first novel, *Burmese
Days*, and in one or two short sketches, such as *Shooting an Elephant*
and *A Hanging*, an early essay which described the really brutal
side of British rule. At the end of his five years in this service,
Orwell went home. He decided not merely to eschew the service
of an imperialism which he had come to hate, but also to try and
do something to expiate his guilt by identifying himself, if not with
the Burmese natives, at least with the oppressed lower classes of his
own country. I quote at length the passage from *The Road to
Wigan Pier* in which he describes his conversion :

" I was not going back to be a part of that evil despotism. But
I wanted much more than merely to escape from my job. For five
years I had been part of an oppressive system, and it had left me
with a bad conscience. Innumerable remembered faces—faces of
prisoners in the dock, of men waiting in the condemned cells, of
subordinates I had bullied and aged peasants I had snubbed, of
servants and coolies I had hit with my fist in moments of rage
(nearly everyone does these things in the East, at any rate occasionally : orientals can be very provoking), haunted me intolerably.
I was conscious of an immense weight of guilt that I had got to
expiate. I suppose that sounds exaggerated ; but if you do for
five years a job that you thoroughly disapprove of, you will probably
feel the same. I had reduced everything to the simple theory that
the oppressed are always right and the oppressors always wrong :
a mistaken theory, but the natural result of being one of the oppressors yourself. I felt that I had got to escape not merely from
imperialism but from every form of man's dominion over man. I
wanted to submerge myself—to get down among the oppressed,
to be one of them and on their side against their tyrants. And,
chiefly because I had had to think everything out in solitude, I had

carried my hatred of oppression to extraordinary lengths. At that time failure seemed to me to be the only virtue. Every suspicion of self-advancement, even to 'succeed' in life to the extent of making a few hundreds a year, seemed to me spiritually ugly, a species of bullying."

It will be seen that Orwell's conversion came from a far deeper experience—emotionally as well as intellectually and physically— than that which made the Spenders and Audens in their college rooms and parental country rectories declare a mental adherence to communism. Orwell's socialism has never been so intellectually elaborated as that of the orthodox leftist writers. It has always been a kind of generalised conception in which the greatest tenet is human brotherhood, and Orwell has shared with most English working-class—as distinct from middle-class—socialists a profound distrust for the subtler shades of Marxist discussion. Indeed, like William Morris, he has never identified himself as a Marxist. On the other hand, his natural caution has always kept him away from the kind of silliness which made the English poets of the time create heroes out of party bureaucrats and, like Day Lewis, write inane verse about feeling small when they saw a Communist! (However, Orwell's attitude had its own failings, which we will discuss later.)

Out of the feeling of the need for expiation arose a desire for participation in sufferings of the poorest. Following this impulse, Orwell went among the tramps and outcasts of London, the really destitute people who fill the doss-houses and the casual wards, who sleep on the Thames embankment and spend their lives tramping the roads from one end of England to the other, who live by begging and a whole variety of occupations, none of which is much more than a cover for mendicancy. For long periods, at times from choice, at other times from necessity as well, he lived among these people on the very periphery of society, the people who had been brought so low that they were pushed right outside the fabric of normal class society and reached a kind of brotherhood where a common misfortune neutralised all differences of origin under its impartial weight.

During the next ten years Orwell took a variety of jobs which all kept him near the poverty line. He worked as a dishwasher in Paris hotels and restaurants, as a private school-teacher, as a book-shop assistant, as a petty grocer in his own account. It was all grist for the literary mill.

A second turning-point in his career came in 1936, when he went to fight as a militiaman in Spain. He admits that his ideas of the issues in the war were then extremely vague. He saw, like most English leftists at the time, a simple conflict between the Spanish people and their Fascist enemies. It was only the accident of his being sent to Spain under the auspices of the I.L.P. and thus finding himself in the Marxist opposition group of the POUM that led him to realise with a peculiar intensity the true nature of the situation within the government, by which the Communists and the right-wing elements were seeking to gain all power to them-selves by the suppression of the genuinely revolutionary elements, such as the anarchists and the POUM. Orwell fought on the Aragon and Huesca fronts, was wounded and returned to Barcelona, to be involved, almost immediately, in the fighting of the May days of 1937, when the Communists sought to deprive the anarchists and the POUM of their positions of advantage within the city. Later, when the great proscriptions began, he had to escape from Spain with the Stalinist police on his heels. In *Homage to Catalonia* he combines a very capable description of conditions on the Spanish fronts and in Barcelona with one of the few clear and honest accounts of the actual events in Barcelona in May 1937, and also an effective exposure of the propaganda lies which were used in the left-wing press to whitewash the Communists.

After leaving Spain, he lived in England and in French Morocco, and when the war began he became an official of the B.B.C. in their Indian service. In a discussion which I had with him at the time he defended his activities by contending that the right kind of man could at least make propaganda a little cleaner than it would otherwise have been, and I know that he managed to introduce one or two astonishing items into his broadcasts. But he soon found there was in fact little he could do, and he left the B.B.C. in disgust to become literary editor of the *Tribune*, at a period when that paper was at its best level during Aneurin Bevan's campaign against Churchill. In the past few years Orwell has become a successful journalist, and the success of *Animal Farm* brought him into the ranks of best-selling novelists. But he remains an important influence among the more revolutionary of the younger English writers, a rallying point for what intelligent anti-Stalinism exists outside the right-wing on one hand and the Trotskyists on the other, and an honest exposer of things he considers evil.

Orwell's work falls into two main divisions. On the one side there are the four novels, and the books of reportage, like *Down and Out in Paris and London*, in which social ideas, although present, cannot be regarded as dominant. And, on the other side, there are a number of books, written mostly since 1936, in which the social motive is more important, but where the æsthetic element enters strongly into the writing and structure, or becomes dominant in long descriptive passages, as in *Homage to Catalonia* or *The Road to Wigan Pier*. To this class belong, beside the books already mentioned, *The Lion and the Unicorn*, a heretical survey of the relationship of Socialism to the English mind, *Critical Essays* and *Inside the Whale*, two volumes of literary-political essays, *Animal Farm*, and a number of uncollected but important essays on various social themes.

In assessing Orwell's work, it might be well to take as a starting point a confession which he made in a recent issue of *Gangrel*, an English little magazine.

" What I have wanted to do throughout the past ten years is to make political writing into an art. My starting point is always a feeling of partisanship, a sense of injustice. When I sit down to write a book, I do not say to myself, ' I am going to produce a work of art.' I write it because there is some lie that I want to expose, some fact to which I want to draw attention, and my initial concern is to get a hearing. But I could not do the work of writing a book, or even a long magazine article, if it were not also an æsthetic experience. Anyone who cares to examine my work will see that even when it is downright propaganda it contains much that a full-time politician would consider irrelevant. I am not able, and I do not want, completely to abandon the world-view that I acquired in childhood. So long as I remain alive and well I shall continue to feel strongly about prose style, to love the surface of the earth, and to take a pleasure in solid objects and scraps of useless information. It is no use trying to suppress that side of myself. The job is to reconcile my ingrained likes and dislikes with the essentially public, non-individual activities that this age forces on us."

This passage of self-analysis is useful because it does give us fairly accurate clues to the nature of Orwell's writing. It indicates the honesty and indignation that inspire it, the concern for certain humanist values, the perception of fraud and the shrewd eye for pretence ; it also shows, perhaps less clearly, the essentially *superficial* nature of Orwell's work, the failure to penetrate deeply into the rooted causes of the injustices and lies against which he fights, and the lack of any really constructive vision for the future of man. To these considerations I shall return. But for the present I will discuss the literary merits of Orwell's work, which, in my opinion, are much more consistent and impressive than the political qualities.

Firstly, Orwell's writing is fluent and very readable. There is probably no writer in England to-day who has gained such a colloquial ease of expression, at the same time without diminishing the quality of style. Even his journalistic fragments, unimportant as they may be from any other point of view, are distinguished from the work of other journalists by their excellent style. In his novels and books of reportage, Orwell has an intense power of description. If one compares *Burmese Days* with, say, Forster's *Passage to India*, the sharper vividness with which the surface aspects of Oriental life are conveyed in Orwell's book is quite impressive. Yet this faculty of description is combined with, and perhaps balanced by, a great economy of effect and wording which gives a clean and almost athletic effect to Orwell's writing. There is no unnecessary emotion, no trappings of verbiage and superfluous imagery, no place—even in the more purple passages—where one can feel that a paragraph is unnecessary or that the book would have been as good if it had been omitted. *Animal Farm* is, of course, the best example of this virtue ; no one else could have given the whole bitter history of the Russian failure in so condensed and yet so adequate an allegory.

But these virtues of economy, clarity, fluency, descriptive vividness, are all *superficial* virtues. They do not make up for a lack of deeper understanding which is evident in Orwell's work. His description of the Eastern landscape and of the attitude of Europeans towards Orientals may be the best of its kind ; nevertheless, one fails to find understanding of the mentality and peculiar problems of Oriental people. Unlike Lafcadio Hearn, Orwell has never tried to think like an Oriental. And, indeed, his work is characterised throughout by a failure to think in other than Orwellian terms, or to create situations out of the imagination. All his novels are more or less autobiographical, in that they deal with the kind of people he has met, or the kind of experiences he has had. Of course, this is not a failing in itself—but in Orwell it is part of an inability to perceive or imagine deeply, and this is perhaps the cause of the failure of the people in his novels to be anything more than caricatures, except when, like Flory in *Burmese Days*, they are true Orwellians, or, like the insurance agent Bowling in *Coming*

Up for Air, they have a kind of schizoid nature, and Orwellise in their thoughts in a way which hardly fits their external, worldly natures. This failure to create three-dimensional characters, with profoundly observed inner lives like the people in Dostoevsky or even Henry James, is a common fault with the liberally-minded type of novelist who is concerned to illustrate some social theme in his work. It is to be found in all the great English radical novelists —Godwin, Dickens, Wells—and Orwell is truly in the tradition of these writers.

There is, for instance, something quite Dickensian in the unlikely straggle of events forming a novel such as *The Clergyman's Daughter,* which is even endowed with that perennial obsession of English radical novelists, the fraudulent private school, and which contains a selection of peripheral characters who, for all Orwell's direct experience of this borderland life, have the simplicity and oddness of true Dickens characters. And the influence of Wells is equally clear, particularly in *Animal Farm,* which contains several echoes of *The Island of Dr Moreau.*[1] It is an interesting point that Orwell should have written good critical essays on the novelists whose work resembles his own, while he fails almost completely to appreciate the virtues of more complex writers like Henry Miller or W. B. Yeats, who are little more to him than examples of the odd perversity of intellectuals who do not subscribe to the radical cause in Orwell's own simple way.

Orwell's political writing is rarely satisfying. Occasional articles, on the borderline of politics and literature, such as his essays on boys' weeklies, crime fiction and political language, are

---

[1] The main points of contact are actually direct reversals. The rule of *Animal Farm* is " Whatever goes upon two legs is an enemy ", the law of *The Island of Dr Moreau* is " Not to go on all fours ". *Animal Farm* ends with the pigs turning to men, *The Island of Dr Moreau* with the manufactured men reverting to animals. There is also the scene in the latter book where Prendick sees the pig-men going on all fours and then upright, which may have entered unconsciously into the plot of *Animal Farm.*

small masterpieces in a limited field. But beyond such bounded fragments of observation, Orwell's social writings rarely justify completely our expectations. They concern " the surface of the earth ", they generalise issues in a way which demonstrates a simplicity of thought that is part of his character and unlikely to change, they never penetrate into the deeper levels of social existence or human experience.

Orwell's rôle is the detection of pretences and injustices in political life, and the application to social matters of a very rough-and-ready philosophy of brotherhood and fair play. He plays, somewhat self-consciously, the part of the " plain man ", and in this fulfils a necessary function. A hundred Orwells would indeed have a salutary effect on the ethics of social life. But the " plain man " always has limitations, and the greatest is his failure to penetrate below the surface of events and see the true causes of social evils, the massive disorders in the very structure of society, of which individual evils are merely symptoms. I have never, for instance, seen or heard Orwell give any sound analysis of the political trends in England to-day, and on such important subjects as money, property and the State he seems to have little idea except the usual vague slogans which have inspired the Labour Party for many generations.

His attitude towards the State is typical. In a recent symposium in *Horizon* on the economic condition of the writer, he said : " If we are to have full Socialism, then clearly the writer must be State-supported, and ought to be placed among the better-paid groups. But so long as we have an economy like the present one, in which there is a great deal of State enterprise but also large areas of private capitalism, then the less truck a writer has with the State, or any other organised body, the better for him and his work. There are invariably strings tied to any kind of official patronage." The inconsistencies are obvious. If, when the State is only par-tially in control, it is a bad thing to be patronised by it, it must be worse when it is wholly in control. And if " there are invariably strings tied to any kind of official patronage ", then the artist will certainly be well and truly strangled when he accepts the patronage of the total State, Socialist or otherwise. Incidentally, this passage is a good example of the obscurity into which Orwell sometimes falls when talking of political ideas. From the first clause one would imagine him an advocate of a total State, whether we call it Socialist or otherwise, but in reality he advocates no such thing. From conversations with him, I gather that he conceives, again very vaguely, something more like a syndicalist federation than a real State in the traditional Socialist model.

There are times when the general superficiality of Orwell's attitude leads him to sincere but unjust condemnation of people or groups, because he has not been able to understand their real motives. His attack on pacifists because they enjoyed the unasked protection of the British Navy, and his " demolition " of Henry Miller for leaving Greece when the fighting started are examples of this kind of injustice. Orwell has never really understood *why* pacifists act as they do. To him passive resistance during the war was at best " objective support " of Fascism, at worst inverted worship of brutality ; he fails to see the general quality of resistance in the pacifist's attitude, the resistance to violence as a social principle rather than to any specific enemy.

Indeed, it is one of Orwell's main faults that he does not seem to recognise general principles of social conduct. He has ideas of fair-play and honesty ; concentration camps, propaganda lies and so forth are to be condemned. But in a more general sense his attitude is essentially opportunist. For instance, he contends seriously that we must have conscription during the war, but that once the war has ended we must resist it as an infringement of civil liberties. During the war we must jail " fascists ", but afterwards we must let them carry on their propaganda at will. In other words, we can have freedom when it is convenient, but at moments of crisis freedom is to be stored away for the return of better days.

A similar opportunist attitude impelled him, in *The Lion and the Unicorn*, to point out the power of patriotism over the English mind, and to claim that Socialists should use this element in popular mythology as a means of gaining popular support. He failed to understand the fundamentally evil nature of patriotism as a producer of war and a bulwark of authority, and also overlooked that patriotism is not far from nationalism and that the union of nationalism with Socialism is worse in its effects than plain reactionary nationalism, as has been seen in Germany and Russia.

Orwell is essentially the iconoclast. The fact that his blows sometimes hit wide of the mark is not important. The great thing about Orwell is that when he exposes a lie he is usually *substantially* right, and that he will always pursue his attacks without fear or favour. His exposures of the myth of Socialist Russia, culminating in *Animal Farm*, were a work of political stable-cleansing which contributed vastly to the cause of true social understanding, and it is for such achievements that we can be grateful to Orwell, and readily forgive the inconsistencies and occasional injustices that accompany them.

If iconoclasm is Orwell's rôle in political writing, then we can hardly expect the opposite virtue ; and, indeed, we find that he has little to say on *how* society can be changed and what it should become. On these points he has largely accepted the Labour Party line, with a few deviations to the left, but he seems to have no clear conception of a Socialist society, beyond a rather vague idea that brotherhood is the essential basis of Socialism. This is, indeed, an important fact which many Socialists seem to have forgotten, but it belongs less to an era of State Socialism than to the Liberalism of the past or the anarchism of the future. And, indeed, while Orwell is by no means an anarchist—although he often joins them in attacking specific injustices—he is very much nearer to the old-style

Liberal than to the corporate-state Socialists who at present lead the Labour Party. This distinguishes him from most of his contemporaries, for the Liberal is a rare suvivor in the atomic age, and a Liberal like Orwell who has developed the necessary vigour of attack is even less common. His old-fashioned pragmatism, his nineteenth-century radical honesty and frankness, his respect for such excellent bourgeois mottoes as " Fair Play " and " Don't kick a man when he's down ", which have been too much vitiated by the sneers of Marxist amoralism, his consideration for the freedom of speech and writing, are all essentially Liberal virtues.

In one of his essays there is a portrait of Dickens which might not inappropriately be applied to Orwell himself.

" He is laughing, with a touch of anger in his laughter, but no triumph, no malignity. It is the face of a man who is always fighting against something, but who fights in the open and is not frightened, the face of a man who is *generously angry*—in other words, of a nineteenth-century Liberal, a free intelligence—a type hated with equal hatred by all the smelly little orthodoxies which are now contending for our soul." The open fighting, the generous anger, the freedom of intelligence, are all characteristics of Orwell's own writing. And that very failure to penetrate to the fundamental causes of social evils, to present a consistent moral and social criticism of the society in which they lived, which characterised the nineteenth-century Liberals, has become Orwell's own main limitation.

VIII

Graham Greene

GRAHAM GREENE stands somewhat aloof among the writers who people the same literary landscape. Like Aldous Huxley in a previous decade, he has retained the respect of intellectuals while adapting a popular form so successfully that his novels have become accepted among circulating library readers and film audiences as good stories even when their moral intention is ignored. Almost alone among his contemporaries, he was little influenced by Communism, but he has never let his just dislike of Marxist ideas and practice lead him into hatred of individual Communists. He has embraced Catholicism in his manhood, yet his work contains none of that hysteria which characterised a previous generation of converts, and he has always shown a feeling for the oppressed and a concern for individual freedom of belief not generally associated with the church to which he adheres.

Nevertheless, he has remained a steadfast Catholic, and his work has been devoted more and more to the evolution, out of Catholicism, of a consistent attitude towards a chaotic world. He is a Catholic propagandist, but this has never prevented him from being a good novelist or an indignant critic of injustice. Paradoxically, his is an essentially humanist attitude; his religion is always made manifest in man.

Greene's novels might be described as a panorama of twentieth-century violence. Except his first book, *The Man Within*, they all portray in one way or another the world-wide struggle of creeds and ways of life which culminated in the last great war. There are many variants of this theme of violent struggle. *The Confidential Agent* describes the intrigues of rival agents of two sides in a country split by civil war, who are both trying to obtain coal in England; *Stamboul Train* ends in the death of a revolutionary who goes back to his own country and is shot by the police at the border; *Brighton Rock* is dominated by two themes of conflict, the underworld strife between gangs of petty crooks, and the pursuit of a murderer by an honest woman with ideas about justice; *The Power and The Glory* reveals the attempt by Mexican Communists to prevent by terror the free teaching of Christianity; and so on in varying scenes and plots down to the last and weakest novel, *The Ministry of Fear*, where the hero, haunted by guilt for killing his wife to prevent her continued suffering from an incurable disease, becomes the unwitting victim and final outwitter of a gang of international spies. Even *The Man Within*, although it is acted in an eighteenth-century setting of smugglers and revenue men, is shown in the same colours of violence and struggle, and its clothing in a past dress merely represents Greene's original desire to evade the urgency of the chaos around him.

But it would be superficial to claim that Greene's novels are concerned merely with displaying the violence of modern life, that they have no better purpose and serve no greater end than an authentic thriller like, say, *No Orchids for Miss Blandish*. Greene has adopted much from the method and form of the thriller, a type of novel which has no justification beyond the appeal of brutality. But his borrowings have been technical merely; there is nothing in his work resembling the sheer amorality of the American pulp thriller. He never in any way accepts violence, but uses the thriller form in order to investigate it, to search for its roots in the human heart, and to subject it to a moral judgment. This approach is shown clearly in a passage from *Journey Without Maps*, his account of travel in Liberia.

"To-day our world seems peculiarly susceptible to brutality. There is a touch of nostalgia in the pleasure we take in gangster novels, in characters who have so agreeably simplified their emotions that they have begun living at a level below the cerebral. We, like Wordsworth, are living after a war and a revolution, and these half-castes fighting with bombs between the cliffs of skyscrapers seem more likely than one to be aware of Proteus rising from the sea. It is not, of course, that one wishes to stay for ever at that level, but when one sees to what unhappiness, to what peril of extinction centuries of cerebration have brought us, one sometimes has a curiosity to discover if one can from what we have come, to recall at what point we went astray."

Greene sees the violence of the modern world not merely as a social phenomenon. For him it is connected with an underlying theological conception of the struggle of good and evil, and until we have grasped the importance in Greene's mind of this struggle of Divine and Satanic influences, it is useless to attempt to understand his work. The working out of this central theme does not, as some critics seem to have assumed, represent the whole of Greene's intention. Indeed, as I hope to show later, his most important contribution to contemporary writing lies outside the Mithraic drama. But at this point it is necessary to understand Greene's preoccupation with evil.

The world we live in contains such a preponderance of evil acts and events that it is difficult to avoid a feeling, however irrational, that evil exists as a real and autonomous force in the universe. It is all too easy to see a positive evil at work every day and in every part of our world. It is difficult to believe in God, but not so difficult to believe in the Devil. The creative aspects of the universe may lie all about us, but it is the dark urges against human love and dignity that move with the greatest noise in our lives and occupy always the central point in our vision.

Once we have become convinced of positive evil, it is not so difficult to learn to believe in good.   Once we have given a name to the violence that surrounds us, it does not appear such a universally bewildering phenomenon, and we can perceive that there are many things in the universe untouched by evil, evading or even resisting it successfully.   We perceive the presence of a positive good co-existent with evil, a good that balances and fights against evil.   And, seeing good and evil present in the world and in ourselves, we are easily inclined to believe in the personification of these qualities, to accept Ormuzd and Abriham, the Devil and afterwards God.   Once we have gone thus far, it is even more easy to become involved in the maze of theological rationalisation and to end by accepting the least credible doctrines of the Roman Church.   It is a cerebral process—in such a religion there is little of the intuitive, less of the mystic, but perhaps for that very reason more of the humanist.[1]

Of his own development in this direction Greene tells us, " I am a Catholic with an intellectual if not an emotional belief in Catholic dogma," and, again, " I had not been converted to a religious faith. I had been convinced by specific arguments of the probability of its creed."   Elsewhere he remarks, " once accept God and the reason should carry you further, but to accept nothing at all—that requires some stubbornness, some courage."

The consciousness of evil entered early into Greene's mind.   At first, in childhood, he was conscious less of evil than of the ubiquity of a " power ", that was present everywhere, but particularly in horrifying things or scenes.   In his journey to Africa, among the animist tribes of the Liberian hinterland, with their magical con-

---

[1] Personally I regard this attitude as the development of a fundamental error that regards evil as a quality existing in its own right.   But this is a personal intrusion, merely to show that the line of reasoning I have endeavoured to explain is one which I do not accept as valid.

ception of a world permeated with a similar " power " neither good nor evil, but menacing, he recovered these early impressions sufficiently clearly to record them.

" It is the earliest dream that I can remember, earlier than the witch at the corner of the nursery passage, this dream of something outside that has to come in. The witch, like the masked dancers, has form, but this is simply power, a force exerted on a door, an influence that drifted after me upstairs and pressed against windows.

" Later the presence took many odd forms : a troop of black-skinned girls who carried poison flowers it was death to touch ; an old Arab ; a half-caste ; armed men with shaven heads and narrow eyes and the appearance of Thibetans out of a travel book ; a Chinese detective.

" You couldn't call these things evil, as Peter Quint in *The Turn of the Screw* was evil, with his carroty hair and his white face of damnation. That story of James's belongs to the Christian, the orthodox imagination. Mine were devils only in the African sense of beings who controlled power. They were not even always terrifying . . .

" It was only many years later that Evil came into my dreams ; the man with gold teeth and rubber surgical gloves ; the old woman with ringworm ; the man with his throat cut dragging himself across the carpet to the bed."

It is significant from this passage that evil for Greene is essentially human, connected directly with man's cruelty or misery.

It was when at school that the reality of evil began to impose itself on his mind, at that age in adolescence when we are all liable to become concerned with the religious emotions and to have visions of God or the Devil. Greene was the son of the headmaster of a small public school. He was also a pupil, and the alternation of the weekday life of school, the realm of evil, and the week-end life of the headmaster's house, the realm of good, gave birth to that duality of attitude to the resolution of which Greene has devoted much of his thought. In *The Lawless Roads* he describes these early experiences.

" One was an inhabitant of both countries : on Saturday and Sunday afternoons of one side of the baize door, the rest of the week of the other. How can life on a border be other than restless ? You are pulled by different ties of hate and love. For hate is quite as powerful a tie : it demands allegiance. In the land of the sky-scrapers, of stone stairs and cracked bells ringing early, one was aware of fear and hate, a kind of lawlessness—appalling cruelties could be practised without a second thought : one met for the first time characters, adult and adolescent, who bore about them the genuine quality of evil."

For such unfortunates, Greene remarks, " Hell lay about them in their infancy," and it was of this hell that his first belief was born.

" And so faith came to one—shapelessly, without dogma, a presence above a croquet lawn, something associated with violence, cruelty, evil across the way. One began to believe in heaven because one believed in hell, but for a long while it was hell only one could picture with a certain intimacy—the pitchpine partitions in dormi-tories where everybody was never quiet at the same time : lavatories without locks : ' There, by reason of the great number of the damned, the prisoners are heaped together in their awful prison . . .' ; walks in pairs up the metroland road, no solitude anywhere, at any time. The Anglican church could not supply the same intimate symbols for heaven : only a big brass eagle, an organ voluntary, ' Lord dismiss us with thy blessing ', the quiet croquet lawn where one had no business, the rabbit and the distant music.

" These were primary symbols : life later altered them : in a midland city, riding on trams in winter past the Gothic hotel, the super-cinema, the sooty newspaper office where we worked at night, passing the single professional prostitute trying to keep the circulation going under the blue and powdered skin, one began slowly, painfully, reluctantly, to populate heaven. The Mother of God took the place of the brass eagle ; one began to have a dim conception of the appalling mysteries of love moving through a ravaged world—the Curé d'Ars admitting to his mind all the impurity of a province : Péguy challenging God in the cause of the damned. It remained something one associated with misery, violence, evil . . ."

It is the particular preoccupation with " misery, violence, evil," that characterises Greene's novels. Other modern novelists are concerned with violence, but for them it is almost a sickness of the heart that makes violence necessary. Hemingway, for instance, with his connoisseur's interest in the bullfight, his gloating over the blood and guts of the arena, has little in common with Greene. For Greene, violence is a symptom of the condition of man, to be examined, to be revealed, but also to be related to the context of a universal struggle between good and evil. Hemingway's world of violence is a dream of black and white images that have no genuine connection with the grey shadows of the living world. But the life of Greene's novels does represent the actual violence and misery of the world in which we live, and recognises that evil is practised by ordinary, weak men and women. Greene enters into the hearts of those who act this drama of hate and love, and pities both the practitioner and the victim.

There are very few of his characters who are wholly evil. All, like the men and women of the world in which we live, are partly good, and none is so good that he is not capable of some lapse of conduct that will bring about evil. Perhaps it would be even more correct to say that they are not in themselves either good or evil, but the agents through whom these powers work, the unworthy and half-conscious vessels that carry grace or the equally precious poison of damnation. In *The Ministry of Fear* Greene says, " the devil—and God too—had always used comic people, futile people, little suburban natures and the maimed and warped to serve his purposes. When God used them you talked emptily of nobility and when the devil used them of wickedness ; but the material was only dull shabby human mediocrity in either case."

It is from these warped, shabby and futile people, from the great half-world of the " seedy " that Greene has drawn the characters to people his Persian drama. Of such it is recorded that Christ formed his ministry.

Greene's novels, up to *The Power and The Glory*, represent a steady development of this theme of the struggle in the world and within the human spirit. It is a war that has no accepted frontiers, where either side will project its forces into the most unexpected sector, where the man who seems evil will bring forth good, where the apparent achievement of good will end in evil. Raven, the killer in *A Gun for Sale*, seems a character dedicated from childhood wholly to evil. Yet circumstances turn him into an avenging instrument against those who used him for a murder to start a war, and his final killings avert the international tragedy. The plot of *It's a Battlefield* is built around a reprieve for a man who killed a policeman in a Communist demonstration. Despite the weakness of the men and women who maintain it, despite the personal and political motives with which it is mingled, the campaign for this reprieve appears to be good in its aim. Yet when, unexpectedly, the reprieve is granted, it appears as a tragedy, because it leaves the convict's wife tied for the rest of her life to a man in prison whom she loves passionately but to whom she cannot hope to be faithful. Ironically, it is also granted too late to prevent Drover's brother from being killed by a car while he is attempting to assassinate the Commissioner of Police. In *Brighton Rock* Pinky, the adolescent murderer, for all his faith in God, deliberately chooses evil. In *The Power and The Glory* the drunkard priest becomes the instrument of God's grace, the agent of good's resistance to evil.

The emphasis is increased from novel to novel, and, until *Brighton Rock*, the struggle is fought in terms of human situations, of plots and thrilling chases, of sensational news stories, of international crime and civil war. In even so remote a novel as *The Man Within* the theme of violence is present, and the human conflict is marked out in the series of betrayals to which Andrews is led, the betrayal of his smuggler comrades to the law, the betrayal of the woman he loves when he allows lust for another woman to persuade him into giving evidence at the trial, and the final expiation when, after one of the smugglers has killed his woman in revenge, he gives himself up as the murderer.

The remaining novels are all comprised within the pattern of violence that lies about us in the modern world. The forces of evil are often represented in the inhuman organisations and purposes that promote such violence—the armaments ring that pays Raven in *A Gun for Sale*, Krogh's financial schemes in *England Made Me*, the reactionary conspiracy in *The Confidential Agent*. Some of the characters are made by their natures to be the instruments of evil, like Raven and Pinky, others are the almost predestined victims, " caught up in other people's darkness," like Anthony Farrant in *England Made Me* and the child Else in *The Confidential Agent*. In a sense, indeed, all his characters are victims of the general tragedy, for to none of them comes earthly happiness or human triumph. The nearest to achievement, the nearest to God, are those, like the priest in *The Power and The Glory*, or Rose Cullen in *The Confidential Agent*, or the other Rose in *Brighton Rock*, who have sacrificed something—life, a secure future on earth, the hope of salvation in heaven—for the sake of love, who have realised trust and have rejected the treachery of a hating world.

Peace comes to the confidential agent, travelling to his death, in a reassertion of confidence in a human being.

" He said : ' I'm an old man.'

" ' If I don't care,' she said, ' what does it matter what you are ? Oh, I know you're faithful—but I've told you I shan't go on loving a dead man.' He took a quick look at her ; her hair was lank with spray. She looked older than he had ever seen her yet—plain. It was as if she were assuring him that glamour didn't enter into *this* business. She said : ' When you're dead, she can have you. I can't compete then—and we'll all be dead a long, long time.'

" The light went by astern : ahead there was only the splash, the long withdrawal and the dark. She said, ' You'll be dead very soon : you needn't tell me that, but now . . .'

" He felt no desire, and no claim : happiness was all about them on the small vibrating tramp. To the confidential agent trust seemed to be returning into the violent and suspicious world."

In the earlier novels the problems are treated in terms of human relationships, of loyalties and betrayals between men, of violence done by and to men in struggles which have their place in the natural world. The Catholic church is hardly mentioned, although Greene had already belonged to it for some years, and the standards of good and evil are those of the kingdom of nature, of ordinary human ideas of right and wrong, of justice and injustice.

But in *Brighton Rock* a profound change appears, for here is brought in the factor of belief. Our world is no longer one of plain right or wrong, of natural justice and injustice. We are introduced to theological conceptions of grace and damnation ; good and evil become three-dimensional because they cannot be considered by human moralities of right and wrong. Because she believes in God's grace, even though she deliberately chooses damnation, Rose, who loves the murderer, is shown to be raised on a higher plane of consciousness than the good-timing Ida, who knows what is right and sets out with a Mosaic insistence to get her revenge for the killing of a man she had met once on a Brighton afternoon. Ida, like the conventional world she represents, has not gone beyond the Judaic conceptions of justice. The girl accepts what she thinks to be damnation because she has attained the Christian conception of grace.

Here we come again to Greene's paradox of the salvation of the damned, represented in the priest's remarks to Rose during her confession after Pinky's death :

"The old man suddenly began to talk—whistling every now and then and blowing eucalyptus through the grill. He said : 'There was a man, a Frenchman, you wouldn't know about him, my child, who had the same idea as you. He was a good man, a holy man, and he lived in sin all through his life, because he could not bear the idea that any soul could suffer damnation.' She listened with astonishment. He said : 'This man decided that if any soul was going to be damned, he would be damned too. He never took the sacraments, he never married his wife in church. I don't know, my child, but some people think he was—well, a saint. I think he died in what we are told is mortal sin—I'm not sure ; it was in the war ; perhaps . . .' He sighed—and whistled, bending his old head. He said : 'You can't conceive, my child, nor can I or anyone—the . . . appalling . . . strangeness of the mercy of God.'"

Pinky, who commits two murders with calculated brutality, who abuses selfishly the devotion of his girl and his friends, is the one character of Greene's creation who seems completely evil. He assuredly is one of those for whom "Hell lay about them in their infancy," and who carried his hell with him ever after. He has almost no redeeming quality, but arouses our pity for his pathetic self-assurance, his precocious cynicism which covers a deep fear of himself, of all his instincts and impulses. Believing in the Catholic dogmas implicitly, the boy deliberately commits one mortal sin after another and rejoices perversely in the thought of his own damnation. "Credo in unum Satanum" he boasts.

Satanism plays a consistent part in Greene's novels. The old priest in *Brighton Rock* declares, "a Catholic is more capable of evil than anyone. I think perhaps—because we believe in him—we are more in touch with the devil than other people." And the priest in *The Power and The Glory* says in prison, "I know—from

THE WRITER AND POLITICS

experience—how much beauty Satan carried down within him when he fell. Nobody ever said the fallen angels were the ugly ones. Oh no, they were just as quick and bright and . . ."

But it would be a mistake to imagine that, because Greene is to some extent " of the devil's party without knowing it," he is a wholehearted Satanist, a hearty partisan of evil. On the contrary, his interest in sinners and the damned seems to arise from his desire for all men to attain salvation.

Yet, for all our pity, we can find little to redeem Pinky. In his whole career and his sordid death, evil seems the triumphant force, consciously driving him to physical destruction and eternal damnation.

If *Brighton Rock* represents the triumph of evil within the human heart, *The Power and The Glory* shows the reverse, the attainment of God's good through the unworthy agency of a " whisky " priest who carries on his work in a Mexican state where the Catholic church is proscribed and a price is put upon his own head. The priest escapes over the border into another state where he will be immune, but returns to his death in response to a call to administer the sacrament to a dying man.

The final spiritual conclusion of *The Power and The Glory* seems to be that within man himself evil and good must always be to some degree intermingled—no man will be wholly good or wholly evil— but the most unworthy man can become the agent by which God's will is carried out and good brought to mankind. In other words, the conflict which entered the Roman Church when it absorbed Mithraic and Manichean dualism has been resolved, and sin is seen, as Christ Himself saw it, to be an essential factor in the development of the human spirit. Man cannot be wholly good, nor is it desirable that he should be without experience of sin, for the greatest good comes often from those who have an intimate knowledge of evil. It will be remembered that Dante reserved a special part of hell for those who had led blameless lives, placing them below those sinners who had the opportunity to pass through purgatory into heaven.

In reaching this conclusion Greene seems to have found himself at the end of his development, or at least at the end of a major line of development. The novels up to *The Power and The Glory* show the steady unfolding of the theme of good and evil. In this last-named book good emerges from evil, like a flower from corruption. The pattern of a world where good and evil are mingled inextricably is completed, and we have reached a destination.

How completely Greene had worked out this theme is seen by a consideration of *The Ministry of Fear*, which succeeded *The Power and The Glory*. This is an "entertainment", the title Greene gives to his lighter novels. But while the earlier "entertainments", like *Stamboul Train*, seem as significant as most of the novels of other writers, and appear to fit into the general pattern of Greene's development, *The Ministry of Fear* has a thinness of quality and plot, a lack of evident purpose, which separate it from the preceding novels. The old theme of good and evil is repeated, and we find many of the devices of technique and plot which occur in the previous novels—the hunted man, the international spy ring, the atmosphere of pervading violence, are all familiar. But this time, instead of serving an end, they appear almost as theatrical devices to form an interesting story, but of little greater significance. The story is certainly exciting, but that is almost all, and, except for one or two faint religious echoes of *The Power and the Glory*, there is no indication of any urgent philosophical purpose. Nor are we aware to any marked extent of the pertinent social criticism which plays such a notable part in the earlier books. More than any other of Greene's books, *The Ministry of Fear* is a simple thriller, and it shows a dangerous tendency to become too much involved in a technique which was admirable when disciplined by a purpose, but which might lead to empty virtuosity when used without any external discipline of intent.

However, it is still probable that Greene will find a new theme of development, or even a variant of the old theme, which will enable him once again to write fruitful novels.

2

Before we proceed from the philosophical to the social aspects of Greene's novels, we should pay some brief attention to the two books of travel, *Journey Without Maps* and *The Lawless Roads*, which act almost as the keys to an understanding of his development. It is in these volumes that most of Greene's autobiographical statements are made, and many references and reflections which greatly assist the interpretation of his novels.

Travels have a great significance in religious imagery, and the psychic life of man is represented in many of the early myths concerning long journeys. Of the first we have only to remember *The Dark Night of the Soul* and *Pilgrim's Progress*, of the second *The Odyssey*, to see the symbolic importance of the idea of journeying in the minds of men who are perhaps no more than a hundred generations from the nomad life.

In a similar way, Greene's journeys are far more than mere travels from place to place, or tours of sightseeing in strange lands. Each has a rich emotional significance, each becomes associated with a further stage in his inner journey of awareness.

Journey Without Maps is concerned with a trip in Liberia, when Greene travelled far into the interior of that little-known country and mingled with tribes who still live at a primitive level of human existence. Among them Greene found much that was attractive after the complicated evil and violence of modern " civilised " life.

" However tired I became of the seven-hour trek through the untidy and unbeautiful forest, I never wearied of the villages in which I spent the night : the sense of a small courageous community barely existing above the desert of trees, hemmed in by a sun too fierce to work under and a darkness filled with evil spirits—love was an arm round a neck, a cramped embrace in the smoke, wealth a little pile of palm-nuts, old-age sores and leprosy, religion a few stones in the centre of the village where the dead chiefs lay, a grove of trees where the rice birds, like yellow and green canaries, built their nests, a man in a mask with raffia skirts dancing at burials. This never varied, only their kindness to strangers, the extent of their poverty and the immediacy of their terrors. Their laughter and their happiness were the most courageous things in nature. Love, it has been said, was invented in Europe by the troubadours, but it existed here without the trappings of civilisation. They were tender towards their children (I seldom heard a crying child, unless at the sight of a white face, and never saw one beaten); they were tender towards each other in a muffled way; they didn't scream or ' rag '; they never revealed the rasped nerves of the European poor in shrill speech or sudden blows. One was aware the whole time of a standard of courtesy to which it was one's responsibility to conform."

Although he could never make real contact, never return, Greene felt a real nostalgia for this lost childhood of the race. He had seen a stage of man's history when, in spite of all the disease and dirt and fear, life was somehow more pure than in the stone forests of Western cities.

" This journey, if it had done nothing else, had reinforced a sense of disappointment with what man had made out of the primitive, what he had made out of childhood. Oh, one wanted to protest, one doesn't believe, of course, in ' the visionary gleam ', in the trailing glory, but there was something in that early terror and the bareness of one's needs, a harp strumming behind a hut, a witch on the nursery landing, a handful of kola nuts, a masked dancer, the poisoned flowers. The sense of taste was finer, the sense of pleasure keener, the sense of terror deeper and purer . . .

" It isn't that one wants to stay in Africa ; I have no yearning for a mindless sexuality, even if it were to be found there : it is only that when one had appreciated such a beginning, its terrors as well as its placidity, the power as well as the gentleness, the pity for what we have done with ourselves is driven more forcibly home."

The effect of Greene's African journey was to make him even more aware of the presence of evil in the world. The misery, the exploitation, the general air of decay and drabness, all combined to give the feeling of a world in which evil was imminent and powerful. In the closing paragraph of a short story, *A Chance for Mr Lever*, Greene remarks :

" The story might very well have encouraged *my* faith in that loving omniscience if it had not been shaken by personal knowledge of the drab empty forest through which Mr Lever now went so merrily, where it is impossible to believe in any spiritual life, in anything outside the nature dying round you, the shrivelling of the weeds."

Returning from this primitive childhood of terror and dirt, Greene found the western world alive with a more active wickedness, the " sense of supernatural evil " replaced by " the small human viciousness " which spreads to embrace a world in war.

From this mood arose *Brighton Rock*, that formidable picture of the jungle of Christian evil. The return to an apprehension of the superabundance of God's grace is represented by another journey, which Greene made to Mexico just before the war, and which is described in *The Lawless Roads*.

In Mexico he found in progress one version of the struggle between the individual and the State which has been going on over the world for the whole of our century. In Mexico this struggle was often maintained by priests of the Roman church, men individually courageous and devoted to the service of their beliefs, which they have often sustained against great persecution at the hands of the authoritarian " communists " who have governed parts of Mexico.

Greene saw Mexico as the epitome of a world where personal

faith struggles against the mechanical and organised mindlessness of an authoritarian society.

" The world is all of a piece of course ; it is engaged everywhere in the same subterranean struggle, lying like a tiny neutral state with whom no one ever observes their treaties between the two eternities of pain and—God knows the opposite of pain, not us. It is a Belgium fought over by friend and enemy alike ; there is no peace anywhere where there is human life ; but there are, I told myself, quiet and active sectors of the line. Russia, Spain, Mexico —there's no fraternisation on Christmas morning in those parts. The horror may be the same, it is an intrinsic part of human life in every place ; it attacks you in the Strand or the tropics ; but where the eagles are gathered together, it is not unnatural to expect to find the Son of Man as well. So many years have passed in England since the war began between faith and anarchy ; we live in an ugly indifference."

Here Greene, like so many others, fails to see that the difference is not between faith and " anarchy ", for anarchy, the condition of being subject to no external authority, is the only state in which a personal faith can be born and nurtured. The authoritarian structure of the church has led him to ignore the fact that *any* kind of government, spiritual or temporal, is liable to become an enemy of a personal and independent attitude to the universe, which is the prerequisite of a true and living faith. This is all the more tragic, because in the same book he shows a sound distaste for temporal authority.

" One thought of the blue-chinned politicians on the balcony, the leaders of the State, with their eyes on the main chance, the pistols on their hips, with no sense of responsibility for anyone at all. . . I remembered the game they were playing at home with counters and dice called ' Monopoly ', the girl of fifteen on the railway-line, a world where the politicians stand on the balcony, where the land is sold for building estates and the little villas go up on the wounded clay with garages like tombs."

I know little of the rights and wrongs of the Mexican quarrel between the "communist" politicians and the Roman church. In their day the church and many of its dignitaries certainly made themselves fat on their pastorate—a fact which Greene does not deny—and the influence of the priests helped to keep the *peons* in ignorance. No doubt to the genuine revolutionaries like Magon the church appeared rightly as part of the structure of oppression, and they fought against it and the corrupt priests for that reason. But the situation is not as simple as that. Not all the priests were corrupt—many were simple and honest men who really believed in their teachings and acted as friends to the poor among whom they lived. On the other hand, the politicians who climbed to power on the pretence of revolution were not opposed to the church as an authority, but as a *rival* authority, and wished to destroy the Catholic faith because they dared not risk the presence of any belief, even among individuals, that might be a danger to their own system of authority. Without taking sides, it might be safe to sympathise with the individual peasant against the organised church and the individual Catholic against the organised State, to condemn both organisations equally and to support the right of both individuals to freedom from external dictation.

In Mexico Greene's imagination was fired by the story of a drunken priest, who had evaded the authorities for many months while continuing to propagate his faith in flight and hiding. The priest was eventually caught and shot, having, for all the apparent unworthiness of his life, been the only man to carry on his mission among the peasants and labourers of the villages of his province. In this story Greene saw a parable of how goodness can come even from a man whose character appears to be unworthy. Out of this he made the plot of *The Power and The Glory* which, as I have already shown, represents the peak of his literary development up to the present time.

3

I have shown that Greene, even in his portrayal of the spiritual struggle of good and evil, is concerned with the actual violence of human life. There is nothing mystical or even truly symbolic about his work. Good and evil are expressed in the lives of men, and it is in the map of a concrete world torn by violence and fratricidal dissension that we see the lines of the spiritual conflict traced most clearly. To Greene it is a moral conflict, even more than a conflict of the soul ; it is centred in the relationships of men, and is manifest in terms of betrayal and loyalty, of cruelty and love.

With such an attitude, it is not surprising that Greene's novels show a developed social consciousness. Greene has been abused by Marxists for lacking this very quality, but that is almost entirely because he does not accept their social criteria, and, although I disagree with many of Greene's ideas—particularly his theological dogmas—I consider that he has a much fuller sense of social values than most of his critics.

Greene's novels form, within obvious limits, one of the most comprehensive surveys of modern social violence that has yet been made in European fiction. They show clearly the nature of the class struggle in modern society, and also go beyond the Marxists to a realisation of that even more fundamental struggle, in progress throughout the world to-day, between the individual and the collective, the common man and the State.

Greene has been called reactionary from all sides, yet it is difficult to see how this impression could have been gained from an honest survey of his work. Always he is in sympathy with the underdog, with the criminal against the society that has warped him, with the rebel against the representatives of authority, with the poor against the rich and the meek against the mighty. In *The Lawless Roads* he quotes with approval the words of St James :

" Go to now, ye rich men : weep and howl in your miseries

which shall come upon you. Your riches are corrupted and your garments are moth-eaten ; your gold and silver is cankered ; and the rust of them shall be for a testimony against you and shall eat your flesh like fire . . ."

" These," says Greene, " are the words of revolution," and it is with something of this levelling spirit of the early fathers that Greene faces the modern world.

In almost every novel we find the exposure of some manifestation of tyranny or exploitation. In *England Made Me* it is monopoly capitalism and international finance, personified in Krogh ; in *Stamboul Train* it is political tyranny in the Balkans ; in *A Gun for Sale* it is the armaments industry with its plots to start wars for the extension of profits ; in *The Confidential Agent*, in spite of Greene's Catholicism, it is the intrigues of the reactionaries in a civil war that smells very much of Spain ; in *The Power and The Glory* it is the intolerance of modern totalitarianism towards any thought that offers a resistance to uniformity ; in every book it is the State, big business, the law, the police, and the whole sophistry of money and power on which contemporary political life is built.

For those who still contend that Greene is a man without social conscience, I will be content with the quotation of one passage from *Journey Without Maps* :

" ' Workers of the World Unite ' ; I thought of the wide shallow slogans of political parties, as the thin bodies, every rib showing, with dangling swollen elbows or pock-marked skin, went by me to the market ; why should one pretend to talk in terms of the world when we mean only Europe or the white races ? Neither I.L.P. nor Communist Party urges a strike in England because the plate-layers in Sierra Leone are paid sixpence a day without their food. Civilisation in West Africa remains exploitation : we have hardly improved the natives' lot at all, they are as worn out with fever as before the white man came, we have introduced new diseases and weakened their resistance to the old—they still drink from polluted

water and suffer from the same worms, they are still at the mercy
of their chiefs, for what can a District Commissioner really know,
shifted from district to district, picking up only a few words of the
language, dependent on an interpreter ? Civilisation so far as
Sierra Leone is concerned is the railway to Pendambu, the increased
export of palm nuts ; civilisation, too, is Lever Brothers and the
prices they control ; civilisation is the long bar in the Grand, the
sixpenny wages."

But Greene's radicalism, his revulsion from the values of a
capitalist civilisation, do not throw him into the arms of some comforting collective creed, some political dogmatism that dries up
all human values and leads by high-sounding words to a result not
much better than the evil state it sought to replace.

" It's typical of Mexico, of the whole human race perhaps,"
he says, "—violence in favour of an ideal and then the ideal lost
and the violence just going on."

And in *The Confidential Agent* the old intellectual D. realises that
the revolutionaries for whom he is fighting are in reality little
nearer a revolutionary attitude to human relationships than their
reactionary opponents.

The struggle in Greene's novels is not that of class against class,
of political organisation against political organisation. It is the
guerilla war of the individual, the isolated man against a restrictive
society. Greene's hero is the man hunted by society, who often at
the same time takes on the rôle of the avenger for the evils which
society forces on the millions of individual men who struggle under
its collective oppression.

This pattern of the lone hero, hunter and hunted at once, occurs
continually in his novels. The Confidential Agent is hunted by
his enemies and by the British police, but when the little servant
girl Else, whom he has pitied and befriended, is murdered by his
pursuers, he himself turns into the hunter and takes his revenge
on K., the teacher who has turned sides for money. Raven, the

killer in *A Gun for Sale*, has murdered a European statesman for an armaments ring, and then is " framed " by his employers when they pay with marked notes and inform the police that the money was stolen in a hold-up. He discovers the trick, and, with the police on his track, goes for his revenge. He exposes the plot, kills the steel magnates, and then is killed at the last moment by his own pursuers. Pinky in *Brighton Rock* hunts and kills the reporter Fred who had betrayed his friend Kite into the hands of a rival gang, but is himself pursued by Fred's friend Ida, and driven to suicide.

The pattern is not unvaried. The priest in *The Power and The Glory* pursues no victim. Dr Czinner is not hunted by any tangible enemy, and yet is driven on by his own feeling of solidarity with the revolutionary workers in his Balkan city to go back and place himself in the hands of his enemies, the Political Police who are awaiting him on the frontier of his country.

In a sense, the fate of Czinner is an anticipation of that of the priest, for both go voluntarily to seek death at the hands of their foes, and in both of them this seeming defeat is a kind of triumph, for the priest by his death wins the conversion of a young boy who had previously been immersed in the creed of the collective party, while the death of Czinner makes an indelible impression on the mind of the chorus girl Coral, and incidentally saves her from becoming the mistress of the unpleasant merchant, Myatt. The triumph of good over evil comes more often and more effectively from non-resistance than from counter-violence ; in the long run the moral victory is more effective than the physical.

This representation of the social struggle as one of the individual against society leads Greene to find his protagonists among those who have already been marked from birth for unhappiness, men and women who live for some reason on the periphery, who are branded by oddness and destined by some original failing to be the misfits who carry on the perpetual war of human rebellion against the inhumanity of the collective. Andrews, in *The Man Within*, is subjected to the mockery of his smuggler father because he prefers a life of thought to one of action, and so comes to hate his comrades. The gunman Raven has a hare lip which makes him repellent to most women ; his youth has been blighted by a hating parent and the hell of a reformatory school. Pinky is a slum child who has struggled into a slightly higher stratum of the underworld and feels inferior in the presence of his sexually mature friends. The clerk, Conrad Drover, in *It's a Battlefield*, is haunted by envy of his physically superior brother. Myatt, the currant merchant, is hypersensitive about his Jewish race. Among the minor characters there is an even more marked eccentricity, which leads them often into becoming types rather than characters. Greene himself, in a revelatory passage of *Journey Without Maps*, says of one of the people he meets :

" Already he was intent on joining that odd assortment of ' characters ' (the Grants and the Kilvanes) one collects through life, vivid grotesques, people so simple that they always have the same side turned to one, doomed by their unself-consciousness to be material for the novelist, to supply the minor characters, to be endlessly caricatured, to make in their multiplicity one's world."

By this strange half-world of odd people, the guerilla fighters against the uniform society, Greene is fascinated, and he has pictured it in many passages. Its characteristic quality he describes as *seediness* :

" There seemed to be a seediness about the place you couldn't get to the same extent elsewhere, and seediness has a very deep appeal : even the seediness of civilisation, of the sky signs in Leicester Square, the ' tarts ' in Bond Street, the smell of cooking greens off Tottenham Court Road, the little tight-waisted Jews in the Strand. It seems to satisfy, temporarily, the sense of nostalgia for something lost ; it seems to represent a stage further back . . .

" It is nearer the beginning ; like Monrovia it has begun to build wrong, but at least it has only begun ; it hasn't gone so far away as the smart, the new, the chic, the cerebral."

Greene's situations frequently hinge round issues of personal loyalty and betrayal, and, generally speaking, the " seedy " are the more deep in their loyalties. Minty, the exiled religious maniac treasuring the memories of his friends, Rose accepting damnation in her love for a murderer, the criminals sharing his cell who refuse to betray the priest, are people whose loyalty is more strong than all the artificial bonds of nations or states. These people have their betrayals also—Conrad Drover sleeps with his condemned brother's wife, Anne gives Raven away to her detective fiancé—but somehow they expiate their failings in a way the slick and the successful never do.

Always, the inward responsibility of the individual to other individuals is shown to be more valuable than blind loyalty to an institution. The priest and the police lieutenant in *The Power and The Glory* have each a loyalty, but the loyalty of the priest is to the salvation of individual men and women, while the lieutenant's is to an abstract plan of happiness, no matter how many lives are lost in its achievement. The barren nature of collective loyalty is shown mordantly in the soliloquy of the Police Commissioner in *It's a Battlefield :*

" By the time he reached the courtyard, he had decided that he did not care for politics. In Northumberland Avenue he said to himself that justice was not his business . . . I've got nothing to do with justice, he thought, my job is simply to get the right man, and the cold washed air did not prevent his thoughts going back to damp paths steaming in the heat under leaves like hairy hands. One pursued by this path and that, and only as a last resort, when there was no other means of ensuring a murderer's punishment, did one burn his village. Justice had nothing to do with the matter. One left justice to magistrates, to judges and juries, to members of parliament, to the Home Secretary."

By such sophistries the Commissioner tries to salve his uneasy conscience.

Mather, the detective in *A Gun for Sale*, immerses himself in a collective activity :

" All over London there were other cars doing the same : he was part of an organisation. He did not want to be a leader, he did not even wish to give himself up to some God-sent fanatic of a leader, he liked to feel that he was one of thousands more or less equal working for a concrete end : not equality of opportunity, not government by the people or by the richest or by the best : but simply to do away with crime which meant uncertainty."

For all the sense of duty, the loyalty to organisations, the Commissioner supports a civilisation that makes the prison and the factory equally the graves of human individuality. Mather becomes the unwitting tool of really big criminals in their efforts to escape the revenge of the petty villain Raven, and the police lieutenant slaughters peasants to save them from believing what they wish.

Yet, although one feels always on the side of the warped and pitiful men and women whom Greene pits against the great and evil forces of society, they are by no means attractive figures. And, what is more germane to our point, they are not always satisfactory as characters in a novel. Greene has a preoccupation with the pathetic and the sordid, so that for almost all his characters life has no real material or even spiritual end, and what happens to them rarely gives real beauty or happiness. Apart from the priest, few leave any great or good works behind them. The quiet anticlimax of each life strips the promise of a future.

Of the way in which Greene distorts his characters, his portrayal of their sexual lives is typical. The statements of some critics that Greene always regards sex with disgust are exaggerated and unjust. The loves of some of his characters are ugly—the affair between Minnie and Conrad Drover, the attitude of Pinky towards Rose, the seductions of Mr Surrogate. But for the most part the sexual adventures are dull and perfunctory rather than disgusting in an active way, and sex clearly plays so small a part in Greene's scheme beside the moral and spiritual wars in which his characters are engaged that he appears to think it requires little attention, except where—as in *Brighton Rock*—it has some important bearing on the moral conflict. The incestuous love of Anthony and Kate Farrant in *England Made Me*, perhaps because it is as perverse as the characters themselves, perhaps because it is doomed never to be fulfilled, is the only sexual episode that plays a really dominant part in one of Greene's books, and it attains a remarkable beauty in the almost Elizabethan tragedy of these two linked souls.

It is perhaps in this frustrated incompleteness of his characters that we see the weakening duality of Greene's outlook. As a Catholic he has certain preconceptions of right and wrong action, of what is and what is not a mortal sin. Yet, as a man of great sympathy with the unfortunate, as a man in that strange position where his reason leans towards traditionalism while his emotions turn towards revolution, Greene is inevitably frustrated in his outlook, and transmits his frustration to his characters.

All his books show, vigorously and indignantly, the way in which society warps the natures of men and women and turns them to bitterness and evil. Theoretically, Greene may recognise original sin, but in his writing the evil in man is always less than the evil without, arising from the collective activities of society. His observations of humanity force him into a revolutionary attitude, and in *The Lawless Roads* he admits his feeling of the need for a dynamic activity that will sweep away the social abuses and inequality which are destroying or injuring the lives of ordinary men and women.

He then practises a curious piece of self-deception by assuming that the real leaders of the Roman Catholic church are revolutionary in outlook, that the " revolutionary " Papal Encyclicals are conceived in all sincerity, and that it is the obstruction of bishops and more-or-less corrupt lower clergy that has prevented the Roman church as a whole from becoming a revolutionary force. This attitude, of course, ignores the way in which the Papacy has, in the recent as well as the distant past, intrigued against freedom and revolution. It ignores the papal agreements with Mussolini, the blessings on the Italian invasions of Ethiopia and Spain, the flirtations with reactionary American capitalism.

The Catholic revolutionary of the type of Eric Gill or Greene always becomes insignificant in his effect because of his reluctance to accept that, whatever the merits of Christian dogmas, the Catholic church as an institution is certainly inspired by no humanist idealism.

In judging Greene as a novelist, we might not at first seem justified in criticising his ideas. Yet when, as is quite clear, his ideas create a perceptible hindrance to the full expression of his literary talents, that criticism becomes necessary.

The Power and The Glory is the best of Greene's novels because he appears there to be approaching, almost somnambulistically, a solution to his problem. The priest is concerned with his holy mission, to maintain the teachings of the church in his province in Mexico. Theoretically the struggle is between two collectivities, the Church and the State, represented by the priest and the police lieutenant. But in fact, while the police lieutenant remains the representative of a collective idea, the servant of the State, the presence of the Church becomes steadily more distant and shadowy, and the priest seems to stand out ever more solidly as an individual, without tangible connections or allegiances, fighting a guerilla war for an idea which he considers right. Instead of being the representative of Catholicism, he becomes more and more the type of the human person fighting against the unifying urges of a power society, and triumphing even in defeat and destruction, because in this battle there are no fronts and the messages are passed on by example to other individuals who continue as rebellious elements

in the total State. This is an underground which is never elimi-
nated, because it has no central committee and no headquarters,
except in the heart of each man who feels the need for freedom.

There are perhaps many and wide differences between Greene
and Eric Gill in their approach to the superficial details of life, but
they have in common their adherence to the Roman church and
their belief in the uniqueness of each human being and his absolute
right to freedom. Both detect the fraud of politics, and seek some
other way of revolutionary change—a change from within that will
allow man to realise his uniqueness. Gill was forced steadily in a
direction where finally his statements were in direct contradiction
to the organisational practice of the Roman church. Just before
his death, he wrote, in a letter to the anarchist, Herbert Read :

". . . in spite of the appearance to the contrary I am really in
complete agreement with you about the necessity of anarchism,
the ultimate truth of it, and its immediate practicality as
syndicalism."

I am not suggesting that Greene will actually declare himself
as Gill did, or that he will take part in any social movement. He
may merely continue to work as a novelist, transmitting through the
medium of his writing the inner conflict between the authoritarian
doctrine of Catholicism and the idea of personal freedom which is
implicit in the true teachings of Christianity. All we can say is
that, up to the present, Greene has steadily developed the theme
of the individual person pitted against society, and that his novels
have come more and more to illustrate the real nature of this conflict in which we are all involved.

But he realises, as we all do, that it is not a struggle to be won with
ease. There are forces within as well as without us that we must
fight, and not least of these is our own deeply rooted fear of freedom,
the childish clinging to our bonds. Before we can change society
around us, we must change the nature of our own hearts, and it
may be a realisation of this that has kept Greene from committing

himself in anything more than the vaguest terms to the discussion of how we shall change society. He perceives within himself " a distrust of any future based on what we are ", and the observer of society whose ideas arise from anything deeper than the repetition of political abstractions, will share that distrust. The re-creation of the man within is a prerequisite of the alteration of society into any pattern that ensures an end of present social evils. And per-haps it is by a cultivation of the personal qualities of men, of their intimate loyalties to each other, of all those unorganised personal contacts that spring up outside any rigid organisation, that we shall proceed the more rapidly towards freedom.

Yet we cannot reach our freedom alone. Greene's priest says :

" I don't know a thing about the mercy of God : I don't know how awful the human heart looks to Him. But I do know this —that if there's ever been a single man in this state damned then I'll be damned too. I wouldn't want it to be any different. I just want justice, that's all."

In the same way, while one man among us is a slave, we are not free. Yet this is an individual, not a collective responsibility, a responsibility we cannot relegate to some state or party for its fulfilment.

Men, compound of good and evil, can still attain Grace, and no man need be damned, no man need give up the hope of freedom. Here there is no revolutionary heroism, no political rhetoric calling us to iconoclastic action, yet we feel that in his own way Greene may be a more genuine revolutionary than many who have been more vociferous in their demands for freedom. For a realisation of the nature of man, towards which Greene has striven, is certainly necessary before he can be made free.

IX

Ignazio Silone

IGNAZIO SILONE has been described as a realistic novelist. Before, however, we judge the accuracy of this description, we must reach a definition of the term "realism", which, like other words classifying literary or artistic works, has in the past been used loosely and without a precise understanding of its meaning.

There are two kinds of writing commonly described as realist. The first is writing concerned with the outward and material manifestations of life, the symptoms rather than the underlying conditions and causes. Man is represented as a creature dominated by his material environment and responding to it in a way which bears no apparent relationship to any universal reality underlying both the environment and the human reactions. Such an approach almost ignores the intellect and negates completely the life of the spirit, nor is it linked to any philosophical conception which integrates the various aspects of life. Thus, the approach embodied in this so-called realism is in fact unrealistic because it portrays not reality but merely a single aspect of appearance.

The second type of "realism" is Socialist Realism. This attempts to support a superficial and materialist representation of life by a Marxist dogma of the nature of history and society. Man is still economic and dominated by environment, still chained to a material and physical universe, and his highest ends are the achievement of material changes in the basis of ownership and social organisation. Again, spiritual reality is ignored, and the intellect recognised only as a means to the achievement of material ends. The philosophical conception underlying these material symptoms is conceived in terms of a universe governed by materialistic laws borrowed from a superannuated system of scientific thought and combined incongruously with a metaphysical and immaterialist theory of history, based on a series of brilliant generalisations which have broken down in practice because in the last resort men are not masses, but individuals reacting in individual ways to the stimulus of historical forces and the operation of natural laws. Even had the Socialist Realists kept honestly to this Marxist conception, their work could have portrayed no true and complete reality. In practice, they added dishonesty to error and became tools for politicians seeking propaganda to aid their struggle for power.

True realism, I submit, must seek to portray life in a manner that will embrace all its aspects, whether manifested physically, intellectually or spiritually. It must reveal to the full extent of the writer's knowledge and ability the nature of human development, and the complex unity of natural law by which it is motivated and governed. The writer who endeavours to show in his work such an integrated view of man and his relationship with the world in which he lives and works, is truly realist.

Ignazio Silone is a realist of this kind. His novels portray with remarkable vividness the life which the people of the Italian countryside lived under the Fascist dictatorship, the miserable hunger of the oppressed peasantry, the slow ruin of the small landowners, and the insecure prosperity in which the intriguing politicians and professional men contrived to live, by destroying their moral feelings and ignoring the sufferings of the poor. But they demonstrate as well that the struggle through which the Italian people are passing is not merely a struggle for material ends, and that it is no isolated event, but rather one aspect of a moral conflict that embraces all mankind. The later novels in particular are concerned with the spiritual developments which mature in the minds of the revolutionary, the isolated liberal, the peasant in whom the power of thought is still not crushed ; there is a steady movement of vision towards a realisation of the manner in which men can attain a life based on natural laws of freedom and mutual trust.

Silone's writing is concerned with social matters. Yet he is not a political novelist, for his writing proceeds steadily towards a conclusion that the regeneration of human society is governed by moral rather than political laws. Even less is he a propagandist, in the commonly accepted sense of the word, which in our day tends to signify a writer who seeks to convert people to an exclusive creed and whose representation of life springs, not from authentic experience but from preconceived dogma. The propagandist, by a meaningless abracadabra of generalisations and false symbols, attempts to induce action which cannot be fruitful because it is based not on concrete temporal realities but on an intellectual abstraction. Silone, on the other hand, is a writer who has sought the truth patiently and has enriched his knowledge from the fruits of his experience. He has attained certain beliefs concerning the life of man, both as an individual and in society, but these have reached him not merely from studying the systems of political theorists, but also from observing the external world and the inner life of man realistically, as he finds them and not as the theorists tell him they exist. By such means, he has developed from a believer in political dogma into an individual thinker striving to realise from direct experience and thought the nature of man's problem and the moral laws by which it can be solved.

To conclude these preliminary definitions, I would add that Silone is at once, and in a real manner, an autobiographical and an allegorical writer. All valuable writing is, in a sense, autobiographical, in that it is based on experience. Silone, however, belongs to the class of writers whose work is directly autobiographical, because it attempts to delineate accurately his own search for the

truth. It is allegorical, in that the events he describes are related
to a moral progression and a social vision as vital as those which are
brought to life in the great and more direct allegories, the writings
of Swift or Kafka.

*   *   *   *

Silone was born in the small town of Pescina, on the edge of
Lake Fucino, which lies in the Marsica province of the mountainous
Abruzzi. The date of his birth is perhaps symbolic. It was the
last May Day of the nineteenth century.

" When I was three months old ", he writes in an autobiographical fragment, " Pescina was partly destroyed by a flood. When
I was fifteen, it was entirely destroyed by an earthquake. Before
the earthquake it had eight thousand inhabitants. Only three
thousand remain to-day.

" In my boyhood Pescina had a bishop, twenty priests, thirty
carabinieri, a convent, and ten lawyers and notaries. It still has
eight churches. Most of the inhabitants are poor peasants."

Of the Marsica and the miserable life of its peasants we are told
in his novels, and particularly in *Fontamara*, from which I quote
this explanation of the causes of its poverty :

" The soil was meagre, dry and rocky. The meagre soil was
divided and subdivided, racked with mortgages. No peasant
possessed more than a few acres.

" Eighty years ago the draining of the Lake Fucino caused the
climate throughout the Marsica to become permanently hotter,
to such an extent that the cultivation of the surrounding hills was
ruined. The olive groves were utterly destroyed. Disease attacked
the grapes, and they did not always ripen. They had to be gathered
at the end of October, before the first snows fell, and they produced
a sharp, acid wine, like lemon-juice. For the most part the same
wretched peasants that produced it were doomed to drink it.

" The soil reclaimed by the draining of the Lake of Fucino was among the richest in Italy, but its exploitation yielded no compensation for these losses. The district had been reduced practically to serfdom. The great wealth it yielded yearly did not stay where it was but emigrated to the capital. A so-called Prince Torlonia owned the 8,000 acres of Fucino, together with a vast expanse of country in the Roman Campagna and Tuscany . . .

" The beet of Fucino is the raw material for one of the most important sugar factories in Europe, but sugar remains a rare luxury for the peasants who cultivate it. It only enters their houses once a year, in Easter cakes. Almost all the corn of the Fucino goes to the city, where it is used to make white bread and cake and biscuits, and even goes to feed cats and dogs ; but the peasants who grow it have to eat maize bread for the greater part of the year. All the peasants get from the Fucino is starvation wages ; wages that allow them to exist, but not to live."

Silone was the son of a small landowner, who worked almost as hard at farming as the peasants and the landless labourers around him. As a child Silone moved among the poor peasants, saw them at first-hand, went to school with their children, and came early to understand and love them. This love of the poor has dominated his actions and given his writings a most beautiful quality of sympathy for human sufferings.

His education was that of a landowner's son whose parents hoped he would embrace the material and spiritual security of the Church.

" I attended junior school at Pescina. On rainy days there were barely enough benches to go round, but on sunny days the classrooms were nearly empty, most of the pupils being engaged in hunting birds or frogs. I passed through the first few grades of senior school at Pescina, as a candidate for the clergy, and remained there up to the earthquake. I completed my schooling in Catholic institutions in various towns in Italy. There were two reasons why I never attended a university. In the first place I was advised not to do so, by the doctors, who gave me very few years to live, and in the second place political work left me very little free time." In spite of the doctors, Silone survived, and this capacity for resisting the probabilities of death may be a physical manifestation of the inner vigour which has maintained him against many disappointments in his search for a true way to mitigate human misery.

His political life absorbed the next ten years. During the war of 1914–18 the peasants of Italy became active in an attempt to gain rectification of the social and economic inequalities which made them poor. Peasant leagues appeared throughout the country; their aim was to gain an equitable distribution of land. Silone, with his sympathy for the peasants, could not stand aside from such a movement, and became one of its active members. When he was seventeen he joined the local Peasant League, and became the secretary of the Federation of Land Workers of the Abruzzi.

" In the same year opposition to the War caused me to join a group of young Socialists, and I was appointed secretary of the Socialist Youth of Rome. A year later I became editor of the weekly *Avanguardia*, which represented the extreme Left of the anti-War movement. In 1922 I was editor of a Trieste newspaper, *Il Lavoratore*, which was three times raided by the Fascists, who were accompanied and protected by the police."

When the Fascists gained power, Silone left Italy, and took up the life of exile which had been the lot of so many great Italian writers, from Dante to Mazzini and beyond. His zeal for political action, however, led him to return, and in 1925 he took up underground work as an agitator. At this time he was a member of the Communist Party. In 1928 he found it virtually impossible to continue his political work without being captured and possibly murdered. He returned to Switzerland, and in Italy he was " denounced (in absence) to the Fascist Special Tribunal for clandestine political activity."

He had already begun to question his political activities and the validity of the Marxist theories on which they had been based. In 1930 his ideas had changed so much that he left the Communist Party, and styled himself an " independent Communist ". For a long time he stood aloof from all the Italian political groups, and his denunciation of politicians and political organisations earned him their hostility.

From 1930 until recently he has lived most of the time in Switzerland, where he has written a number of books, of which four have been published in England. They are a series of three novels, *Fontamara*, *Bread and Wine* and *The Seed Beneath the Snow*, and a full length dialogue on fascism called *The School for Dictators*.

* * * *

In discussing Silone's writings, I intend to deal firstly with his three novels, which represent his progression as an individual thinker searching for the values that govern the liberation of man.

Fontamara, his first novel, written during 1930, is intended primarily as a simple story to show the life of the poor in Fascist Italy, and, although it is by no means a piece of direct propaganda and has certain interesting undertones of intention, it is much less complex and less elaborately written than his two later works.

Fontamara is a miserable village in the hills above Lake Fucino. Its inhabitants are peasants of the poorest type, " the heirs to generations of poverty ". They hate the authorities, the landlords, the carabinieri, the townspeople and the Piedmontese. They evade paying taxes, and distrust the Government almost by instinct. Nevertheless, the fact that each is the owner of a miserable portion of infertile land makes them cautious and conservative. Their attitude is changed by the series of events described in the story.

The peasants are tricked by a Fascist official into signing a petition asking for the diversion of their stream away from the peasant fields into a piece of land which the *podesta* of the nearest town has just bought cheaply. A number of women go into the town to try and gain redress for their grievance. Once again they are tricked, this time by a lawyer posing as The People's Friend, who persuades them to accept a poor compromise.

Afterwards the village is attacked by Fascist militia, who arrive when the men are in the fields, break up the homes and rape the women. The most conservative and torpid of the villagers are shaken by the series of outrages which have been committeed against them :

" What was quite clear was that the militia had come to Fontamara and raped a number of women. But they had done so in the name of the law and in the presence of a police commissary, and that was not so clear.

" At the Fucino they had put up the rents of the smallholders and lowered the rents of the big proprietors. That was clear. But the proposal to do this had been made by the representative of the poor peasants and that was not so clear.

" Each one of our misfortunes, examined separately, was not new, for similar misfortunes had often happened in the past. But the way they befell us was new and strange.

" The whole thing was absolutely beyond our understanding."

The peasants are finally disillusioned when they realise that the arrangement made for the diversion of the stream means that their fields will be completely dried up because so little water will be left to them.

" All the same, no one was resigned to the loss of the water. No one was resigned to the loss of his entire crop. No one could reconcile himself to the prospect of winter without bread or soup.

" ' If there's no justice against thieves, we've reached the end of all things,' said Ponzio Pilato.

" ' When the law has broken down and the first to violate it are those whose business it is to enforce it, it's time to go back to the law of the people,' the old cobbler said one night.

"'What is the law of the people?'

"'God helps him who helps himself,' said Baldissera."

At this time Berardo Viola, a landless peasant, goes to Rome in the hope of earning some money. He falls in with the Mystery Man, a young revolutionary who had once saved the peasants from an *agent provocateur*, and is arrested with him. In prison Berardo tells the Mystery Man of the troubles of the Fontamarese, and then sacrifices himself by declaring that he is the real Mystery Man. He is tortured to death by the Fascists. The Mystery Man himself is set free, and immediately goes to Fontamara, where he provides the peasants with the materials for a duplicated paper to tell the grievances of the country people. The peasants make their newspaper and distribute it in the surrounding villages. The same day Fontamara is invaded and the peasants, except the few who escape into the hills, are massacred.

Fontamara can be considered from two aspects. As a portrayal of the evils of Fascism, it is confident and successful, both artistically and as a representation of factual truth. But as propaganda for a party or for any definite course of action, it is virtually useless, because it is already impregnated with those doubts concerning the rôle of the revolutionary agitator which become so prominent in the later novels. Whether or not Silone intended it, the Mystery Man appears as a bringer of evil to the peasants, as a partner, however unwilling, with the Fascists in the perpetration of their final misery. He saves them from the trouble which their enemy, the *agent provocateur*, would have brought them, and precipitates them into an even worse desolation by an action which he at least should have known would end in tragedy. One feels, in fact, very little kindness for the revolutionary in this instance; all one's sympathy goes to the peasants, ground between the upper and nether millstones of rival systems of politics. Nevertheless, from the point of view of the social agitator, *Fontamara* already raises a problem which must sooner or later have troubled the conscience of every sincere revolutionary who had a real feeling for the people. How far is the revolutionary justified in leading the poor into action which he knows will bring them an immediate increase in suffering, even if he believes that in the long run such action will precipitate their freedom ? How much truth is there in the revolutionary casuistry that the people must be induced to rebel against their masters and suffer for their rebellion so that they may be taught the true character of the ruling class, and by this means be brought to overthrow its tyranny ? The question might be put in the words of the survivors of Fontamara :

" After so much strife and anguish and tears, and wounds and blood, and hatred and despair—what are we to do ? "

It is a question which as yet Silone is content merely to pose rather than to answer, for *Fontamara* is a book concerned first of all with the tragedy of the peasants, and only indirectly with the problems of the revolutionary.

* * * *

In the two later novels the revolutionary becomes the central figure, and the complex structure of Italian social life is the background against which is enacted the physical struggle of the revolutionary to keep his outward freedom, and the mental struggle through which he develops from a materialist party dogmatist into an individual thinker whose view of society becomes moral and universal rather than political and sectarian.

Bread and Wine opens with the arrival in the Marsica of the agitator Pietro Spina, ill with consumption after months of hiding. A peasant fetches a doctor who was at school with him in his youth, and who has temporised with the Fascist régime. Sacca, the doctor, speaks of the disillusionment of his class. His description fits not only Italy, but all countries caught in the toils

of a society based on authority and war ; Spina's answer has an
equally universal application :

"Sacca held one of his hands and talked of the illusions, the
disappointments, the wretchedness, the lies, the intrigues, the nausea
of his daily life.

" 'All our life is lived provisionally,' he said. 'We think that
for the time being things are bad, that for the time being we must
adapt ourselves, even humiliate ourselves, but that it is all temporary,
and that one day life, real life will begin. We get ready to die, still
complaining that we only have one life, and spend the whole of it
living provisionally, waiting for real life to begin. And thus the
time passes. Nobody lives in the present. Nobody has any profit
from his daily life. Nobody can say : on that day, on that occasion,
my life began. Even those who enjoy all the advantages of belonging to the government party have to live by intrigue, and are
thoroughly nauseated by the dominant stupidity. They too live
provisionally, and spend their lives waiting.'

" 'One must not wait,' said Spina. 'In exile one spends one's
life waiting too. One must act. One must say : Enough ! from
this very day.'

" 'But if there is no liberty ? ' said Nunzio Sacca.

" 'Liberty isn't a thing you are given as a present,' said Spina.
'You can be a free man under a dictatorship. It is sufficient if you
struggle against it. He who thinks with his own head is a free man.
Even if you live in the freest country in the world, and are lazy,
callous, apathetic, irresolute, you are not free but a slave, though
there is no coercion and no oppression. It's no use begging it
from others.' "

Through Sacca's arrangements, Spina goes disguised as a priest
to recuperate at an inn in the foothills of the Appenines. There,
living among people who trust him because of his disguise, he is
able to see intimately into the lives and minds of the country people.
Resting from the hard political struggle, he has leisure to test his

[164]

ideas and his motives. He begins to doubt the whole conception of life which has dominated his action up to the present time.

In the two girls whom he encounters and who become devoted to him are represented the two influences which attack his beliefs. Bianchina is the desire to enjoy freely the physical, wordly side of life. Christiana is the desire for spiritual fulfilment. Both make him realise how much he has become lost in subservience to political dogma. His doubts are expressed in a passage which he writes in his notebook :

" Is it possible to take part in political life, to devote oneself to the service of a party, and remain sincere ?

" Has not truth, for me, become party truth ? Has not justice, for me, become party justice ?

" Have not party interests ended by deadening all my discrimination between moral values ? Do I, too, not despise them as petty-bourgeois prejudices ?

" Have I escaped from the bondage of a decadent Church only to fall into bondage to the opportunism of a party ?

" What has become of my enthusiasm of that time ? By putting politics before everything else, before all other spiritual needs, have I not impoverished, sterilised my life ? Has it not meant that I have neglected deeper interests ? "

This is a situation that must inevitably face the revolutionary who has not allowed himself to become completely crushed by political dogma. It is, moreover, a critical situation which, unless it results in the positive assertion of spiritual and moral values, will lead to the eventual inner destruction of any moral or æsthetic sense the revolutionary may possess. The revolutionaries who fail to assert their moral values become the betrayers of the revolution, the Stalins and the Robespierres.

Such changes in attitude are never achieved immediately, nor does an intellectual enlightenment usually result in a sudden change in action, for there are still emotional loyalties which drag heavily on the subject of such a conversion. Thus Spina tries to throw aside his doubts by returning to political action. He finds discontent among the young people of Fossa and tries to convert them to his political creed. Yet in talking to them he defeats his own ends and shows his lack of faith in the dogmas he still pretends to hold :

" There are many distinctions that are distinctions of words only. There are many alliances that are alliances of words only. In no century have words been so perverted from their natural purpose of putting man in touch with man as they are to-day. To speak and to deceive (often to deceive oneself) have become almost synonymous. So far has this process gone that I, wishing to speak to you sincerely and fraternally, with no other object in mind than that of understanding you and making myself understood by you, if I begin to search for the right words, remain in perplexity, so false, equivocal, hackneyed and compromised they are. Therefore it is perhaps better to keep silent and to trust the silence."

As in *Fontamara*, his attempts at political action end in tragedy for others. A student he urges to work for the party is killed by the Fascists. Bianchina, whom he recommends to go to Rome, becomes a whore. He himself is discovered and has to escape into the mountains, but Christina, who follows him for love, falls a prey to the wolves among the mountain snow. In the same way are the spiritual and physical lives destroyed in the man who is ruled by the abstractions of dogma.

*   *   *   *

The Seed Beneath the Snow continues Spina's adventures and his spiritual progress. A large portion of the book is devoted to an intricate and successful description of the corruption and tragedy in the life of the Italian middle class, but as this is still in fact the background against which Spina's struggle is enacted, I have chosen to ignore it for reasons of space. From a literary criterion, this is the most successful of Silone's books. The structure is more closely integrated, the characterisation more rich. There is greater beauty

of imagery and language, and the slightly overdone gruesomeness
of the earlier novels is tempered by a more friendly mellowness.

Nearly a half of the book is used to describe the rural society,
in which only a few retain their integrity. The rest are too much
engrossed in the intrigues necessary for power, or even for safety.
Then, against this elaborately worked background is introduced
Spina's experience as he hid for his life in a miserable donkey's
stable on the mountain, told to his grandmother, who has saved him
and taken him into her house.

Here, from the devotion of a dumb peasant lad who came every
day to sit with him, he realises the value of companionship, and
comes nearer to the poor than he was ever brought by his political
actions :

" How can I possibly give you an idea, Grandmother, of the
simple, silent, deep friendship between us ? I could barely see the
dark hulk of his heavy body and hear his deep slow breathing, but
there was a certain affinity between his body and the bodies of the
other objects in that cave—the donkey, myself, the mice, the
trough, the straw, the packsaddle and the broken lantern—a
communion, a brotherhood whose discovery flooded my heart with
a new feeling which perhaps I should call peace or even happiness.
. . . I feel now as if I had never really been myself before, as if
I had been playing a part like an actor on the stage, wearing a mask
and declaiming prepared speeches. This life and this civilisation
of ours seem to me a theatrical, conventional, lying sham. . . .

" I have come to think that the quiet, the peace, the happiness,
the well-being, the homeliness, the companionship which I found
in that stable derived from a contact with simple, true, difficult,
painful forms of life, immune from the plague of rhetoric."

Spina experiences what is known as a " change of heart ",
transmitted with all the vividness of a mystical experience. He
realises in the symbiotic unity of nature a meaning and a pattern
which are expressed humanly in brotherhood and companionship.

[167]

In observing the processes of nature, he sees, moreover, an earnest of the growth of truth and freedom among men. This is the " seed beneath the snow : "

" At first I feared that the seed was already dead but, after I had carefully cleared away the earth around it with a straw, I discovered a slender white tongue like a stalk of grass coming out of it. My whole being, my whole heart came to centre around that little seed, Grandmother. I was in despair because I didn't know how to keep it alive : even now I'm not sure that I did the right thing. To keep out the cold and to replace the shelter of the board which I had removed, I covered it with a little earth ; every morning I melted some snow over it to provide it with water, and, to give it heat, I breathed on it. That clod of earth with its tiny, weak, exposed yet living, hidden treasure came to hold for me the mystery, the familiarity and the sacredness of a mother's breast. . . My own existence, I knew, was as precarious and as exposed to danger as that of the seed abandoned beneath the snow, and yet it was as natural, as vital as life itself, not an image, a pretence or an imitation of life, but life itself, at its sorrowful and dangerous source."

Spina's experience is now involved in the discovery of brotherhood. With his grandmother he finds a new relationship based on their common faith in spiritual realities. Then his dumb friend comes to the town where he is hiding. Spina leaves his grandmother's house and joins Infante, the dumb boy, and Simone the Polecat, a peasant who gives them refuge. With Infante and Simone he discovers a relationship more deep and comradely than any he had ever enjoyed before. He realises in this experience why his political activity was futile :

" . . . All in all, I must have been acquainted with several thousand persons in the Party more or less and known a few dozen among them a little better. But in fifteen years I never knew a soul as well as I know you and Infante. I used to think it was my fault, but I came to see that the same thing was true of the others.

To tell the truth, they didn't hold much with friendship in the Party; there was something suspicious about it, as if it might engender the formation of cliques and gangs. For this reason I should even rightly admit that friendship, in the true and human meaning of the word, was regarded and despised as a remnant of bourgeois individualism."

Later, Spina flees to a town in the mountains, accompanied by Faustina, a beautiful and intelligent girl who in this book embodies the qualities represented by the two girls in *Bread and Wine*. She represents the union of spiritual and physical happiness and fulfilment. With Faustina he discusses the change that has occurred in his philosophy :

" It was more painful for me than I can tell you, Faustina, after I had come back from exile abroad in order to work and fight against the dictatorship, to spend almost a whole year in inactivity here in the country, rusting away, all because I was going through a spiritual crisis. But this much I learned at my own expense : that before we can give something of ourselves to others, we must first possess ourselves. A man who is spiritually a slave cannot work for true freedom. To look after one's own soul no longer seems to me a waste of time or, as I once used to say pontifically, a sign of bourgeois decadence. When all is said and done, there is no better and more necessary occupation than man's effort to know himself and the meaning of his life on earth. Everything else must follow, as the cart follows the horse. I now feel that the two fundamental motives of my existence came out of this spiritual crisis stronger than ever ; the rejection of our present social order and attachment to the poor, two motives which are but one. . . My love for the poor must have come down to me from a previous existence ; I can imagine myself armless and legless but not without my feeling for them. This love for the poor has been my salvation ; were it not for this, Faustina, I might have wound up as a Government orator."

This is Spina's final credo, on which his fate is cast. He has left the abstraction of political dogma, the artificial cage of party practice, and entered upon the intimate reality of direct knowledge between men. On this only can the society he desires be built, patiently and with love.

The change in his ideas is symbolised in the ending of the book. This time Spina asks and gains no sacrifice of others to achieve his objects. The political machine demands its victims, but the loving man gives himself for friendship. Spina has planned to leave Italy and live abroad with Faustina, thus achieving the end of his conflict and the gaining of complete physical and spiritual happiness. But Infante commits a murder and Spina lets himself be led away into prison in his place. Thus the man who seeks to save mankind by moral values has a task as much burdened by hardship and self-sacrifice as that of any political martyr who gives himself for the illusions of a mass dogma.

*　　*　　*　　*

We have seen, both in Silone's life and in his novels, a developing sense of the reality of moral and spiritual values and the futility of any attempt to change society that is not derived from a conception of morality. But, because Silone has not been explicit in his novels as to the exact nature of the social programmes he would advocate, we must not consider that he has retired into a mysticism that has no contact with social facts. On the contrary, his realisation of the need for a moral basis for social action springs in part from his own experience as a political worker and his ever-present desire for a life which will relieve the poor and the oppressed from their miserable fate.

It is in *The School for Dictators* that we find Silone's social attitude most clearly expressed. Primarily, this book is an analysis of the nature and methods of Fascism, and as such, although it is probably the best book of its kind that has been written, it is not of immediate interest. In this article we are concerned with the glimpses we gain from it of Silone's view of a free society.

Silone's social creed is essentially and thoroughly libertarian. Elsewhere, he calls himself an "ethical socialist", but fundamentally his ideas are not widely different from those of the anarchists.

His social attitude is based on a passionate belief in freedom :

"If I may for one moment abandon the rôle of cynic that I have assumed in these conversations, I will frankly confess that I *only* believe in miracles. Other things I have no need to believe, because I see them. But I believe in the miracle of liberty, although I see all the things that are opposed to it."

It is in such a belief in freedom, irrational because it is above reason, that Silone's creed, like that of the anarchists, becomes truly religious. Faith, as well as reason, is necessary for the achievement of harmony among men. In the last resort, every great revolutionary, every great social thinker, has found his energy in a faith that went beyond his reasoning powers, in a belief in qualities and potentialities of man for which the material world can afford no proof.

Moral teachings have often been derided by politicians as being unrealistic. Yet it is just because most politicians are not actuated by moral values that their own efforts have been so harmful to the interests of humanity : " . . . a genuine knowledge of social reality does not suffice if it is not supported by a strong moral sense."

It is in fact only by the realisation and revelation of the natural laws concerning humanity that social knowledge can be imparted, and only by the spreading of knowledge can communal felicity be attained. With such knowledge, politics as we know it becomes redundant, for :

"Is not a certain ignorance of the laws that govern human society at the very basis of all politics ? "

Silone's criticism of existing political institutions, whether of the State or of parties attempting to take over the State, is directed towards both their methods and their ends. He attacks the domination of machine and technique, the predominance of the means over the end :

" Machines, which ought to be man's instrument, enslave him, the state enslaves society, the bureaucracy enslaves the state, the church enslaves religion, parliament enslaves democracy, institutions enslave justice, academies enslave art, the army enslaves the nation, the party enslaves the cause, the dictatorship of the proletariat enslaves Socialism. The choice and the control of the instruments of political action are thus at least as important as the choice of the ends themselves, and as time goes on the instruments must be expected to become an end for those who use them. Hence the saying that the end justifies the means is not only immoral ; it is stupid. An inhuman means remains inhuman even if it is employed for the purpose of assuring human felicity. A lie is always a lie, murder is always murder. A lie always ends by enslaving those who use it, just as violence always enslaves those who use it as well as their victims. What is the story of Fascism but that of an instrument which became an end in itself and imposes itself upon those who wanted to use it ? "

" Technique aims at the mechanical use of men, while liberty considers the human personality as sacred. A technique of the progressive stupefaction of the masses exists. A technique of liberty does not and cannot exist."

Liberty can only arise organically, from free companionship among men and the growth of trust and brotherhood. It cannot be imposed from without, but must be gained by each man, individually and in co-operation with his fellows.

On social organisation, Silone's ideas may be epitomised as, firstly, the use and control of the means of production by the workers themselves, and secondly, a federalist social structure based on local functional autonomy.

" Socialism means socialisation. Nationalisation, whether partial or total, is not socialism. Why ? Capitalism has separated

labour from the ownership of the means of production.   Under
the feudal system the two were united.   Socialism aims at reuniting
labour and the means of production on the technical and social
level that has been made possible by modern industry, taking the
latter out of the hands of private individuals and the state and giving
it to the labouring community.   Fascist ' Socialism ' is not of this
nature, hence it is not Socialism, but a bogus form of Socialism, a
substitute for it, a fake.   All that the totalitarian state does when it
intervenes in production remains, and is bound to remain, within
the confines of capitalism.   The success of the fake is aided by the
fact that even many so-called Socialists have lost the notion of
Socialism and confuse nationalisation, and even any kind of state
intervention in production, with Socialism."

In 1942, Silone wrote a statement of his philosophical position,
and I can do no better than leave the final summary of his social
beliefs to be spoken therefrom :

" The struggle between socialism and fascism will not be decided
by war, the truth being that wars in general decide nothing.   It
may well be that fascism will be conquered by force of arms, and
nevertheless will develop in the victor states—perhaps even with
a democratic or socialist mask, under the form of a ' Red fascism '.
History is made by men, not by social determinisms, and I confess
that I am not pessimistic.

" In summing up, I stand for : (1) an integral federalism and
(2) an ethical conception of socialism.   Federalism is often recommended these days as a penalty for defeated nations.   But it would
not be a penalty ; it would be a triumph for our cause.   As for the
ethical conception of socialism, it does not demand a new morality ;
all we have to do is to recognise its true potentiality. . . .

" We have all heard it said that the masses will not fight except
for material things, and hence must always be guided by mediocre
ends and mediocre people.   I believe, on the contrary, that the
masses have rejected the leadership of the democrats and the

socialists because it was middling and muddling. If mediocrity were good enough for the masses, the Social Democrats would never have lost their influence over the German workers. It is precisely because the masses suffer from a feeling of mediocrity that they refuse to accept mediocre leaders. The Church won the hearts of the masses in the days when it offered them the boldest and most difficult aims. It lost its spiritual leadership when it became prudent and conservative.

"There is still another myth to be refuted. It is that in all countries where the means of expressing opinions are monopolised by the State, men can no longer think freely or boldly. But the truth is quite the contrary; that the greatest, the most audacious thoughts on liberty have come from nations where liberty had ceased to exist. The human mind will never let itself be transformed into a machine. Human liberty and human dignity are conceptions that will never perish."

Here, as in the rest of Silone's writings, we find a developed social insight which can only be gained by relinquishing the dogmas of political orthodoxy and rediscovering by individual experience the simple and difficult truths of brotherhood and mutual trust among men, the veritable seed beneath the snow from which will rise the harvest of freedom.

(*Note.* Since this article was written Silone has returned to political life, and worked actively in the Socialist Party. The exact reasons for his return to this form of action, which he tacitly condemned in his most recent books, is not yet apparent, and I have chosen to leave this essay as it was written rather than attempt to adapt it to fit actions of whose cause I am unaware. I still consider that what I have written stands good as an interpretation of Silone's writing, and that his subsequent conduct does not necessarily invalidate any of the criticisms of the political attitude which he has made in his books.)

X

Arthur Koestler

ARTHUR KOESTLER's life and development have followed, in many ways, the same general pattern as those of Silone. He too started as a Communist, having been born in a country that came under a reactionary dictatorship. He too experienced close and direct contact with the brutality of totalitarian régimes, and his works are saturated with the physical experience of struggle against such brutality. He too came gradually and painfully to realise that the Communist Party was in reality as totalitarian as the régimes it opposed, and that its methods and philosophy could only do harm to the cause of freedom and socialism. Like Silone, he finally left the Communist Party, and has since devoted himself so much to the task of exposing the Stalinist myth that he ranks with George Orwell among the writers in England most hated by the Communists. Finally, he, as well as Silone, has turned away from doctrinaire, " scientific ", managerial socialism, in the hope of finding an ethical basis for his social beliefs. His most recent actions seem to show that he has failed to establish any such basis at all securely in his mind.

On the other hand, Koestler differs quite profoundly from Silone on a number of important points. Firstly, while feeling a deep *intellectual* solidarity with the workers, he has never achieved the same emotional identity with the lives of the poor which breathes through every page of Silone's works. Unlike Silone, he never

seems to have acted as an agitator among the workers, and certainly
has lived too much the middle-class life of the international journalist to have been in real contact with them for any long period of
time.   Consequently, he tended at first to have bourgeois illusions
about workers, rather than a deep and intimate knowledge such as
Silone shows for his poor Italian peasants and labourers.   When
Koestler did come into a close and prolonged contact with real
workers in large numbers, it was in the French concentration camp
of Le Vernet, and he found it the disillusioning experience which
comes sooner or later to any intellectual who has idealised the
working class, unless he remains insulated from real contact with
them all his life.   With a man like Silone, who has always loved the
poor for what they are, faults and virtues all complete, it would be
impossible to imagine any such disillusionment.

Out of this lack of roots among his own people, has arisen the
shifting, expatriate character of Koestler's work.   Silone remained
always an Italian writer, concerned with his own people ; in exile
he stayed in Switzerland, as close to Italy as he could, and the
books he wrote were always concerned with Italy and the life of
its people.   He was an internationalist, but with that richer inter-
nationalism which is rooted deeply in the feeling of a real regional
life, of the actual lives of the men and women of his own arid native
hills.   Koestler has none of this.   He has become the perpetual
exile, more exile by far than the Herzens, Bakunins and Kropotkins
of an earlier age who, for all their participation in international
movements, always looked back on Russia with nostalgia and the
hope that it would somehow achieve the dawn of freedom for
which they had worked.

Koestler, in his early books at least, represents the rootless inter-
nationalism of a revolutionary consciousness which has thrown away
the nationalism that mingled varyingly in all forms of nineteenth-
century revolutionism, and has failed to realise the regional consciousness which is its true substitute.   His books exhibit little

concern for the plight of his own country. All Silone's books are
devoted to the life of the Italian people. But Koestler's four
novels show no unity of this kind. *The Gladiators* is set in ancient
Rome, *Darkness at Noon* deals with Russian dictatorship, *Arrival
and Departure* portrays the lives of expatriates in Portugal ; some
of the earlier experiences of the hero are actually concerned with
political activity in Hungary, but they are definitely subordinated
to the main theme of his typically refugee problems, his conflict
whether to leave Portugal for the comparative ease of life with his
mistress in America, or to go to England and fight against Germany. Finally, his last novel, *Thieves in the Night*, adopts one of the
synthetic nationalisms of the nationless ; just as in an earlier period,
Koestler accepted the *ersatz* nationalism of glorifying Russia as the
worker's fatherland, he now adopts Zionism, the creed of an artificial nation, as a substitute for his own lack of a native regional
consciousness. Equally significantly, although he evidently had
interesting experiences in his younger days in Central Europe,
there is almost no reference to them in his writings ; his two books
of reportage, *Spanish Testament* and *The Scum of the Earth*, are
concerned with Spain and France respectively. Lastly, Koestler
has allowed himself to become absorbed into English culture in a
way which no other whose native tongue was not English has been
able to do since Conrad. All these efforts to cut himself away
from his home, to thrust exploringly into other countries and ages,
to find adoptive homes in Russia, in Spain during the Civil War,
in France on the eve of collapse, in war-time England, in Palestine
racked by strife, mark Koestler as a wanderer cursed with some kind
of compulsion that prevents him from ever turning back to his own
native environment, or, however much he may try, gaining roots
in another country. It is significant that he should only seek a
spiritual home in countries that are made unsure by strife and danger,
as if an irresistible sense of doom led him from one such country to
another. All this is closely connected with the preoccupation with

violence that becomes evident in a closer examination of his various
books.

A final, and vitally important, point of difference between Silone
and Koestler lies in the nature of their writing. Silone is, perhaps
more than any of his contemporaries, a complete novelist. He aims
at expounding ideas in his novels, but he does not subordinate his
works to this aim. His novels, instead of being expositions of intellectual ideas, act on all levels of consciousness—physical, emotional,
intellectual, spiritual. He does not merely represent the disorders
of the world to-day. He shows first of all the timeless tragedies
and comedies of humanity, the deep basic elements of life. This is
why I would call him a true and complete novelist.

Koestler, on the other hand, deals firstly with ideas ; not general
humanist ideas so much as ideas on the nature of man's contemporary crisis. Unavoidably, his political preoccupations lead him
to subordinate all else, and consequently his work is shallow on the
physical, emotional and spiritual levels. His characters sometimes
act unreally because their deeds have no reason beyond the political
pattern of the book. His writing is locked in the prison of contemporary events ; it has no wider reference, and for this reason,
he should be regarded more as a brilliant journalist of fiction than
as a real novelist.

This is not to deny that Koestler has gifts. Indeed, if I may
venture on a second comparison, he reminds one strongly of Aldous
Huxley in the years of his youthful and never fulfilled promise.
There are the same acute perceptions of the characteristics of a
person or a situation, the same negative gifts of scepticism and
iconoclasm, the same display of an apparently encyclopædic knowledge, the same failure to build with all these qualities any really
satisfying work of literature or any convincing social vision. Koestler
is in one respect even more gifted than Huxley, in that his political
sense is more acute, and is reinforced by an empirical knowledge
of political activity from the inside which enables him to put this

sense to good use in the exposure of pretences. Yet, for all the brilliant execution of the works which he has so far produced, none of them has yet shown him as a writer of really positive value.

Koestler's first book published in England, *Spanish Testament*, pretends to be little more than a journalistic description of his experiences in Spain during the Civil War. The earlier part is unremarkable, even among the books of war correspondents, and shows little of the acuteness of analysis which one has later come to expect from Koestler. At that time he was still more or less attached to the Communist Party, and he supported the current Popular Front line with what seems, reading between the wavy lines of his reports, to have been a singular lack of conviction. He was obviously uneasy, but not yet ready to speak openly on the betrayals which he probably knew even then were happening in Spain.

The latter part of the book, in which he deals with his imprisonment, is much more convincing, and shows all the brilliant presentation of atmosphere which we have come to associate with Koestler —what George Orwell calls " the nightmare atmosphere which is, so to speak, his patent . . ." Koestler just escapes a summary shooting, and then lies in prison for months under the threat of death, hearing his fellow prisoners shot in batches every night and expecting his own turn to come any day. In this book the feeling of violence is already evident. Yet it is a book that deals naturally with violent events and experiences, and one would not be justified in drawing attention to this fact if Koestler's later works did not perpetually show a more than usual consciousness of the presence and enormity of violence in human life.

As descriptions of prison life go, Koestler's is one of the best and most terrifying. Perhaps it does not reach so tenderly into the depths as Dostoevsky's *House of the Dead*, but more than most other books it shows the perpetual and almost extra-human cruelty of the metamorphosis that imprisonment inflicts on ordinary men.

I have rarely read a more concise and telling description of the sustained horrors of prison life than the following brief passage :

" Guilty or innocent, the prisoner changes form and colour, and assumes the mould that most easily enables him to secure a maximum of the minimal advantages possible within the framework of the prison system. In the world outside, now faded to a dream, the struggle is waged for position, prestige, power, women. For the prisoner these are the heroic battles of Olympian demi-gods. Here inside the prison walls the struggle is waged for a cigarette, for permission to exercise in the courtyard, for the possession of a pencil, for a bath or a shave. It is a struggle for minimal and unworthy objects, but a struggle for existence like any other. With this difference, that the prisoner has only one weapon left to him ; cunning and hypocrisy developed to the point of reflex action. Of all other means he has been deprived. The hearing and sense of touch of a man who has been blinded are intensified ; there is only one direction in which the prisoner can evolve—that of increasing artfulness. In the hot-house atmosphere of his social environment he cannot escape this fateful transformation of his character. He feels his claws growing, a furtive and dejected, an impudent and servile, look creeps into his eyes ; his lips become thin, sharp, Jesuitical, his nose pinched and sharp, his nostrils dilated and bloodless, as in the death-mask of the poet who wrote the *Inferno*. His knees sag, his arms grow long, and dangle gorilla-like. Those who uphold the theory of ' race ' and deny the influence of environment on the development of the human being should spend a year in prison and observe themselves daily in a mirror."

It was out of the nightmare of Spain, with its betrayals, its prisons and its violence, that there grew up Koestler's first English novel, *The Gladiators*. After leaving Spain, he began to lose his faith in Communism ; he had time to reconsider the events, to realise the errors of all the revolutionary groups, to see the failure

of any insurrectionary method yet attempted to achieve the revolutionary object desired. What he was observing—only he did not
bring himself to admit it—was that destruction of a revolution which
follows inevitably as soon as authority and governmental institutions are allowed to grow again, as they were even by the anarchists
in Spain.

From this disillusionment with his experience in Spain, and
equally with the failure of the Russian revolution to produce anything better than what he now realised was a ruthless dictatorship,
Koestler wrote his story of the collapse of a slave rebellion in
antiquity. It is an interesting allegory of modern political trends,
but it fails as a novel, because, firstly, it does not state the main
problem in contemporary human terms, and, secondly, cannot
present a convincing picture of the age in which the real rebellion of
Spartacus—whose actual historical details are still barely known
to us—took place. Not that Koestler himself is to blame,
for, as Orwell says, " Nowadays the present and the future are too
terrifying to be escaped from, and if one bothers with history it is
in order to find modern meanings there." But such an inevitably
biassed way of looking at history is unlikely to produce a really
satisfying work of historical fiction—and Koestler's classical proto-
types of the Russian revolutionaries are unconvincing, partly
because their motives do not fit their age, and partly because their
creator is as little aware as they of the real causes of their failure—
the corruption of power that has ruined every revolutionary movement to the present day. In this book the theme of violence once
again appears, in the hideous shadow of the cross, on which the
surviving rebels are finally hung to die.

Koestler's next book is *The Scum of the Earth*, which describes
his experience when, for a few months, he was kept prisoner in the
notorious French internment camp of Le Vernet. Here were
interned a strange collection of anti-fascists whom the French police
chose to remove from circulation at the opening of the

so-called war against fascism. As Koestler describes them :

" They were partly the last Mohicans of the International Brigade and partly politically active exiles from all countries under Fascist rule. The French Sureté Nationale, which had never ceased to be an instrument of the Bonnet-Laval policy and which had had Vichy all bottled and ready for sale since September, 1939, decided that the first thing to do in a war against Hitler was to lock up all the notorious anti-Hitlerites. To make this private anti-Left pogrom of the Sureté more palatable to the public, the ' Scum ' was given a fair sprinkling of about twenty per cent of genuine criminals, pimps, dope peddlers, nancy-boys and other types of the Montmartre underworld.

" But the remaining eighty per cent of us, whom they had thrown on the dung heap, were those who had started the present war on our own as far back as 1930 and even earlier, who had drunk of Mussolini's castor oil and had lain on the torture-racks of the Siguranza in Bucarest and sat on the Ghetto benches of Lvov and known the steel whips of the S.S. in Dachau ; who had printed secret anti-Nazi leaflets in Vienna and Prague and, above all, had fought through the prelude to the Apocalypse in Spain."

In Le Vernet, Koestler learnt two important and bitter lessons. He discovered the hollow pretences of democracy, that the much-vaunted freedom of democratic France could in practice be as cruel as any dictatorship. And he found that the workers whom he had previously tended somewhat naïvely to idealise, could be as despicable and as treacherous as any other class. He began to perceive the great dilemma of the genuine revolutionary—that no rapid progress to social liberation can be made until the masses have become awakened and educated to their responsibilities, and that, on the other hand, such awakening and education are in themselves largely conditional on a certain degree of material social progress that will remove the workers from the immediately numbing influence of want and suffering, and give them enough respite to think about their lives and discover their moral responsibilities to society.

Koestler's second novel, *Darkness at Noon*, is undoubtedly his best. It represents his first direct approach to the problem of Russian Communism, and an honest effort to probe the mysteries of the Russian purge trials of 1936–38.

It is the story of the arrest of an old Bolshevik on a faked charge of counter-revolutionary activities. The central character, Rubashov, is said to have been modelled on Karl Radek. Rubashov is taken away to a prison of the GPU, where he undergoes a process of steady wearing-down, first at the hands of an old comrade Ivanov, and then under one of the new ruthless officers, Gletkin, a man who has none of the idealism of the old Bolsheviks, but represents the ruthless policeman type which has been dominant in Russian affairs for the past ten years and is to-day represented by such nationally powerful figures as Beria and Malenkov. At last Rubashov is brought to the point where he can resist no longer ; he confesses what his persecutor desires, and is finally condemned and shot. As he awaits death, he recalls the scenes of his life as a Comintern bureaucrat, the intrigues among the parties of other countries, the merciless betrayal to hostile authorities of party men and women considered unfaithful to Russian interests, the general corruption that comes from an easy acceptance of the philosophy of ends justifying means.

This is the best of Koestler's novels, yet even here he is still rather the brilliant journalist of fiction, entering fully into the spirit of the contemporary social phenomenon, than the constructive artist in whose work some living quality can be apprehended growing out of the ruins of tragedy and evil. This book, in fact, reveals a mental duality from which many of our contemporary intellectuals are suffering to-day. They realise the evils which result from a particular authoritarian system and can envisage them with a remarkably destructive clarity, but this very clearness of

perception often springs from the fact that they are still fundamentally in the state of mind which produces the evils they regard
with such honest horror.

In its crudest form, this duality gives rise to the malady of
Trotskyism, where the opponent of Stalinism sees the source of the
evil in personal terms—had it not been for the corrupt aims of
certain individuals, Bolshevism as it arose in the revolution would
have produced paradise. The system in itself is sacred, and is
bound to succeed if the right people apply it. At the other end of
the scale we get the people who realise fully that no good can arise
from an authoritarian system of government, yet who have insufficient faith in man to see any alternative to authority. These retire
to the ivory tower, become spurious mystics like W. B. Yeats, or
literary fascists like Ezra Pound. Koestler, who is one of the most
talented of the independent Left intellectuals of this country, is a
much more subtle case than the people who occupy these extreme
positions. He realises all the faults in authoritarian societies up
to the present, he has sufficient concern for mankind to make him
continue in spite of this fact to hope for a social system that will not
partake of these faults, yet he has not made that ultimate act of
faith in the potentialities of man which results in the final rejection of authority as the pattern of social relations and the acceptance
of a libertarian co-operation as the basis of the administration of
society.

The duality in *Darkness at Noon* becomes more evident if we
regard the book from two different points. As a description of the
nightmare life of prisons it is excellent. Koestler has drawn fully
on his own experiences, and had he been content to write a novel
based on the horrors of the Russian prison system he would probably
have produced a real work of art. But he had to superimpose an
intellectual framework—an attempt to explain why the old
Bolsheviks finally made public confessions of almost all the acts of
which they had been accused. And here, it seems to me, Koestler

shows the lack of that deep psychological penetration which is the mark of a really good novelist, as distinct from a fictional journalist. He adopts what appears the least likely of all the explanations that have been given for the confessions. He suggests that they were made because the men in question were so steeped in party loyalty that they had eventually to accept their own death and discredit as a final gesture for the good of their cause. Personally, I find it difficult to believe that this was so in the case of men like, for instance, Bukharin, and I consider most unconvincing the mental processes by which Rubashov in the book came to accept his guilt inwardly, as well as acknowledging it outwardly to end his persecution. It is impossible not to share the incredulous disgust of the Tsarist officer who is Rubashov's neighbour in prison, when one reads of the smugness with which the latter regarded his surrender.

Undoubtedly the most impressive scene in the book is that in which Bogrov, a former comrade of Rubashov, is taken to his death while his fellow prisoners drum a last salute on their cell doors as he passes :

" Along the corridor came the low, hollow sound of subdued drumming. It was not tapping nor hammering ; the men in the cells 380 to 402, who formed the acoustic chain and stood behind their doors like a guard of honour in the dark, brought out with deceptive resemblance the muffled, solemn sound of a roll of drums, carried by the wind from the distance. Rubashov stood with his eyes pressed to the spy-hole, and joined the chorus by beating with both hands rhythmically against the concrete door. To his astonishment, the stifled wave was carried on to the right, through No. 406 and beyond ; Rip Van Winkle must have understood after all ; he too was drumming. At the same time Rubashov heard to his left, at some distance still from the limits of his range of vision, the grinding of iron doors being rolled back on their slidings. The drumming to his left became slightly louder ; Rubashov knew that the iron door which separated the isolation cells from the

ordinary ones, had been opened. A bunch of keys jangled, now the
iron door was shut again ; now he heard the approach of steps,
accompanied by sliding and slipping noises on the tiles. The
drumming to the left rose in a wave, a steady, muffled crescendo.
Rubashov's field of vision, limited by cells Nos. 401 and 407, was
still empty. The sliding and squealing sounds approached quickly,
now he distinguished also a moaning and whimpering, like the
whimpering of a child. The steps quickened, the drumming to
the left faded slightly, to the right it swelled.

" Rubashov drummed. He gradually lost the sense of time and
of space, he heard only the hollow beating as of jungle tom-toms ;
it might have been apes that stood behind the bars of their cages,
beating their chests and drumming ; he pressed his eye to the judas,
rising and falling rhythmically on his toes as he drummed. As
before, he saw only the stale, yellowish light of the electric bulb in
the corridor ; there was nothing to be seen save the iron doors of
Nos. 401 and 407, but the roll of drums rose, and the creaking and
whimpering approached. Suddenly shadowy figures entered his
field of vision ; they were there. Rubashov ceased to drum and
stared. A second later they had passed.

" What he had seen in these few seconds, remained branded on
Rubashov's memory. Two dimly lit figures had walked past,
both in uniform, big and undistinct, dragging between them a
third, whom they held under the arms. The middle figure hung
slack and yet with doll-like stiffness from their grasp, stretched out
at length, face turned to the ground, belly arched downwards.
The legs trailed after, the shoes skated along on the toes, producing
the squealing sound which Rubashov had heard from the distance.
Whitish strands of hair hung over the face turned towards the tiles,
with the mouth wide open. Drops of sweat clung to it ; out of the
mouth spittle ran thinly down the chin. When they had dragged
him out of Rubashov's field of vision, further to the right and down
the corridor, the moaning and whimpering gradually faded away ;

it came to him only as a distant echo, consisting of three plaintive vowels : ' u-a-o '. But before they had turned the corner at the end of the corridor, by the barber's shop, Bogrov bellowed out loudly twice, and this time Rubashov heard not only the vowels, but the whole word ; it was his own name, he heard it clearly : Ru-ba-shov.

"Then as if at a signal, silence fell. The electric lamps were burning as usual, the corridor was empty as usual. Only in the wall No. 406 was ticking : ARISE, YE WRETCHED OF THE EARTH."

Here, in this scene, we have two of the important elements of Koestler's work portrayed vividly. Firstly, there is the ability to reconstruct and adapt convincingly scenes actually experienced, combined with a lack of real imaginative power—the characteristics that distinguish the fictional journalist from the real novelist. And we have also violence appearing as the key theme of the book—for this scene strikes one immediately as the deepest centre of life in the whole book.

Koestler's next novel, *Arrival and Departure*, is another study in motives. It is, in a sense, a psycho-analytical treatise on the revolutionary mind, and the theme of violence and guilt for violence becomes increasingly more insistent. There are also significant autobiographical elements which make it an interesting book to the student of Koestler's mind, although as a novel it is unsatisfactory and much inferior to *Darkness at Noon*.

The hero is a young Hungarian who was formerly active in the Communist Party but has since become disillusioned. He escapes to Portugal, where he intends to enlist in the British forces in order to fight against the Nazis. But he finds the obstacles and bureaucratic delays are greater than he anticipated. Expecting nothing from the British, he begins despairingly to try and get a visa for America. While he is still waiting, he reaches the end of his resources, and then encounters a woman psychologist who had known him at home. She gives him hospitality in her flat ; there he has an affair with a French girl, and between the temptations of Love, represented by Odette, and Reason, represented by the psycho-analyst, he begins to lose his urge to fight for the Allies, and thinks even more steadily of departing for America. Odette leaves, and then he is prostrated by a psychological breakdown which deprives him of the use of a leg. A long process of analysis follows, in which are revealed, firstly the story of his revolutionary activity and his persecution at the hands of the secret police at home, and then, as the guilt and violence motive that underlies his entry into revolutionary activity, his childish hatred of his brother and his desire to cause him violent physical harm.

He is cured, and intends to start for America. The psychologist has left before him, and while he is waiting for his boat he encounters a young Nazi who criticises the Left and tempts him to work for the Nazis. He refuses, but the temptation is part of a series of circumstances that make him change his mind about going to America. Later he finds a letter from Odette to the psychologist that shows there was a Lesbian attachment between them, and that to Odette he was only an amorous incident. The final stroke comes when he is on the ship ready to depart, and the young Nazi greets him effusively before a group of refugees. He suddenly wonders where his actions have led him, and leaves the boat just as it is about to depart. He goes back to the British Consulate, and the last scene shows him being parachuted as a British agent into his own country.

It is an unconvincing book, and does not show at all thoroughly *why* Peter makes his final change of mind. He is disillusioned with Communism, and with Britain as well, and the facts that he cannot answer Bernard's criticisms of the Left and that he has been disillusioned with Odette seem hardly sufficient to send him into a war. The only explanation appears to be that his analysis has not in fact exorcised his sense of guilt or his preoccupation with violence. This seems a scanty peg on which to hang a novel.

It is clear, however, that Koestler had been influenced by that strange book of Richard Hillary, *The Last Enemy*, which describes the curious fatality that led this young man on to his death with no apparent faith in the cause for which he fought, or any really adequate reason to die. Hillary actually appears in a thinly disguised form in *Arrival and Departure*, as the badly burnt airman whose presence plays on Peter's conscience and is a contributory factor in his decision to join the British forces. Undoubtedly young men like Hillary do present a most interesting problem of motives, but it seems to me that Koestler, in trying to mingle it somewhat arbitrarily with the distinct problem of revolutionary disillusionment, has failed to produce a clear or satisfying book.

The Gladiators, Arrival and Departure, Darkness at Noon, all found Koestler deeply concerned with the various dilemmas of revolutionary action. And these dilemmas, with the consciousness of the equivocal position in which he, as well as others like him, found himself in a world where revolution is necessary, but seems always more difficult, led him to write the essays which form *The Yogi and the Commissar*.

This book is an attempt to investigate thoroughly the position of the revolutionary intellectual and to prescribe some line of development that might lead to more constructive results. It conveys an impression of real honesty, and is written with clarity and a display of knowledge. Its documentation is not always accurate, as when Koestler states that Nechaev " lived for a number of years chained to the wall of a humid cell and when his comrades succeeded in establishing contact and offered to liberate him, refused because he preferred them to concentrate on more important tasks. But later, in the emigré atmosphere of Geneva, he became involved in the most squalid quarrels and died an obscure nobody."

In fact, Nechaev never left his humid cell, and the squalid quarrels took place many years before his death in prison. However,

I am sure this error is an honest one, arising from a slip in research or possibly from the confusion of Nechaev's life with that of some other Russian revolutionary.

The book also suffers from a certain disjointedness, because it is compiled from articles which have been written over a number of years, and some of which have only a very tenuous relationship to the main theme.

Koestler sees the dilemma of the intellectuals expressed in the extremes of the Yogi and the Commissar. The Commissar believes in Change from Without, and that man's condition can be made perfect by a mere alteration in economic conditions. He believes that the end justifies the means, and thus enters upon a degeneracy of values in which at last he becomes dominated by the means and suffers a brutalisation and corruption which are destructive both to himself and to his end. The Yogi, at the other end of the spectrum, seeks Change from Within, but in the failure to communicate his own mystical uplift, attains a condition of inaction which admits the continuance or even the increase of physical evil without protest or resistance. " The Yogi and the Commissar may call it quits."

Koestler, it can be seen, hovers uneasily between, seeing the good in each of them, yet unable to reconcile these apparently contradictory tendencies. The duality from which he suffers is shared by many of his generation, and has resulted in that unfortunate lack of direction which has led so many of our intellectuals into compromise positions, into defending the lesser evil. Koestler puts their position when he says :

" The collapse of the revolutionary movement has put the intelligentsia into a defensive position ; the alternative for the next few years is no more ' capitalism or revolution ' but to save *some* of the values of democracy and humanism or to lose them all ; and to prevent this happening one has to cling more than ever to the ragged banner of ' independent thinking '."

But surely this is only another way of admitting the victory of the Yogi !

It is in reality this duality of Yogi and Commissar, of ideal and practice, of Ends and Means, that is at the root of the faults in modern social thought. The politician becomes the slave of his means, the visionary planner achieves nothing because he is blinded to anything but his end. Both neglect the fact that in *reality* there is no such duality. The means is part of the end, the practice of the ideal, and it is for this reason that reformist policies, and attempts to achieve revolutionary ends by the use of corrupt institutions, are bound to fail. Koestler seems to realise this fact in a philosophical sense when he talks of the Gestalt theory of " wholeness ".

However, *The Yogi and the Commissar* is undoubtedly a very valuable book, for it does bring into the open issues which too many revolutionary intellectuals fear to face, because any admission they make on these questions may mean abandoning some of their refuges from reality and their cherished illusions about themselves. Not the least important part of the book is the section entitled " Explorations ", where Koestler carries out a lengthy and capable analysis of the rise of the Soviet myth, and a critical survey of the structure of Russian Communist Society. This section has great documentary importance, and illustrates the kind of work in which the writer's journalistic gifts can be turned to the best advantage.

The Yogi and the Commissar revealed Koestler's dilemma. His latest book, *Thieves in the Night*, may almost be said to have resolved it in an arbitrary and defiant manner. Koestler comes down heavily on the side of the Commissars, and decides at last that the end does justify the means. He chooses what seems at first sight a singularly weak case on which to base his decision.

Thieves in the Night is concerned with the activities of Jewish terrorists in Palestine. It tells the story of an English half-Jew Joseph, who is made conscious of his race through an embarrassing incident in his adolescence, and who finds himself in Palestine, about to become a settler in one of the new Hebrew communities. We are told the story of the foundation of the commune, its defence against Arab terrorists, and its rapid success, through much hard work, in making fertile the barren hills on which it is built. During this time Joseph begins to establish tenuous contact with terroristically-inclined Jews ; at first he disagrees with their attitude, but later, when his personal difficulties in the community lead him to adopt work that takes him into the cities, when he realises how the Jews of Palestine are being betrayed by the British Government and how the frontiers of that pre-war world are being closed against the refugees from racial terrorism, when he sees that Jews who try to land on what they regard as their own sacred soil are imprisoned and put aside to be deported, he begins to change his opinions. His decision to co-operate with the terrorists is precipitated by an act of violence which once again forms the keypoint of the book.

In the community there is a Jewish girl from Central Europe, Dina, with whom Joseph has been in love for some time, but who has developed a violent phobia against physical contact with men because of her experiences in the hands of the Nazis. For this reason, Joseph's love goes unsatisfied, and he finds a substitute in Ellen, another community girl, but continues to hanker after Dina. Then, one evening when he is away from the community, Dina is attacked as she is riding home to the settlement, and murdered in a particularly brutal way by Arabs from the neighbouring village.

This event impels Joseph to contact the terrorist organisation. He is introduced into its elaborate ritual and conspiratorial discipline, and his particular grievance is satisfied when the terrorists kill the headman of the Arabs who murdered Dina, fulfilling the barbaric Old Testament law of " a life for a life ".

Joseph tries to work for the organisation, but he is allowed to take part in only one of their expeditions, and then is reserved for propaganda work. He continues to live the double life of a community official and a subsidiary terrorist.

The book ends with Joseph assisting at the foundation of a new settlement. He lives over in his mind his own experiences as an early settler, and reflects on the difference of Jewish nationalism from that of other races :

"Nationalism ? Nonsense . . .—Joseph repeated to himself.— This earth means something different to us than Croatia means to the Croats or America to the Americans. They are married to their countries ; we are searching for a lost bride. We are homesick for a Canaan which was never truly ours. That is why we are always foremost in the race for Utopias and messianic revolutions, always chasing after a lost Paradise. Defeated and bruised, we turn back towards the point in space from which the hunt started. It is the return from delirium to normality and its limitations. A country is the shadow which a nation throws, and for two thousand years we were a nation without a shadow . . ."

In the hands of a novelist who could write with real understanding and dispassion, this plot might have been the skeleton of an excellent novel. With Koestler it becomes the framework of a pamphlet in fiction—a pamphlet extolling the use, in a cause supported by Koestler himself, of all the ruthless methods used in other countries by the Commissars.

There is no possibility of doubting Koestler's support of the terrorists. Their actions are not shown as part of a tragic struggle in which all sides are acting against the true interests of human solidarity, which is what an unbiassed judgment would make of the present nationalistic struggles in Palestine. On the contrary, the terrorists are quite obviously the heroes of the book. Everyone else—Arabs, British, the moderate and internationalist Jews—is described with contempt. But the terrorists are displayed always as men who are ready heroically to sacrifice even their internationalist principles, who are ready to commit any act, no matter how violent or soul-destroying, for the sake of the Jewish nation. To make trebly sure, Koestler goes so far as to dedicate his book to Vladimir Jabotinsky, the nationalist leader who introduced Jewish fascism into Palestine.

Since it is clear that the terrorists express Koestler's view on the Palestine question, it may be profitable to examine his latest development by a series of short quotations from their statements, which Koestler evidently supports with a certain conviction.

1. *From the diary of Joseph after the murder of the Arab headman :*

" In war we act on the principle that the blame is homogeneously distributed among the individuals who constitute the enemy nation and hence that it makes no difference which particular individual is killed. Civilised warfare is as promiscuous in the choice of its targets as an Arab blood-feud—which Europeans regard as a barbarity ; and in three-dimensional war even discrimination between ages and sexes disappears completely. The only difference is that the laws of the tribal blood-feud are more honest and explicit in treating the adversary as a homogeneous, collectively responsible unit.

" ' The Arabs ' have been waging intermittent tribal war against us for the last three years ; if we want to survive we have to retaliate according to their accepted rules. By throwing bombs into Arab markets the Bauman gang performs exactly the same inhuman military duty as the crew of a bomber plane ; the only difference is that the latter do it from the comparative safety of a few thousand feet in the air."

2. *A statement of Bauman, the terrorist leader :*

" We have to use violence and deception, to save others from violence and deception."

3. *A conversation at the end of an initiation ceremony where boys are admitted into the terrorist gang in an elaborate ritual in which they swear* " *not to rest until the nation is resurrected as a free and sovereign State within its historic boundaries, from Dan to Bersheba* " :

[194]

" Later, when Joseph took his leave from Bauman in the corridor Bauman asked him :

" ' What did you think of it ? '

" ' I thought,' said Joseph, ' that I did not envy you. I would rather obey than command.'

" ' Who would not ? ' said Bauman."

From these statements, one is led by an insidious logic into the sneaking admiration for the achievements of the Commissars which Joseph feels after his initiation into the terrorist organisation :

" It was curious, Joseph reflected as he continued his walk towards Zion Circus, now dark and deserted, it was strange indeed that political imaginativeness was nowadays only to be found among extremist movements of the tyrannical type. Nazis, Fascists and Communists seemed to hold the international monopoly of it. It was not due to their lack of responsibility, as the envious democracies pretended, for these movements remained equally imaginative in their methods after they had ascended to power. One would have expected that a democratic structure would leave ampler space for the display of originality than these rigidly disciplined bodies ; and yet the opposite seemed to be true. Apparently submission to discipline and boldness of vision were not as incompatible as was generally assumed. Those who denied the freedom of ideas were full of ideas and ingenuity ; while the defenders of free expression were dull and pedestrian with hardly an idea worth expressing."

This is the last stage in the development of a man who has once been deceived by totalitarian ideas, has rejected them, and then, having failed to recognise any better way, or to preserve any faith in human responsibility, has come full circle and returned by another path to all the doctrines of political expediency he once rejected.

Koestler's career is an illustration of the fact that scepticism alone will not lead us anywhere. To progress, we must have at least faith in man, and it should be the function of the intellectual to nurture a humanist faith that will stand on its own against all authority, whether political or intellectual, temporal or spiritual. Then only will men walk erect in the daylight, and not go as thieves in the night.

XI

Kafka and Rex Warner

In comparing the symbolism of Kafka and Rex Warner, and in estimating the influence of the elder on the younger writer, we have to bear in mind from the start the essential difference in nature between the symbolism used by the two novelists.

Kafka's symbolism is ambiguous and Protean—with all the clues at our disposal we are never sure what he is aiming to teach or portray, and his symbols can, within wide limits, be interpreted by every reader according to his predilections. The struggle he has shown of man against his environment, is real, on a physical or a spiritual plane, for everyone who is likely to read his books, and his very vagueness makes it easy for anyone to read his own problems, his own struggle, into the life of K. or Kafka's other central figures.

Warner's symbolism, on the other hand, is simple and direct, applicable within narrow limits, and aiming at the creation of a clear-cut allegory to illustrate certain defined facets of the human struggle.

The accepted interpretation of Kafka's writings, taken largely on the authority of Max Brod, is that they have a strictly religious significance, and are intended to portray the dualism of the universe which divides " the orders of Nature and of Grace ". This may indeed be the meaning which Kafka himself attributed to his allegories, the primary conscious meaning, but Kafka's work is so heavily loaded with subconscious tendencies that we should be unwisely hasty if we took a meaning that seems *primâ facie* obvious either to the author or to the reader. In order to gain some idea of the wide applicability of Kafka's writings, we should examine the circumstances that influenced him and gave him the peculiar feeling of isolation from any proximate continent of reality, which we find in all his works.

For, taken in their literal and most simple sense, Kafka's writings, and particularly his type-novel *The Castle*, represent the solitary man struggling to wrest from his environment some kind of reality and security. Some of the aspects from which we can view this simple statement of literal interpretation and which may assist us in assessing its value, are given in the following paragraphs.

Kafka was a consumptive, who spent much of his life in sanatoria, and whose ill-health continually inhibited his joining in the active life of the world around. People in such circumstances usually feel their difference from other men with great poignancy, and their work is frequently much influenced by it. I was recently sent some poems by a young consumptive, from which one gained a feeling of inescapable loneliness very similar to that one gets from K.'s failure to make any real contacts with the people around him during his life in the village.

Kafka was a Jew, and therefore came of a race with an ingrown feeling of isolation in a hostile world. I have not heard that he experienced any great degree of direct persecution, but even in Jews who have lived normally among their neighbours there will remain a memory of hostility and a feeling of difference based on the racial theories of Jewish orthodoxy. When a race has been isolated and persecuted intermittently for twenty centuries, it is unlikely that any of its members will feel completely at ease even in an apparently friendly environment.

In connection with Kafka's Jewish race we must also recollect the journey symbolism in his work—the journey to America, the setting of K.'s struggle against the Castle as the penultimate stage of a journey by a vagrant, the departure of the explorer in *The Penal Settlement*, etc. This symbolism can be paralleled by the continual presence of the journey in the historical traditions of the Jews, the great race of wanderers. The series is long—there are the Bedouin wanderings of Abraham and Isaac, the exodus from Egypt and the long desert journey to the Promised Land, the journeys into exile in Babylon, the dispersal after the Roman sack of Jerusalem, and, last of the series in Kafka's day, the breaking up of the ghettos in Europe and the dispersal of the Jews among the Gentiles as neighbours and fellow-citizens in a—comparatively—liberal world.

To the Jews also, we in the West owe the idea of the invisible and elusive God, to be compared with the elusive Castle which K. can never enter or make contact with, except by indirect means. Moses encountered God as a voice speaking from the cloud, but, as St Paul, the last of the great Jewish prophets, remarked, " No man hath seen the face of God ". This saying, with its undertone of defeat, represents the high point of the Hebrew effort to attain unity with God, which was carried on by the Jewish mystics in the Caballah, to which it is likely Kafka had access and in which we find the distinction between the orders of justice and of grace mentioned in the inaugural essay.

That Kafka had strong mystical leanings is obvious. We know that he was influenced by the unorthodox and destructive mystic Kierkegaard, and it is likely that his mysticism was another determinant of his frequent use of the journey symbol. The journey of the soul is a common mystical concept, appearing in ancient religions in the journey of Osiris, in the East in the journey of Tripitaka, in Christianity in the legend of Christ's journey into Egypt, and, among more recent religious writings, expressed crudely by Bunyan in *Pilgrim's Progress* and, more subtly, by St John of the Cross in *The Dark Night of the Soul*.

The last of the tentative indications I shall give is that Kafka lived most of his life in a subject territory of the old Hapsburg

Empire, whose bureaucracy was extensive and notoriously pompous. On a farcical plane the authoritarian structure of the empire was satirised unmercifully by Jaroslav Hasek in *The Good Soldier Schweik*, and we can see that the evasive, vast and dictatorial assemblage of authorities in *The Castle*, even if it were not meant to represent the bureaucracy of the empire, was at least very much influenced in its form by the fact that Kafka lived under such a régime and probably observed its working and methods with a certain hostile cynicism.

These are suggestions which may help in our study of Kafka. I do not contend that any or even all of them will give a full explanation of what Kafka had to say, but I think that between them they give us a good idea of the reason for his feeling of isolation from reality, of struggle against his environment, and also explain why he expressed these feelings in the form of the dialectical struggle of the wanderer against established authority.

Kafka's work represents, as, indeed, does every serious work of the imagination, an attempt to reach the ultimate reality of the natural world, to grapple with the unknown and, by its conquest, to reach freedom.

In human terms this is represented in the struggle of man against authority, against the domination of cosmic or earthly rulers, and it is this, admittedly limited, aspect of Kafka that appeals to me personally, as expressed in one of K.'s remarks to the villagers regarding their relationship with the Castle :

" Fear of the authorities is born in you here, and is further suggested to you all your lives in the most various ways and from every side, and you yourselves help to strengthen it as much as possible."

K. struggles continually against the authorities in order to gain access to the Castle, in other words to make himself one with authority, the father. That is why, after the last remark, he qualifies it with the words : " Still, I have no fundamental objection to that; if an authority is good why should it not be feared," because he himself hopes one day to enter into the Castle, to wield the authority against which he now struggles, and so, he thinks, to become free. While he tries to placate the authorities, he at the same time hates them, and when their representatives, the assistants, come into his power, he treats them with contempt and brutality. His hostility is also expressed in a manner which could be taken as illustrative of an important contention of modern psychology, when he appropriates to himself the mistress of Klamm, who for him represents authority, and thus repeats the classic symbol of defeating the father in the affections of the mother, as a substitute for taking his freedom in defiance of authority.

The final important characteristic of Kafka's work is his confirmed pessimism. K. does not attain the Castle, nor, even in the projected ending of the uncompleted novel, does he gain more than a qualified recognition from the Castle authorities. Interpreted according to our tastes, this can be taken to mean that for men there is no possible unification with God, no fullness of freedom, no fulfilment of the personality. The world of reality and the world of man run along parallel lines—the thought of their meeting is an illusion of mental perspective. It is further significant that, not only does K. not reach the Castle—he does not even know what the Castle really is. In the growing scepticism of this novel one is reminded of the reports of certain Western mystics who have gone along the ways of Eastern mysticism to *samadhi* and return with bleak disillusion to tell that they have found nothing at the end of their spiritual journey.

To return to the comparison of Kafka and Rex Warner. The imputing of influences is a hazardous duty for the critic, and I would say, first of all, that the direct influence of Kafka on Rex Warner seems to me more tenuous than is generally supposed. There seems to have been some direct influence—we find certain concepts in common—but I do not think in the motivation of Warner's books we can fairly attribute any more influence to Kafka than to, say, *Gulliver's Travels*.

What, therefore, seems more profitable is to consider them as parallels rather than to consider Warner as derivative from Kafka. To an extent they use a similar set-up and similar symbols. The conflict between man and his environment is common to both of them, and in one at least of Warner's books the journey symbolism is retained. Warner isolates one of the possible lines of meaning which we get from the consideration of Kafka's books, and develops it along a defined and narrow path. By this I do not mean that Warner took the idea from Kafka. It would be sufficient to suppose that the two writers, living in the same period of history, will have similar problems, and that their solution will also partake of a certain similarity.

With Warner there is relatively little chance of doubt as to his intentions, and the undertones of interpretation we can read into his work are limited, almost, one feels, deliberately limited by the conscious manipulation of technique to reach disciplined ends in which the conscious intent of the writer will be paramount. There is no transcendentalism in Warner's work, no authentic mysticism, in spite of some of his Marxist critics. All his values take their validity from their application to human relationships. The drama is played entirely on an earthly plane, and there is no chance that any of the characters are gods in disguise.

At the outset we find a similarity between Warner and Kafka, in that both use the village or the country as the base from which the central character sets out to struggle against the opposite, authoritarian influence represented by the Castle, the city or the aerodrome. At the same time all the protagonists imagine that what they wish to attain can be reached through the antagonistic influence. K. wishes to enter the Castle, the brothers see the city as a way to the Wild Goose, Roy sees the aerodrome as the means to gain power, discipline and, through these, freedom. The Wild Goose is freedom, and Roy in entering the aerodrome hopes to gain freedom from the old ties of his family and Bess, and also the wider freedom which the Air Vice-Marshal promises his followers they will attain through the conquest of power.

In Warner the village and the city-aerodrome can be taken as representative of two opposing ways of life. The village is the life of natural man, the city-aerodrome is the mechanised and regimented life of the modern total state, fundamentally unnatural and grounded on abstractions.

Both the brothers and Roy hope to gain their objective of an extension of life by exchanging the village for its antithesis. Unlike K., who never makes contact with the Castle, the brothers reach the city, Roy enters the very heart of the aerodrome, the Air Vice-Marshal's office. Here, in all cases, disillusionment awaits them ; city and aerodrome represent, as they realise, the death rather than the attainment of their desires. The Wild Goose, which is the god of the city, is a stuffed one—in the city, moreover, David loses his sex and Rudolph his sight. The Air Vice-Marshal talks of freedom, but the power by which he proposes to attain it turns mercilessly upon the people with whom he has had the most human relationships—a son and two of his late mistresses are the victims of his ruthless struggle to establish his domination. Roy realises that, with all its disorder, the life of the village is more desirable than that of the aerodrome :

" Yet I began to see that this life, in spite of its drunkenness and its inefficiency, was wider and deeper than the activity in which we were constricted by the iron compulsion of the Air Vice-Marshal's ambition. It was a life whose every vagueness concealed a wealth of opportunity, whose uncertainty called for adventure, whose aspects were innumerable and varied as the changes of light and colour throughout the year."

In both *The Wild Goose Chase* and *The Aerodrome* the heroes realise that, not only will the city or the aerodrome fail to bring them the freedom they desire, but that these influences are destroying, in the village, the very roots of humanity from which their freedom must grow.

They commence the struggle against authority. In *The Wild Goose Chase* George becomes the leader of a revolutionary army, Rudolph a revolutionary poet. In *The Aerodrome*, from which are purged the crudities of symbolism one finds in the former book, the Flight Lieutenant preaches a sermon in which he tells the villagers that the aerodrome has only done them harm, while Roy accepts a technical breach of the rules of the aerodrome, for which he is not directly responsible, as a possible means of escaping to a recommencement of his life with Bess.

In the struggle with authority, Warner repeatedly uses symbolism recognised by modern psychology as pertaining to such a conflict. In the final showdown in *The Aerodrome*, Roy discovers that the Air Vice-Marshal is both his and the Flight Lieutenant's father, so that the two men struggling against authority are also sons struggling against the father. The sexual competition with the father also appears in a similar manner to that already noted in Kafka. In *The Wild Goose Chase*, George, after he has chased away the king, lives for a time by the underground lake with Marqueta, who was formerly the king's mistress. In *The Aerodrome*, both the Flight Lieutenant and Roy become lovers of Eustachia, who was formerly the mistress of the Air Vice-Marshal.

In the struggle with authority the heroes win. The city is captured, and the king driven away. The Air Vice-Marshal is killed on the eve of attaining his great ambition, when his plane crashes owing to the sabotage of the Flight Lieutenant. But the heroes realise that the mere overthrow of tyranny is not the attainment of their real desires. As George stands at the celebration of the capture of the city, the dome of the Anserium breaks apart and the Wild Geese fly overhead in a splendid procession. Roy realises that the death of the Air Vice-Marshal and his own sub-sequent liberation mean only the beginning of the development of his life and his relationship with Bess. When dominion is ended, freedom has yet to be made positive.

The Aerodrome shows a significant advance in Warner's sense of social reality, because, while in *The Wild Goose Chase* George actually assumes power in the city, Roy makes no attempt to set himself in the place of the dead Air Vice-Marshal, but instead merely uses his liberation to return to the life he really desires. In other words, this is a recognition of the social truth that not the assumption but the destruction of authority—whether in the world or in the mind—is the beginning of freedom. A symbolic anticipa-tion of this conclusion is, indeed, contained in *The Wild Goose Chase*, when Marqueta, the king's former mistress, whom George has appropriated, withdraws herself from him by committing suicide, and leaves him to return to Joan, who represents the human values symbolised by the village.

The main difference between Kafka and Warner would, if this analysis is reasonable, be that, while both are concerned with man's struggle with authority, Kafka works along a broad way which embraces the cosmic as well as the human relationship and, in this progress whose contact with shadowy powers admits of no tangible result, comes to a pessimistic conclusion in which man attains nothing he struggles for. Kafka, for all his religious interests and mystic affiliations, is in the end sceptic and defeatist. Warner, on the other hand, proceeding on the narrow and defined way of human relationships, reaches the optimistic conclusion that it is possible for man to attain freedom and to fulfil himself.

" It might be said that we anticipated, both of us, that now at last the circle of sin might be broken, that, with what we knew, we might live to avoid murder and deception."

Restricting himself to the human world, Warner has the faith which Kafka did not reach.

[205]

It is for this reason that I feel one at least of Warner's novels, *The Aerodrome*, to be ultimately more satisfying than any of Kafka's. Kafka's work, with its cosmic implications, is unfinished in more than one way, because Kafka never attained a whole view of the vast world of relationships he strove to embrace. Warner attains a completeness and validity of his own precisely because his world of relationships is limited to that of humanity and its proximate, physical environment.

XII

The English Hymn

I

In the nineteenth century, the age of the industrial revolution, of the birth of State education and the rise of middle-class democracy, the hymn had its heyday and reflected as faithfully as any other form of writing the nature of the society that produced it. In the hymn we find the needs and ambitions, the hopes and despairs of both the rich and the poor reflected. Their loneliness, their yearning sexual hunger, their desire for protection, for power, for an unflawed happiness—all are represented with varying felicity by the many hymn-writers who flourished from the Methodist Revival to the religious decline that marked the end of the nineteenth century.

To every social class and to every kind of man the hymns made their appeal. There are the magnificent literary achievements of Charles Wesley and Bishop Heber, and the doggerel rhymes with music-hall tunes by which the Salvation Army made its appeal to the sentimentality of the uneducated and unintellectual masses. There are the hymns which glorify the existing order and make the rich feel secure in their wealth, and those which appeal to the poor by promising a " happy land, far, far away " where in Zion the saints will feast in the glory of God and human injustice will be no more. There are hymns of a seafaring nation, hymns of an imperialism that spreads from " Greenland's icy mountains to India's coral strands ", and the martial hymns of a century of predatory war when even religion marched in uniform and counted its gains like an invading conqueror. And, behind all these, there were the quiet personal hymns, the hymns of a debased mysticism, where Christ spoke to the sinner, not through the pomp of liturgy, not in the garments of a conqueror, but intimately, as a still, small voice within the spirit, giving not the future and apparently physical kingdom of heaven where

> . . . they who with their Leader
> Have conquer'd in the fight,
> For ever and for ever
> Are clad in robes of white,

but the peace of heaven within the tranquil and fulfilled spirit.

What we never find among the hymns of the churches and sects are any that proclaim the march to the earthly millennium for which earlier Christians, the Anabaptists, the Diggers, the Fifth Monarchy Men, strove so bitterly. While in the seventeenth century religious upheavals were intimately connected with movements of social insurrection, in the nineteenth century the division between the two became, except for a few instances, complete. The revolutionary vision of the Kingdom of God on earth, the one valuable and dynamic concept which Christianity gave to the world, was replaced by a heavenly and immaterial kingdom, a Zion of elusive comforts that was to be the common man's substitute for the classless society on earth. The poor, patient here, would become saints in glory when they had crossed the Jordan of death. Where revolutionary ideas appeared, they had been transformed to suit their innocuous religious substitute. Bishop Heber, describing the Son of God going forth to a spiritual (or theological?) war, protrays him as bearing a " blood-red banner ", borrowed from the symbolical stock-in-trade of the social revolutionary. But Bishop Heber would have been the last to find a social revolutionary con-

tent in Christ's teaching. That was left to an unpopular set of
eccentrics, like Kingsley, whose ideas had almost no effect on the
hymn-writing of the century.

Nevertheless, hymn-singing became so universal a social custom
that it was bound to reflect ideas and impulses which may not
consciously have been in the minds of the writers. Religious
people sang hymns not only in their churches, but often at home
around the piano in the parlour and even as they went about their
work. People who were not particularly religious would be
attracted by the catchiness of a hymn-tune or the emotionally
moving nature of its content. Even in our own day we have had
the spectacle of great crowds at football Cup Finals—hardly the
kind of assemblies to be regarded as religious in a conventional
manner—singing with great feeling the hymn which perhaps more
than any other reflects the loneliness and need for comfort of the
ordinary man—Lyte's " Abide with me ".

> Abide with me ; fast falls the eventide ;
> The darkness gathers ; Lord, with me abide !
> When other helpers fail, and comforts flee,
> Help of the helpless, O abide with me.
>
> Swift to its close ebbs out life's little day ;
> Earth's joys grow dim, its glories pass away ;
> Change and decay in all around I see ;
> O Thou who changest not, abide with me.

Would it be possible to appeal more closely to the feeling of
insecurity which haunts the common man in a world of unemploy-
ment and periodic wars ?

When hymns passed from the religious to the irreligious, it was
natural that their content should tend to change, and as the driving
urge of the evangelical movements diminished, the hymns they had
made popular assumed secular forms, became absorbed, by means

of parody, into vulgar popular song. As the evangelical preachers took popular tunes and set hymns to them, so the irreligious took catchy hymn tunes and sang their own humorous verses. Many of the soldiers' songs of the 1914–18 war were set to hymn-tunes— a well-known example is " When this —— war is over " to the tune of " What a friend we have in Jesus ".

Eventually the uses of hymns were perceived by the demagogic leaders of political parties and of pseudo-revolutionary movements. They began to write " revolutionary " songs which were similar in form and often in content to the popular hymns of the day. The pre-occupation with the blood of Christ, which appeared in so many of the revivalist hymns, was paralleled almost exactly in Connolly's " The Red Flag ", where he talks of the flag having been dyed in the blood of the martyred socialist dead. In America many hymn-tunes were taken over whole by the radicals, and from the adoptions arose such familiar songs as " Pie in the Sky " and " Alleluia, I'm a Bum ". The most interesting example in this *genre* is the Horst Wessel song of the Nazis, which is said originally to have been composed as a Salvation Army hymn, to have been taken over by the Communists, and finally to have appeared as the most celebrated of Nazi songs.

2

The evolution of a hymn that would appeal to the ordinary man by the exploitation of the emotions and circumstances of his daily life began with Charles Wesley. During the Middle Ages the Roman Church had its hymns, but they were usually in Latin and were liturgical songs of praise or devotion which can have made little appeal except to the initiated. During the Reformation, hymns were almost completely replaced by metrical versions of the Psalms, most of which were dull in sentiment and pompous in expression. Hymn-singing was reintroduced among the dissenters early in the eighteenth century, mostly through the efforts of Issac

Watts, a poet of talent who left a number of celebrated hymns, including " O God, our help in ages past ". But the hymns of Watts, like those of the mediæval monks, were songs of praise for the converted rather than appeals to the common man, the sinner in the street, the factory and the gin shop. This situation was favoured by the prevalent Calvinist belief in Election, or the pre-destined choice of those who will be saved, which then influenced not merely the dissenters but also many of the Anglican clergy, and which formed an influence antagonistic to missionary effort. The poor man and the sinner, according to this doctrine, were so by the will of God, and could be no other. The effort to save them was doomed to failure and therefore need not be made.

Calvinism was the doctrine of the middle class, the lawyers, the merchants and the new landowners who had risen in the Reforma-tion and consolidated their power during the Civil War and the Glorious Revolution of 1688. It gave them a comfortable justifica-tion of their wealth and social position, and kept the poor in their place on the other side of the barrier that on Judgment Day would eternally divide the sheep from the goats.

But the lower classes were in a state of discontent against the social and theological domination of the *bourgeoisie*. Already in the Civil War the movement had reached formidable proportions by the rise of the Levellers, the Diggers and the Fifth Monarchy Men, all of whom aimed at some degree of revolutionary social change. Now the economic changes that began the Industrial Revolution were throwing up the lower middle class, the shopkeepers, factory owners and their like, as an articulate class whose power was growing steadily. Parallel with the economic changes and the new shift in the class basis came a change in the religious mood of the people. They were no longer content with a theology that divided the saved from the damned, as the economic system had divided the rich from the poor. They remembered that Christ came to save sinners, and demanded a religion that would enable sinners to rise

to salvation, as the new economy enabled many of the poor to rise
to comparative material wealth.

The men who came forward to smash the tyranny of Calvinism
were John and Charles Wesley. They attacked violently the
doctrine of Predestination, and declared that the kingdom of
heaven was open to all, provided only they repented of their sins,
and received God into their hearts. In accordance with their
beliefs, they left the churches, where they could preach only to the
converted, and went out into the market-places and the streets in
order to call the unsaved to repentance. In the environs of London,
among the rough tin miners of Cornwall, the colliers of Staffordshire
and the industrial workers of Manchester and Birmingham, they
and their disciples held great open-air meetings at which they
attempted to arouse enthusiastic acceptance of religious teachings.
Sometimes they were attacked by bands of hooligans and driven
away or even injured in the scuffles. At other times they were
persecuted by the local magistrates or other representatives of the
ruling class. But it is significant that they were always regarded
with favour by the more astute central authorities at Westminster.
This shows a surprising sense of reality among the ministers of the
Hanoverians, for there is no doubt that the Methodists, by the
revolutionary tone of their theology, managed to create a popular
movement which diverted discontent away from the political
channels and enabled the social changes to take place without the
danger of a general popular revolution which would have made it
difficult for the ruling class to adjust itself to the new circumstances.
Wesley, of course, was as Tory in his politics as he was libertarian
in his theology.

In spite, however, of local hostility among the populace or the
magistrates, the evangelistic pilgrimages of the Wesleys were frequently greeted with enthusiasm and resulted in a nation-wide
movement which later spread to America, where it achieved equal
success. The achievements of the preachers were due largely to

the personal courage and the intimate eloquence with which they made their testimony to their great audiences. But they were also helped by the introduction into the meetings of mass singing and particularly of the hymns of Charles Wesley.

Even to-day the most widely sung hymns are those of Wesley, and this long period of popularity demonstrates the success of the appeal that Wesley made to the emotions of men. His hymns were not liturgical in any strict sense; they were not primarily songs of praise. More than anything else they were expressions of the most intimate psychological needs of the people who sang them. Like no other hymn writer before or since, Wesley entered into the hearts of the men and women to whom his appeal was made, and voiced his sentiments as they would have done, had they his consummate poetic technique.

He understood the loneliness that afflicts every man, particularly the social outcast. He preached an evangel that proclaimed the universality of God's love, and in this he identified himself with the solitary and the guilty.

> Outcasts of men, to you I call,
> Harlots, and publicans, and thieves!
> He spreads His arms to embrace you all;
> Sinners alone His grace receives:
> No need of Him the righteous have.
> He came the lost to seek and save.

> Come, all ye Magdalens in lust,
> Ye ruffians fell in murders old;
> Repent, and live; despair and trust;
> Jesus for you to death was sold;
> Though hell protest, and earth repine,
> He died for crimes like yours and mine.

Charles Wesley, in spite of the uneasy protests of his brother

John, left no side of the emotional nature of man untouched by his appeals. He saw the love of God as universal and therefore did not fear to express it in erotic imagery, such as

> Jesu, Lover of my soul,
> Let me to Thy bosom fly.

One of his most beautiful hymns is in fact an adaptation of an erotic song to Venus from one of Dryden's plays. The original runs :

> Fairest Isle, all isles excelling,
> Seat of pleasures and of loves,
> Venus here will choose her dwelling,
> And forsake her Cyprian groves.

Wesley's lines give us in this instance a means of judging the hymn-writer as a poet, for they are more felicitous and musical than the verse that prompted them.

> Love divine, all loves excelling,
> Joy of heaven, to earth come down ;
> Fix in us thy humble dwelling,
> All Thy faithful mercies crown.

Many of Wesley's hymns, such as " Soldiers of Christ, arise ", translate into religious imagery the martial sentiments that were endemic in a century of comparatively distant wars. By imagining themselves soldiers even in a spiritual sense, the stay-at-home middle classes were able to displace a good deal of the half-conscious guilt they must have felt at the idea of others fighting to defend their interests.

But there was also a more direct sado-masochistic strain in Wesley's hymns. The doctrine of the atonement by the blood of the god is of course an ancient one, going back before Christ into the cult of Mithras and the even older fertility rites. And at all times of evangelistic revival, when the emotions of the people have been roused into hysterical fervour, there is always an atavistic return to this primal religious concept. Even political parties have their cults of blood, which are derived from the same emotional need. The references to bloodshed in Wesley's hymns are numerous :

> (1) His blood procured our life and peace
> And quench'd the wrath of hostile Heaven.

> (2) For what you have done
> His blood must atone.

> (3) His blood atoned for all our race
> And sprinkles now the throne of grace.

> (4) Sprinkled with the blood we lie
> And bless its cleansing power.

The list could be extended by many further instances.

Behind all these dark emotions there looms the great shadow of guilt. Wesley realised that only by admitting it, by giving way to it, could men rid themselves of the sense of guilt, and in some of the lesser known hymns he freely identifies himself with sin.

> Sin, and shame, and guilt, and pain,
> And hell and I are one.

But it would be unjust to emphasise too much Wesley's concern with these darker emotions of the masses. He also gave them hymns which provided an exuberant release of joy and sheer good spirits in such boisterous hymns of praise as " Blow ye the trumpets, blow ", or " Soldiers of Christ, arise ".

Nor should we neglect the literary interest of many of Wesley's hymns. Much that he wrote was mechanical and insignificant, as was perhaps inevitable in a man whose great industry produced no less than 7,300 hymns during his active life. Nevertheless, he did much towards breaking down the poetic conventions his period had inherited from the Augustan age, and for his experimental

technique and imagery he must be regarded as a precursor of the
Romantic movement.   Nor were his greatest hymns without a
considerable poetic merit.   " Lo !   He comes with clouds descend-
ing ", for instance, contains two of the most memorable verses in
English poetry :

> Every eye shall now behold Him,
>   Robed in dreadful majesty ;
> Those who set at nought and sold Him,
>   Pierc'd and nail'd Him to the Tree,
>   Deeply wailing,
>   Shall the true Messiah see.
>
> Those dear tokens of His passion
>   Still His dazzling Body bears,
> Cause of endless exultation
>   To His ransom'd worshippers :
>   With what rapture
>   Gaze we on those glorious scars !

3

English hymn writing after Wesley developed on the lines he
had already indicated, and almost all the devices which he had used
for reaching the emotions of men were repeated by his successors.
On the other hand, little new was discovered that had not already
been used by his resourceful talent.

Almost immediately, hymn-writing tended to split into two
movements—one liturgical and more or less literary ; the other
evangelistic and emotional, concerned with the kind of song which
would arouse the feelings of great masses of people assembled in
revival meetings.

The hymns that survived from Wesley's immediate following
are mostly the literary hymns of devotion and praise.   The Olney
hymns of Newton and Cowper, such as " Hark, my soul, it is the

Lord ", " God moves in a mysterious way " and " How sweet the name of Jesus sounds ", appealed intimately to the already devout, and many of the hymns which appeared at this time carried a suggestion of mysticism. Men like Doddridge and Toplady, however, wrote a type of hymn that had a wider appeal. Toplady, indeed, touched more deeply than even Wesley on the most intimate need of the lonely human being, with the " womb " symbolism of his

> Rock of ages, cleft for me,
> Let me hide myself in Thee ;
> Let the Water and the Blood,
> From thy riven side which flow'd,
> Be of sin the double cure,
> Cleanse me from its guilt and power.

That, however, the ranting type of popular hymn had already appeared was evident by John Wesley's concern with the decline of hymn-writing into doggerel. He was particularly shocked by what he regarded as the coarseness of the Moravian hymns. These, of which some are extant, show a remarkably vivid strain of amatory and sadistic symbolism. They were particularly concerned with the anatomical details of the Crucifixion, such as the hole in Christ's side, which seems always to have a strongly sexual significance for a certain type of Christian (as in Toplady's hymn). One of the most interesting of these eccentric Moravian hymns runs thus :

> Ye Cross's air-birds, swell the notes
>   Of the sweet Side-hole Song,
> That Fountain's Juice will clear your throats,
>   And help to hold it long.
> Each Day and Year will higher raise
> The Side-hole's glory, love and praise :
> Hallelujah ! Hallelujah !
> To the Side *Gloria* !

But it was in America, about 1800, that a real movement of popular hymnody began. In that year commenced the Camp Meeting movement, started in Kentucky by the Presbyterians, but soon taken over by the Methodists, whose more emotional technique of preaching and singing made the greater appeal to the unlettered people of those distant farming districts. The Camp Meetings were gatherings at some central meeting-point of people from a very large rural area. They encamped in tents and covered wagons formed into a hollow square, with a rude pulpit and long seats arranged in the centre. A number of evangelists would exhort the people to repentance and hymns would be sung by the great concourse. At first these were Methodist hymns.

" But with the tumultuous enthusiasm that soon developed, the old hymns were felt to be too sober to express the overwrought feelings of the preacher and the throng. Spontaneous songs became a marked characteristic of the Camp Meetings. Rough and irregular couplets or stanzas were concocted out of Scripture phrases and every-day speech, with liberal interspersing of Hallelujahs and refrains. Such ejaculatory hymns were frequently started by an auditor during the preaching and taken up by the throng, until the meeting dissolved into a singing ecstasy, culminating in a general hand-shaking. Sometimes they were given forth by a preacher, who had a sense of rhythm, under the excitement of his preaching and the agitation of his audience. Hymns were also composed more deliberately out of meeting, and taught to the people or lined out from the pulpit." [1]

Most of the original Camp Meeting hymns have been lost. But in later years a more literary form, based on the popular ballad styles, went by this name, and was used extensively in revival meetings during the ensuing decades. Not only the literary forms, but also the actual tunes of popular songs were used. As one of the hymns expressed it :

[1] Benson, *The English Hymn.*

> Enlisted in the cause of sin,
>> Why should a good be evil ?
> Music, alas ! too long has been
>> Press'd to obey the devil.

The Camp Meeting hymn itself had little influence on hymn-singing in England. But it was important for three reasons. First, it was the precursor of the " Negro Spiritual " and thence of a great part of the rich tradition of Negro song. This, of course, lies beyond the limits of the present article. Secondly, it prepared the ground for the later and much more widespread Gospel Hymn, which had great popularity on both sides of the Atlantic. To this we shall return. Thirdly, it had interesting offshoots among the many American sects which flourished at the time. Of these the most interesting, perhaps, were the Adventists and the Mormons. The hymns of the Adventists, who looked for the second coming of Christ in 1843, were fully in the rude Camp Meeting tradition. Their favourite song began :

> You will see your Lord a-coming
>> To the old church yards
> With a band of music
>> Sounding it through the air.

The Mormons, on the other hand, during their long pilgrimage across the deserted West and the brief years of their holy city on the Great Salt Lake, cultivated a surprisingly high literary standard. Some of their best hymns were among the most accomplished in the language.

> In thy mountain retreat, God will strengthen thy feet ;
>> On the necks of thy foes thou shalt tread ;
> And their silver and gold, as the Prophet foretold,
>> Shall be brought to adorn thy fair head.
> O Zion ! dear Zion ! home of the free,
>> Soon thy towers shall shine with a splendour divine,
> And eternal thy glory shall be.

4

Meanwhile, in England there had taken place a substantial change in the status of the hymn. Orthodox Churchmen like Heber, Milman and Montgomery had realised the value of hymn-singing as an aid to church ritual. They attempted to set a higher literary standard, both by writing hymns themselves and by preparing books of hymns for use in churches. As a result of their efforts, hymn-writing became respectable, the Church adopted hymns as a recognised part of its liturgy, and a whole series of liturgical writers emerged which persisted to the end of the nineteenth century.

Of these, Bishop Heber was undoubtedly the most able. He was an accomplished poet, who derived from the Romantic movement, among which he had a number of personal contacts. His poems were even occasionally tinged with a suggestion of the paganism that finds a place in that movement, as when he described Christ as " Brightest and best of the sons of the morning "—a phrase which in another setting might well have been used to describe Apollo. His best hymns were equal to those of Wesley in their felicity of appeal.

Holy ! Holy ! Holy ! all the saints adore Thee,
    Casting down their golden crowns around the glassy sea ;
Cherubim and Seraphim falling down before Thee,
    Which wert, and art, and evermore shalt be.

Yet his appeal was limited and seemed to avoid deliberately that universal call to the human emotions which Wesley strove to achieve. This limitation was accepted by the liturgical writers who followed him, and for this reason the hymns of men like Keble and Faber became singularly bookish and emasculate.

Heber was one of the earliest of the great missionaries of the nineteenth century who acted as emissaries of the British Empire, the forerunners of trade gin and syphilis, the rifle and the whip.

In his most famous hymn he puts the most fatuous and yet most frequently repeated argument of the self-justifying Imperialist, the theme of the White Man's Burden :

> From many an ancient river,
>   From many a palmy plain,
> They call us to deliver
>   Their land from error's chain. . . .
>
> Can we whose souls are lighted
>   With wisdom from on high,
> Can we, to men benighted,
>   The lamp of life deny ?

On the bloody pavements of Amritsar, Bishop Heber's work came to fruition !

But the ruling-class view of the universe was most clearly defined by Mrs Alexander in 1848, when she attempted to reassure a world shaken by revolution with her immortal statement on the divinely-appointed class structure of society :

> The rich man in his castle,
>   The poor man at his gate,
> God made them high and lowly,
>   And order'd their estate.

By the end of the century an even more blatant expression of the nationalist, imperialist and aristocratic nature of the Church's outlook was made in such hymns as that of Frederick William Newman for St George's Day.

> Blazon'd on our country's banner,
>   England bears the true knight's sign.
> Lord, our fatherland empower,
>   That, endued with strength divine,
> She may evermore with courage
>   Bear the standard that is Thine.

. . .

Jesus, Lord, Thou mighty Victor,
Thy all-glorious name we praise ;
THOU ART WITH US, GOD ALMIGHTY . . .

5

The tendencies within the Established Church only reflected those in society outside. As the ruling class used the State Church to express their own domination in society, so the lower orders used unorthodox religion as a means to express discontent with their present lives and a desire to achieve something better. It is significant that the great revivals of the latter half of the nineteenth century arose and flourished at the same time as the movement of social discontent which was manifested in the First International. It is further significant that these revivals, like that of the Wesleys, had a reactionary social attitude and used a pretence of revolutionary theology to draw the workers away from dreams of the social revolution to chiliastic visions of the immaterial heaven after death.

The characteristic hymn of the revivals was the Gospel Hymn. This was in a sense the descendant of the old Camp Meeting hymn, in that it was based on popular tunes, was set in a form similar to the ballad or music-hall song, and was well adapted to emotional singing by large audiences in crowded halls or great open-air meetings. The evolution of these hymns began in the late 1840's, among the evangelists associated with the newly formed Y.M.C.A. The Gospel Hymn was first used extensively in the Praise Services organised by Eben Tourjée in Boston in 1851. In the following twenty years a great number of Gospel Hymns were published, under the names of composers like William Bradbury, Asa Hull, Robert Lowry and William Fischer. But the evangelists who made the Gospel Hymn really popular in both England and America were Dwight Moody and Ira D. Sankey, who brought the evangelical movement to a culmination in the 1870's with the great success of their revival campaigns on both sides of the Atlantic.

The Gospel Hymn, in spite of its great popularity and of the way in which it remained for many years a familiar social phenomenon, was in almost every respect a decline on the types of hymn which preceded it. Unlike the songs of the first Methodist revival, and particularly those of the Wesleys, it made no pretence of literary worth, subtlety of emotional appeal or profundity of thought. Its style was crude, its thought banal and superficial, and its emotional appeal was made on the most elementary level. On the other hand, it lacked the compensating spontaneity of the Camp Meeting Hymn or the Negro song. It was manufactured by professional hacks whose level of performance was no higher than that of the writers of penny novelettes. Its sole virtue was usually the catchiness of the tune, and without this rub-a-dub music the Gospel Hymn would certainly not have achieved any great popularity. It is significant that, when the emotional revival years were past, it lived only in parodies whose verses were usually superior to the original. Like their political descendants of to-day, the evangelists of the Gospel Hymn period gave the workers too little credit for intelligence and set their appeals at so low a mental level that their success was bound to be superficial and transitory.

A mass of sentimental and almost meaningless hymns, characterised by an unpleasantly cloying amatory attitude towards Christ, has to be sifted to find anything of great interest. Of two types, however, there remains a certain nucleus sufficiently significant to show the emotional driving forces of the movement. First, there are the hymns where the sentimental attitude towards Christ becomes definite in the sadistic concern with the atoning blood and the anatomical details of the Passion. One of the most expressive of this class is " There is a fountain " :

[223]

> There is a fountain filled with blood,
>> Drawn from Immanuel's veins,
> And sinners plunged beneath that flood
>> Lose all their guilty stains !

Chorus. Hallelujah to the Lamb
>> Who died on Mount Calvary !
>> Hallelujah ! Hallelujah ! Hallelujah ! Amen !

(Note the refrain which was customary in the Gospel Hymns and which derives from the Camp Meeting days.)

Other and more famous hymns of this type are " I'm depending on the Blood " and " Are you washed in the Blood of the Lamb ? "

The concern with Christ's wounded side, which we have already noticed in the Moravian hymns, appears again.

> Oh, now I see the cleansing wave !
>> The fountain deep and wide ;
> Jesus, my Lord, mighty to save,
>> Points to His wounded side.

Chorus. The cleansing stream I see, I see !
>> I plunge, and oh, it cleanseth me !
>> Oh, praise the Lord ! it cleanseth me ;
>> It cleanseth me, yes, cleanseth me.

An even more macabre note is reached in another hymn :

> Dost thou know at thy bolted heart's door to-night
>> The Saviour in meekness doth stand,
> And longs for admission ? pray listen now
>> To the knock of the nail-pierc'd hand.
>> Heed the knock of the nail-pierc'd hand,
>> Heed the knock of the nail-pierc'd hand ;
>> Swing the door open wide,
>> Bid Him enter and abide,
>> Heed the knock of the nail-pierc'd hand.

In such hymns as these we get some idea of the strength of the feeling of guilt from which the people who sang them sought release.

Secondly, there are the hymns concerned with a better world. They are numerous. On the whole, they are the most virile of the Gospel Hymns and have a vivid strain of Biblical imagery. They show how strong was the force of social discontent which stirred in this movement. But the better world is never here and now. It is always in " The Sweet By-and-By ", where

> There's a land that is fairer than day,
>   And by faith we shall see it afar ;
> For the Father waits over the way,
>   To prepare us a dwelling-place there.

In this " Beulah Land " the poor and the unhappy find wealth and peace at last.

> I've reached the land of corn and wine,
> And all its riches freely mine ;
> Here shines undimm'd one blissful day,
> For all my night has passed away !

The faithful expressed with naïve certainty their intention of reaching this heavenly land of compensation for earthly miseries. " We're marching upward to Zion " they shouted with enthusiasm, and sang :

> When the trumpet of the Lord shall sound, and time shall be no more,
>   And the morning breaks, eternal, bright and fair ;
> When the sav'd of earth shall gather over on the other shore,
>   And the roll is call'd up yonder, I'll be there.

Heaven is always beyond the river of death. There is no earthly paradise, and nowhere do we find the hymn-writers telling us to fight and march for a Kingdom of God on earth. All the advice that can be offered for this life is

Work, for the night is coming,
  Work thro' the morning hours ;
Work while the dew is sparkling ;
  Work 'mid springing flowers ;

Work while the day grows brighter
  Under the glowing sun ;
Work, for the night is coming
  When man's work is done.

It is significant that the Gospel Hymn, for all its popularity, represents the last phase of the hymn as an important element in the life of the people or as a living literary form, just as the Revival that made it formed the last great upsurge of public religion in the lives of the people. Never was any religious movement shown to be more socially blind, and therefore more morally bankrupt. The sound of " Shall we gather at the river ? ", played thinly by a tiny Salvation Army band in an unheeded corner of a busy street, seems particularly ridiculous and incongruous in a twentieth-century city. Yet one could hardly find a better symbol for a religion that has deliberately and consistently betrayed and negated the belief in social responsibilities and the dynamic of revolutionary thought which its own founders brought into the western world.

XIII

Henry Bates on the Amazons

When Henry Bates went to the Amazons in 1848—the year of Revolutions—there were no steamers, and that terrifying sea of a river was traversed only by canoes and *cubertas*, the minute sailing craft of the country. All along the thousands of magnificent miles of water there were barely a dozen minute cities and towns, a few score hamlets of Indians and mameluco half-castes, and a few hundred isolated plantations or huts lying along sheltered creeks, or on little coves beside the main river or its almost equally great tributaries. Only the banks were inhabited. The forests and campos of the interior were left to the monkeys, and on the higher waters of some tributaries travelling was dangerous because of the wandering hordes of food-gathering Indians who had been made hostile by the unprincipled deeds of Brazilian traders. Between the rare habitations, the tangled and majestic forests stretched in lofty monotony, often for hundreds of miles unbroken, edged with graceful palms and corded with woody lianas and the hanging air roots of brilliant epiphytes. Their inhabitants were howling monkeys and jaguars, bright-winged toucans and barbets, beautiful coral snakes and heraldically fantastic ant-eaters. In the turgid waters the alligators were so numerous that their hides clanked together like armour when they crowded into the bays at the frightening approach of the first god-alligator of a steamer. On to the widespread sandbanks at low water the big river turtles scrambled in millions to lay their eggs in deep pits dug with their flippers. And every reach of the river had its own special insect pest, to remind men of the impartiality of nature's exuberance.

Man lived in these great forests as an insignificant being, far less numerous and hardly more important than humming birds or the giant toads as big as cats. Everything dwarfed him. The forest trees towered hundreds of feet over his head. The river was so wide that sometimes its farther bank was invisible on a clear day ; at best little more than a black line could be seen to represent the lofty forests on the distant horizon. On its waters raged storms as fierce as those of the sea, and the navigator of the great reaches needed a skill of his own to avoid disaster on those strong and often tumultuous waves. The throb of the tides from the far Atlantic reached many hundreds of miles inland at the dry season in the flat lands of the river's lower course. But in the upper parts the level of the water rose thirty feet at each wet season, covering the great sandbanks and islands, and flooding into the jungle until the forest roads became canals up which the people travelled for many miles in their canoes or even larger boats. The whole was a great domain of wild nature in which men had only the scantiest bridge-heads from which to build up their conquest of this enormous land.

Indeed, in the Amazonian life, man was at that time no more important than many other animal forms. There were the great communities of ants whose ordered armies marched in marauding columns over the land, driving from their track every living thing —including man—that had the power to move away from their hostility. Some of these ants, of a blind species, built covered roads across the thickets and campos, made of fragments of earth keyed into real arches without the use of cement. There were the troops of apes which roved the country and whose mode of life was hardly more primitive than that of the miserable food-gathering Indians, who were indeed sometimes forced to imitate the monkeys by raiding the plantations of their settled neighbours. There were the armies of turtles which inhabited the river and the inland pools in their millions. There were the alligators, commoner than pike in an English river. There were the fierce jaguars which prowled by night up to the edges of the towns and villages and even into the outskirts of Para itself. And, lastly, there was the terrifying anaconda or *sucuraya*, the great water serpent which grew to a length of more than forty feet. This great snake had inspired the natives of the river banks with so much awe and terror that they had woven around it the legend of a fabulously large serpent, " many score fathoms in length, which appears successively in different parts of the river " and which they called " *ai Md'agoa*—the mother, or spirit, of the water ".

In such surroundings men had little sense of their own grandeur and were content to live simply and without great achievements. The native Indians were inspired with little curiosity concerning the world in general or the processes of nature, and Bates remarks uneasily that they had apparently little idea of God and less desire to consider the basis of the universe. The majority of the population were mamelucos, descendants of mixed unions of Portuguese whites and Indians, and, while they had perhaps more enterprise than the Indian, they shared his lack of concern with the world beyond the great river, and showed none of the questing enthusiasm which had brought their Portuguese ancestors to this land or sent them voyaging along the coasts of Africa with Prince Henry or round the Cape with Vasco da Gama. Even the *élite* of the few towns, officials and priests, had little knowledge of what went on beyond their own neighbourhood, and there was nothing extraordinary in the small town dignitary who thought the world lay all along a greater Amazons and solemnly asked on which bank of the River Paris lay. More unusual was the young mameluco clerk in a remote village of the Tocantins, who showed Bates a whole well-thumbed library of Latin classics, Virgil, Terence, Cicero, Livy, in his " mud-plastered and palm-thatched hut ". A man of learning was indeed rare, and the priests, with two exceptions so noteworthy that Bates mentions them by name, were distinguished for loose living rather than for deep reading.

Yet, for all their lack of knowledge and ambition, or perhaps because of it, the majority of the people of the Amazons seem to have lived in those days relatively carefree and happy lives. Some of the Indians, it is true, were forced to work for hard official taskmasters, but these must have been very few ; most of the people had their own holdings and lived independent peasant lives. In terms of cash they were undoubtedly poor. But the satisfactions of most of life's needs lay near at hand. The fertile forest soil, even where, as in most instances, it was ill tended by the lazy proprietors, grew a sufficiency of vegetables and fruits and, in particular, such staple foods as bananas and *mandioca*, a poisonous root, from which was prepared, when the noxious juice had been squeezed out, *farinha*, the regional equivalent of flour. The forests contained an abundance of nutritious wild fruits and, while there was little live-stock, and therefore no great supply of butcher's meat, the rivers swarmed with fish and turtles, and the taste of the people for meat was sufficiently catholic for them to eat even monkeys and alligators. All of these meats Bates tried and most of them he found palatable. He even went farther than the inhabitants and experimented with such out-of-the-ordinary foods as ant-eater which, in spite of prejudice, he found good. Used to the heavy flesh-eating of Victorian England, he found the diet of fish, fruit and vegetables somewhat inadequate and consequently had a persistent desire for meat which he could never fully satisfy. But it must be remembered that Bates led a life too energetic for the climate in which he chose to work, and the break-up of his health doubtless came from over-exertion in tropical heat rather than from deficiency of food. For the people of the Amazons, who never exerted themselves more than they desired, the diet was probably adequate.

Of the other needs of this simple life, the greater part were satisfied by products of the rivers and forests around them. The bark of various trees, for instance, could be converted into rope, mats, and the hammocks which served as beds and couches ; it could serve as an excellent substitute for cigarette paper and at a pinch could be made into garments. The oil from turtles' eggs was fuel for lamps. Houses were built of the wood and mud of the ground on which they stood. Boats were cut from forest trees, or, by the poor food-gathering Indians, made of bark tied roughly together with lianas. Each peasant, besides being a farmer, was usually fisherman and hunter, carpenter and boatbuilder.

A few crops, such as cacao, were grown for sale or, more often, barter. For the same purpose the poorer half-castes and the Indians gathered sarsaparilla, rubber, Brazil nuts and turtle oil. These were exchanged with wandering traders for such goods as could not be grown or made at home—cheap flintlock guns and their ammunition, tobacco, cloth, metal implements and, perhaps most desired of all, *cashaça*, the rum of the country. Money rarely entered into these transactions.

Bates describes many households and plantations which he visited during his travels. Here are some examples which give an idea of the leisured simplicity in which these people lived as a result of what Bates calls " the incorrigible nonchalance and laziness of the people ". This is the picture of a cacao plantation near Obydos :

" We landed at one of the cacao plantations. The house was substantially built; the walls formed of strong upright posts, lathed across, plastered with mud and whitewashed, and the roof tiled. The family were mamelucos, and seemed to be an average sample of the poorer class of cacao growers. All were loosely dressed and bare-footed. A broad verandah extended along one side of the house, the floor of which was simply the well-trodden earth, and here hammocks were slung between the bare upright supports, a large rush mat being spread on the ground, upon which the stout matron-like mistress with a tame parrot perched on her shoulder, sat sewing with two pretty little mulatto girls. The master, coolly clad in shirt and drawers, the former loose about the neck, lay in his hammock smoking a long gaudily-painted wooden pipe. The household utensils, earthenware jars, water-pots and saucepans, lay at one end, near which was a wood fire, with the every-ready coffee pot simmering on the top of a clay tripod. A large shed stood a short distance off, embowered in a grove of banana, papaw, and mango trees; and under it were the ovens, troughs, sieves, and all other apparatus for the preparation of mandioca. The cleared space around the house was only a few yards in extent; beyond it lay the cacao plantations, which stretched on each side parallel to the banks of the river. There was a path through the forest which led to the mandioca fields, and several miles beyond to other houses on the banks of an interior channel. We were kindly received, as is always the case when a stranger visits these out-of-the-way habitations; the people being invariably civil and hospitable. We had a long chat, took coffee, and on departing one of the daughters sent a basket full of oranges for our use down to the canoe."

This shows what a normal plantation anywhere on the Amazons would be like. Some were poorer, some more prosperous and efficiently worked, but there was an essential similarity in the living circumstances of the people of the river, whether they were mameluco, white, negro or civilised Indian. This can be seen if we quote another description of the home of a pure-blooded Passé Indian, many hundred miles further up the river, in the neighbourhood of Ega:

" I was rather surprised to find the grounds around this establishment in neater order than in any *sitio*, even of civilised people, I had yet seen on the Upper Amazons; the stock of utensils and household goods of all sorts was larger, and the evidences of regular industry and plenty more numerous than one usually perceives in the farms of civilised Indians and whites. The buildings were of the same construction as those of the humbler settlers in all other parts of the country. The family lived in a large, oblong, open shed built under the shade of the trees. Two smaller buildings, detached from the shed and having mud-walls with low doorways, contained apparently the sleeping apartments of different members of the large household. A small mill for grinding sugar-cane, having two cylinders of hard notched wood ; wooden troughs, and kettles for boiling the *guaràpa* (cane juice) to make treacle, stood under a separate shed, and near it was a large enclosed mud-house for poultry. There was another hut and shed a short distance off, inhabited by a family dependent on Pedro, and a narrow pathway through the luxuriant woods led to more dwellings of the same kind. There was an abundance of fruit trees around the place, including the never-failing banana with its long, broad, soft green leaf-blades, and groups of full-grown *Pupùnhas*, or peach-palms. There was also a large number of cotton and coffee trees. Amongst the utensils I noticed baskets of different shapes, made of flattened manatta stalks, and dyed various colours. The making of these is an original art of the Passés, but I believe it is also practised by other tribes, for I saw several in the houses of semi-civilised Indians on the Tapajos."

When Bates arrived at this *sitio* he found an old woman " distilling spirits from *carà*, an eatable root similar to the potato, by means of a clay still which had been manufactured by herself," and a young woman " scalding and picking fowls for the dinner, near the fire on the ground at the other end of the dwelling ". Later he was taken through the woods along a path which terminated at a plantation of mandioca. " There were probably ten acres of cleared land, and part of the ground was planted with Indian corn, watermelons and sugar-cane." The standard of living of such people must have been appreciably higher than that of the contemporary English factory worker or agricultural labourer.

In contrast with such pictures of comparative prosperity, one must remember that Bates did encounter settlements of poor hunting Indians who lived miserably in filthy hovels and on scanty food. But such conditions were endured by a dwindling minority even among the Indians, who showed signs of having degenerated from a higher state of barbarism by their use of that ingenious and highly specialised weapon, the blow-gun.

The inhabitants of the settlements and *sitios* along the river were by no means always tied to their field work. Frequently they went on group fishing or hunting expeditions, when they would spend several days or weeks away from home along the river or at the inland pools within the forest, which swarmed with fish and turtles. The people of the towns were equally fond of making such expeditions and leaving their normal habits to camp out for a time in the country. For instance, every year it was the custom for the whole population of Ega to travel many miles down the river to certain sandbanks at the season when the turtles laid their eggs, when a great communal digging took place, during which the people enjoyed a pleasantly Bohemian outdoor life away from their normal (though very light) cares and responsibilities. Farther down the river Bates came upon similar camps of people who had left their towns just for a change of air and habits. He describes one which he encountered near Patos, on the Tocantins, 150 miles from Para :

" We found here several families encamped in a delightful spot. The shore sloped gradually down to the water, and was shaded by a few wide-spreading trees. There was no underwood. A great number of hammocks were seen slung between the tree-trunks, and the litter of a numerous household lay scattered about. Women, old and young, some of the latter very good-looking, and a large number of children, besides pet animals, enlivened the encampment. They were all half-breeds, simple, well-disposed people, and explained to us that they were inhabitants of Cametà, who had come thus far, eighty miles, to spend the summer months. The

only motive they could give for their coming was that ' it was so
hot in the town in the *verao* (summer) and they were all so fond of
fresh fish '. Thus these simple folks think nothing of leaving home
and business to come on a three-months' picnic. It is the annual
custom of this class of people throughout the province to spend a
few months of the fine season in the wilder parts of the country.
They carry with them all the *farinha* they can scrape together, this
being the only article of food necessary to provide. The men hunt
and fish for the day's wants, and sometimes collect a little india-
rubber, sarsaparilla, or copaiba oil, to sell to traders on their return ;
the women assist in paddling the canoes, do the cooking, and sometimes fish with rod and line. The weather is enjoyable the whole
time, and so days and weeks pass happily away."

These fishing, hunting and holiday expeditions were usually
undertaken by groups of people, and communal practices seem to
have been regular wherever sufficiently large groups of people were
gathered. Bates describes one interesting form of mutual aid
practised on the Tapajos, a large tributary of the Amazons :

" All the heavy work, such as felling and burning the timber,
planting and weeding, is done in the plantation of each family by
a congregation of neighbours, which they call a ' pucherum '—
a similar custom to the ' bee ' in the backwoods settlements of North
America."

Except in one or two towns where stilted Portuguese habits
survived, the intercourse of the people was free and open. Bates
was impressed at the beginning of his travels by this frankness of
habits.

" The easy, lounging life of the people amused us very much. I
afterwards had plenty of time to become used to tropical village
life. There is a free, familiar, *pro bono publico* style of living in
these small places, which requires some time for a European to
fall into. No sooner were we established in our rooms, than a
number of lazy young fellows came to look on and make remarks,

and we had to answer all sorts of questions. The houses have their doors and windows open to the street, and people walk in and out as they please ; there is always, however, a more secluded apartment, where the female members of the family reside. In their familiarity there is nothing intentionally offensive, and it is practised simply in the desire to be sociable."

The lazy freedom of life, the readiness to co-operate in work and pleasure, the open frankness of intercourse, were made possible by and indeed probably arose from an almost complete lack of organised authority, both of institution and idea, and a great freedom from economic exploitation. The provincial government, away in Para, extended an authority which was tenuous in the extreme and which interfered hardly at all in the lives of the people. The army stayed in the capital and there was no regular police force. Conscription and direct taxation did not exist. Landlords and rent were almost unknown, except in the larger towns, for the river banks and the forest were free for all, without even the formality of an official claim as in most newly-opened countries. What a man grew or caught was his own—he had to pay no tolls to any parasitic individual or organisation. No organised state existed, and nationalist feeling was yet unborn.

Combined with this freedom from material oppression was also freedom from the domination of ideas. The Church had comparatively little influence, except in Para, and Bates does not appear to have encountered any pronounced prejudices against his rationalistic Protestantism. There was no apparent discrimination of race or colour—whites, negroes, mamelucos, and civilised Indians mingling on a basis of complete equality. Nor was there any xenophobic hatred of foreigners—Bates was accepted by all people in whatever part of the Amazons he travelled, and the experience of other Europeans seems to have been similar.

Respectability—in the nineteenth century English sense—was not greatly valued, except by a very few pure white families in two or

three of the larger towns.   People of all races got drunk perio-
dically, and the few serious differences which Bates experienced
with the inhabitants seem to have arisen only when he rather primly
refused to join their drinking bouts.   Habitual drunkenness, on
the other hand, was rare.

In sexual matters there was a great deal of freedom.   In Para
Bates found much furtive promiscuity.   On the higher reaches,
however, there was a more open and healthy freedom, particularly
before marriage.

" Most of the half-caste women on the Upper Amazons lead a
little career of looseness before they marry and settle down for life ;
and it is rather remarkable that the men do not seem to object
much to their brides having had a child or two by various fathers
before marriage.   The women do not lose reputation unless they
become utterly depraved, but in that case they are condemned
pretty strongly by public opinion.   Depravity is, however, rare
for all require more or less to be wooed before they are won."

One is reminded vividly of the attitude of primitive peoples in
the South Seas and in Africa to sexual intercourse among young
people.

In this free life there seems to have been little or no dissension
among the people as individuals.   Indeed, there was little cause
for it, as any man could have free access to the means of life,
and need not be dependent upon another for gaining food and
shelter.   Therefore the crimes artificially induced by a property
society were infrequent, and the uninhibited nature of the river
life in general led to a rarity of violent incidents.

Among these people Bates moved as a curiously incongruous
figure, a Victorian and a near rationalist, bespectacled and passionately concerned with furthering the progress of science.   His
achievement as a naturalist was considerable—he discovered
8,000 new species of animal life, made the first intensive study of
mimicry among insects, and collected data which contributed to the

development of evolutionary theory. But it is not the naturalist who appeals to us as we read his sole literary work, *A Naturalist on the River Amazons.* It is the observant and appreciative traveller, who had the necessary humility to move freely among simple people and live among them a life like their own. For a Victorian Englishman, Bates had a remarkable faculty of acceptance. Only occasionally is he the moralist. Drunkenness and sexual freedom he reports almost without comment. Concerning laziness he is rather more censorious, but in that he had at least the excuse of being an energetic man himself. But he is angry only on the rare occasions when he encounters instances of the ill-treatment of poor Indians by their civilised neighbours.

He appears to have taken part freely in the life of the people. He hunted and fished with them, joined in their social life and drank with them in moderation. Of his sexual life, unfortunately, we gather nothing except for a few diffident references to the attractiveness of certain of the women he encountered. On the whole he enjoyed the free and easy life of the river and its people. That he stayed there eleven years shows how the land held him.

Yet he underwent many hardships and the delights of his residence must be balanced against these, as he himself describes them :

" I suffered most inconvenience from the difficulty of getting news from the civilised world down river, from the irregularity of receipt of letters, parcels of books and periodicals, and towards the latter part of my residence from ill-health arising from bad and insufficient food. The want of intellectual society, and of the varied excitement of European life, was also felt most acutely, and this, instead of becoming deadened by time, increased until it became almost insupportable. I was obliged, at last, to come to the conclusion that the contemplation of Nature alone is not sufficient to fill the human heart and mind."

At last, in 1859, when his health had broken completely, Bates returned to England. Already, the old free order of life was beginning to break up. The steamers had started to run up the river, taking with them their loads of government officials and traders, and already some of the people had begun to taste the evils of money and power. To-day, no doubt, the rot has penetrated deeply, and the values of money and power are as important among the Amazonians as they are among the English. Nevertheless, it is valuable to have been left a record of how well men can live in freedom from all the abstractions that beset our modern life.

XIV

The Peroxide Saint

My childhood was spent in an atmosphere of evangelical religion, and some of my earliest memories are of dry-skinned, bearded men who would speak in the church on a Sunday to appeal for funds to convert the benighted heathen, and would afterwards appear at my grandfather's house in the afternoon to eat a large tea and discuss the collection. They were fanatical, seedy and generally rather unpleasant men, but the stories they told of their adventures with hostile heathens and the odd weapons or fragments of beadwork which they sometimes exhibited were always fascinating.

This was my only direct contact with missionaries. I found them somewhat frightening, and often felt a certain guilty sympathy for the sinful and naked pagans of whom they talked with such insulting compassion. In their accounts of discussions with the unconverted, the arguments of the " natives " seemed so clear and sensible and those of the missionaries so much like the specious arguments which my elders used against me when I asked questions about God, that I found myself almost always on the side of the heathen. So I was often impolite to these outlandish visitors, and would then be fined a week's pocket-money, for my grandmother's missionary box. Thus my prejudice against the missions was always being fed and increased.

I say this, because my attitude towards missionaries has never changed in any important respect. The antagonism which arose from personal assessment and childhood reasoning, persists, and has only been confirmed by all I have learnt of the effect of missionary activities in breaking up the traditional organic life of primitive societies. Probably no other class of European, even the slave trader, has done so much to destroy indigenous cultures or to break down the economic and social patterns of tribal life which were often based on a sense of co-operation and mutual aid superior to anything that occurs in modern Western civilisations.

One of the results of the missionary cult at my home was the presence of a number of curious books concerning the activities of these destructive evangelists, and by far the most illuminating of these was the autobiography of John G. Paton, perhaps the most formidable of all the missionaries—a great self-publicist, a fervent destroyer of native customs and beliefs in the Polynesian islands to which he was sent as one of the great plagues of the Victorian Jehovah, and in all respects a phoney saint who has long awaited a deserved place among the great charlatans canonised by the lime-lights of Hollywood. With his bleached hair and beard, his sanctimonious fervour for clothing the naked and his superb ability to raise large sums of money by holy demagogy for the Lord, he appears as a magnificent symbol of the Victorian conception of militant religion.

Paton came of a poor Scottish family in one of those villages of the Cheviots which declined during the enclosures of the agricultural revolution from a prosperous township into a poor hamlet. He went to Glasgow as a youth, having decided he was called to the Lord's work, and toiled there for a time in poverty as a school-teacher and a city missionary. Finally, he was moved by the Lord and the imagined " wail of the perishing heathen " to offer himself as a Missionary for the South Seas. His friends tried to dissuade him, but Paton was always an obstinate man, and their persuasions were unavailing. To one old man, who prophesied that he would be eaten by the cannibals, Paton replied, in complete solemnity :

" Mr Dickson, you are advanced in years now, and your own prospect is soon to be laid in the grave, there to be eaten by worms ; I confess to you, that if I can but live and die serving and honouring the Lord Jesus, it will make no difference to me whether I am eaten by cannibals or by worms ; and in the Great Day my resurrection body will arise as fair as yours in the likeness of our risen Redeemer."

A man who could say this without laughing at himself was certain to carry through his plans from sheer insensitivity, and in 1857, he landed on Tanna, an island of the New Hebrides whose inhabitants had a bad reputation for frightening missionaries.

" My first impressions drove me, I must confess," he tells us, " to the verge of utter dismay. On beholding these natives in their paint and nakedness and misery, my heart was as full of horror as of pity. Had I given up my much-beloved work and my dear people in Glasgow, with so many delightful associations, to consecrate my life to these degraded creatures ? "

Nevertheless, Paton stayed, and proceeded with much tenacity and real courage to preach the creed of what he called his " Jehovah God ". At first the natives received him with friendliness. They sold him land on which to build a house—payment being made in various trade goods, such as hatchets and cloth, and appropriated any odd articles he left lying about within their reach. Some of the chiefs, for what appear to have been largely political motives, even pretended to be interested in his teachings, and, while he did not interfere with their way of life, the Tannese did not object to his talking about a new God. What, after all, did one more god mean among so many ?

But Paton's spiritual pride was not content with tolerance. He regarded the whole complex of tribal customs and beliefs as the products of the devil. That he never made any attempt to understand these beliefs is shown by the scandalous misrepresentations of tribal life with which his Autobiography abounds. But, after all, the Reformed Presbyterian Church had sent him out, not as an anthropologist but as an apostle, not to understand but to destroy.

He proceeded to preach the Gospel with a bigot's fervour, regardless of its relationship to the people to whom he addressed himself. Had he done nothing more he might have been left in peace. But, instead, he began a policy of steady interference with the daily lives and customs of the people. He deliberately broke taboos, he interfered in the comparatively innocuous wars between the tribes, he tried to prevent the natives from maintaining some of their most treasured customs, he attempted to persuade them to burn their sacred images and objects. He made the wearing of shirts and the abandonment of traditional adornments a condition of admission to the Christian faith, and when the friendly Tannese arranged a great feast in his honour and performed their native dances for him, he responded with a churlish exhibition of disapproval.

After a period of this kind of behaviour, it is not surprising that the Tannese began to tire of Paton's oddities, and when a series of misfortunes befell them, in the form of epidemics, storms and poor crops, they decided that the presence of such an outlandish figure must be offending their own gods. Accordingly, they did their best to rid themselves of this guest who had made such a poor return for their hospitality. At first they tried persuasion, but Paton turned a deaf ear. Then they tried threats and warnings, but still without any effect. Finally, while their obligations as hosts would not allow them to harm him in any way, they decided to resort to scaring him in such a way that he would imagine they intended to kill and eat him.

This they did partly by repeating to him stories of plots against his life, and partly by making hostile demonstrations outside his house. Paton, a highly-strung man with an active imagination, responded quickly to this kind of treatment, and firmly believed to his last day that many times it was only the direct intervention of Jesus that saved him at the last moment from violent death.

" One day," he tells us, " while toiling away at my house, the war chief and his brother, and a large party of armed men, surrounded the plot where I was working. They all had muskets besides their own native weapons. They watched me for some time in silence, and then every man levelled a musket straight at my head. Escape was impossible. Speech would only have increased my danger. My eyesight came and went for a few minutes. I prayed to my Lord Jesus, either Himself to protect me or to take me home to His Glory. I tried to keep working on at my task, as if no one was near me. In that moment, as never before, the words came to me—' Whatsoever ye shall ask in my name, I will do it '; and I knew that I was safe. Retiring a little from their first position, no word having been spoken, they took up the same attitude somewhat farther off, and seemed to be urging one another to fire the first shot. But my dear Lord restrained them once again, and they withdrew, leaving me with a new reason for trusting Him with all that concerned me for Time and Eternity."

From this and other accounts of similar incidents it is clear that the Tannese were in fact anxious not to treat Paton with violence, and did all they could to induce him to depart by the only means at their command, after persuasion had failed, that of frightening him. In all this they showed much more forbearance and patience than did most white men in their actions towards the South Sea Islanders.

Eventually, after an epidemic of measles introduced by sandalwood traders had decimated the population, the feeling against intruding whites became really strong, and Paton was finally smoked out when the Tannese set fire to his church and house.

He departed with a poor grace, and took his story of ill usage to the British naval authorities, who sent H.M.S. *Curacoa* to the island on a punitive expedition. The missionaries sailed with the expedition, and in this pleasant little joint action by the Church and the State, the island was shelled, several villages and many

canoes were burnt, and nine Tannese were later killed through dis-
covering an unexploded shell. After this, the Tannese were
naturally less friendly towards the whites, and gained a great
repute as killers of traders and missionaries. With the
story of Paton's activities in one's mind, it is difficult to condemn
them.

The missionary's activities were next directed towards a much
smaller island, a coral atoll called Aniwa. Here he was once again
received with friendliness, and began his interference with the
tribal life of the natives. This would probably have had the same
result as his deeds on Tanna, if he had not been able to enact a
spurious miracle, which convinced the unscientific Aniwans that
Jehovah God was really more powerful than their own fetishes.
The only water supply on Aniwa, at the time of Paton's landing,
was accumulated rainwater. A drought occurred, and Paton
decided to combine a theological with a practical purpose by
announcing to the natives that his God would make rain come out
of the ground. They were all sceptical, and when he began to
dig a well, even the converted decided that he was mad. But
Paton persisted, with a great deal of patter about Jehovah, until,
to the astonishment of the whole population, he struck water.
The drought was ended, and the ascendancy of Jehovah was assured.
Paton, with characteristic dishonesty, maintained throughout that
the water was a special gift of Jehovah, who had sent it in answer
to his prayers. Afterwards, in his Autobiography, he was to repeat
the story, with great self-satisfaction at this somewhat cheap trick
by which he won Aniwa for Jesus.

There were still a few recalcitrant villages and individuals. One
chief, in particular, maintained a very capable rationalist argument against Paton's fundamentalist Christianity :

" It's all lies you come here to teach us, and you call it Worship !
You say your Jehovah God dwells in Heaven. Who ever went up
there to hear Him or see Him ? You talk of Jehovah as if you had

visited His Heaven. Why, you cannot climb even to the top of one of our cocoa-nut trees, though we can and that with ease! In going up to the roof of your own Mission House, you require the help of a ladder to carry you. And even if you could make your ladder higher than our highest cocoa-nut tree, on what would you lean the top? And when you get to its top, you can only climb down the other side and end where you begin! The thing is impossible. You never saw that God; you never heard Him speak; don't come here with any of your white lies, or I'll send my spear through you."

But, after the miracle of the well, Paton had the power of numbers behind him, and he was always willing, after a coy display of reluctance, to lead an armed horde of Christians to terrify any village that still maintained hostility to the worship. In this way the opposition was rapidly liquidated, and even the Chief who put such logical arguments against Christianity found it politic to become an active adherent of the new order. Led by their chiefs, the Aniwans embraced the new faith and burnt and broke their idols in an iconoclastic fervour.

From this time Paton's reign was absolute, and he was able completely to break down the old tribal cultures and customs. He induced the natives to give free labour for the building of churches and schools, as well as to provide produce to be sold in order to gain funds for their own conversion. He forced the naked into cheap shirts and trousers, and by this action alone set in motion a complex series of changes in their lives, which Tom Harrisson has detailed in *Savage Civilisation*.

" Economically the mission natives were firmly yoked to the trader and to copra or sandalwood production, so that they might get clothes; they were supplied with the poorest clothes that rot quickly in this rotting climate; hygienically, clothes could not be kept clean within the native standard of living, so that skin disease, tuberculosis and parasites benefited. Psychologically a new element of shame and secrecy was introduced into the open, balanced physical approach of sexes."

Paton retired from his Aniwan triumph to spend the remainder of his life raising funds for the missions. He became the missionary equivalent of the hot-gospellers, Sankey and Moody. He moved into high society, and played at politics, demanding that the British should occupy the South Sea Islands to keep out the French and their Catholic missionaries. Too late, he realised the exploitation by trader and blackbirder which his own inroads into native culture had helped to foster, and when the era of the recruiters for the Queensland labour market was almost ended, he began to denounce them in round terms of abuse. He spent his last years in long and triumphant tours of Britain, America and the Dominions, making thousands of emotional speeches to large audiences whom he impressed with his patriarchial appearance and tearful manner, and building himself an enormous legend, where many better men, even among the missionaries, went completely unknown. He died, canonised in the opinion of canting Christendom, in 1907.

Paton was certainly more dishonest and more self-assertive than many other missionaries. Yet he remains in his actions and in their effect typical of his profession. With the best of intentions, often with courage and genuine self-sacrifice, the missionaries set out on a systematic destruction of the native cultures of all the primitive nations of the world. Their ostensible object was to improve the lot of these peoples by rescuing them from error and ignorance, but the practical result of their actions was that the converts gave up their native systems of values and became prey to all the physical evils, the disease, the economic exploitation and the spiritual emptiness which form the negative side of European life. In return they gained the promise of salvation beyond death, the nebulous kingdom of heaven in the sky.

We can judge the work of the missionaries only by comparing the populous and prosperous South Sea Islands before their advent, as described by Herman Melville in *Typee*, with the disease-ridden and declining peoples, existing in thraldom to the trader, the missionary and the soap combines, who are their successors to-day. For their part in this degradation of a group of beautiful and independent races, the missionaries stand condemned, and among them Paton was probably the most deserving of such censure.

THE END